CUSTOMER & USER EXPERIENCE MAPS
STEP-BY-STEP GUIDE

2ND EDITION

Robert A Curedale
Copyright © 25 February 2019 by Robert A. Curedale
All rights reserved. Published by Design Community College Inc.

The publisher and author accept no liability, regardless of legal basis. Designations used in this book may be trademarks whose use by third parties for their own purposes could violate the rights of the owners. The author and publisher have taken great care with all texts and illustrations in this book. The information contained within this book is strictly for educational purposes. If you wish to apply ideas contained in this book you are taking full responsibility for your actions. There are no representations or warranties, express or implied, about the completeness, accuracy, reliability, suitability or availability with respect to the information, products, services, or related graphics contained in this book for any purpose. Any use of this information is at your own risk. The author has made every effort to ensure the accuracy of the information within this book was correct at time of publication. The publisher and author do not assume and hereby disclaims any liability to any party for any loss, damage, or disruption caused by errors or omissions, whether such errors or omissions result from accident, negligence, or any other cause.

All rights reserved. No part of this publication may be reproduced, distributed, or transmitted in any form or by any means, including photocopying, recording, or other electronic or mechanical methods, without the prior written permission of the publisher, except in the case of brief quotations embodied in critical reviews and certain other noncommercial uses permitted by copyright law. For permission requests, write to the publisher, addressed "Attention: Permissions Coordinator," at the address below.

Design Community College Inc.
PO Box 1153
Topanga CA 90290 USA
info@dcc-edu.org
Designed and illustrated by Robert Curedale
Cover color graphic and artwork designed by Robert Curedale
ISBN-10: 1-940805-46-5
ISBN-13: 978-1-940805-46-7

CUSTOMER & USER
EXPERIENCE MAPS
STEP-BY-STEP GUIDE
2ND EDITION

ROBERT CUREDALE

PUBLISHED BY DESIGN COMMUNITY COLLEGE INC.
LOS ANGELES https://dcc-edu.org

CONTENTS

INTRODUCTION

01 SERVICE DESIGN   13
1. Growing use of the term service design
2. Largest us private employers 1960 vs 2010
3. Private sector employment
4. 1948 To 2010 % of total private employment
5. The growth of services
6. The evolving focus of design practice
7. Bells stages of economic development
8. Preindustrial society
9. Industrial society
10. 1900 To 1950
11. Postindustrial society
12. Why service design is one of the
13. Fastest-growing areas of design
14. Servitization
15. Types of product service systems
16. Why servitization?
17. Strategic rationale
18. Challenges for servitization
19. Implementing servitization
20. From goods-centered to
21. Customer-centered solutions
22. Service industry growth in China
23. Percentage of China's GDP from services 1970 to 2030
24. Why design services?
25. The design ladder
26. The design ladder in relation to success in export
27. Average growth in turnover
28. Storytelling
29. The big questions
30. Story structure
31. Narrative
32. An effective story
33. Plan your story
34. Audience
35. Context
36. Focus on what's important
37. Be visual
38. Ask for feedback from your audience
39. Challenges
40. Effective design balances
41. People's needs, business needs, the best technology and consideration of the environment
42. Human needs
43. Shoshin
44. Service design spaces
45. Spaces for creative work Haworth recommendations
46. Tacit knowledge
47. Qualitative research
48. Questions to consider
49. Thinking styles
50. Abductive thinking
51. Deductive thinking
52. Inductive thinking
53. Critical thinking
54. Design thinking
55. Divergent and convergent thinking
56. Research triangulation
57. Primary research
58. Secondary research
59. Why use mapping methods?
60. Craft a better user experience

61. Improve your business performance
62. Design ethnography
63. Some disruptive trends
64. Empathy
65. Experience design
66. Human needs
67. Segmentation
68. Personas
69. Origin of personas
70. Persona template
71. Types of personas
72. Primary personas
73. Secondary personas
74. Stakeholders
75. Exclusionary personas
76. Biographical information

02 APPLYING MAPPING METHODS IN YOUR ORGANIZATION 69
1. Moderating groups
2. Roles
3. Assistant moderator
4. Moderator
5. Group behavior
6. Constructive group behaviors
7. Destructive group behaviors
8. Intervention
9. Time management
10. Keep the interview on track
11. What methods did you use to research your customers?
12. Which internal departments were represented in your mapping team?
13. Use the interview guide
14. Do not rush the discussion
15. Moderator skills
16. Building rapport
17. Listening to discussion participants
18. Teams
19. Diversity
20. Who sponsored your most recent mapping project?
21. Empowerment
22. Facilitation
23. Which research method was most effective for journey mapping?
24. Collective intelligence
25. Which software tools have you used to create journey maps?
26. Cross pollination
27. Cross-disciplinary collaboration
28. Everyone contributes
29. What methods did you use to research your customers?

03 DESIGN PROCESS OVERVIEW 96
1. The design phases
2. Process map
3. The double diamond process model

04 DISCOVERY
1. The discovery process 105
2. Bias
3. Research plan
4. Question matrix
5. Activity map
6. Anthropump
7. Behavioral map
8. Benchmarking
9. Benefits map
10. Boundary shifting
11. Camera journal

CONTENTS 5

12. Open card sort
13. Closed card sort
14. Benchmarking matrix
15. For product design
16. Day in the life
17. Dot voting
18. Emotion cards
19. Five whys
20. Fly-on-the-wall
21. Focus groups
22. Ideation decision matrix
23. Consensus matrix
24. Interviews
25. Planning interviews
26. Challenges
27. Planning
28. Conducting the interview
29. Interview guide
30. Problem definition
31. Problem interview script
32. Welcome
33. Background information
34. Tell a story
35. Problem ranking
36. Customer's world view
37. Wrap-up
38. Document results
39. Interview guide
40. Interview consent form
41. Interviewing methods
- Contextual inquiry
- Group interview
- Guided storytelling
- Man in the street
- Naturalistic group
- One-on-one interview
- Structured interview
- Photo elicitation
- Unstructured interview
- Telephone interview
42. Mixed method research
43. Observation
- Covert observation
- Direct observation
- Indirect observation
- Non-participant
- Participant observation
- Overt observation
- Structured observation

44. User stories
45. What-how-why method
46. WWWWWH

05 EXPERIENCE MAPS 166
1. What is an experience map?
2. History
3. How to build an experience map
4. Coffee shop experience map
5. Air travel experience map
6. Experience map exercise

06 GLOSSARY 192

07 INDEX 210

08 COURSES & OTHER TITLES 226
1. Other DCC titles
   235

09 BIBLIOGRAPHY
1. About the author

20TH CENTURY DESIGN	21ST CENTURY DESIGN

INDIVIDUAL DESIGNERS	DESIGN TEAMS

PRODUCTS	SYSTEMS OF PRODUCTS, SERVICES AND EXPERIENCES
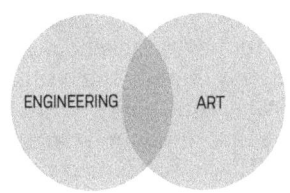	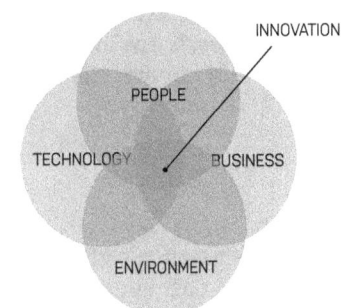

DESIGN INSPIRATION FROM IMAGES OF THE WORK OF 20 FAMOUS DESIGNERS IN EACH DESIGN DISCIPLINE	DESIGN INSPIRATION FROM RESEARCH AND THE UNMET NEEDS OF-END USERS
3D DESIGN SKILLS SKETCHING MODELMAKING CAD	**4D DESIGN SKILLS** IDENTIFYING UNMET NEEDS EXPERIENCE MAPS SERVICE BLUEPRINTS INTERVIEWING SCENARIOS CO-DESIGN VALUE NETWORKS

INTRODUCTION

In this book is described one of the most powerful tools available to craft superior experiences for your customers. It can transform your organization, and dramatically improve your customer satisfaction and your bottom line. Many goods and services are not truly distinctive. An experience map is a customer-focused process map that focuses on the nature and quality of the experience from the perspective of your customer. An experience map progresses through the service steps as a customer would experience them as they happen.

> **Companies that excel at customer experience grow revenues 4-8% above the market."**

Source: Bain & Co.

This edition has been reworked extensively from the first edition with an increased page count to make it, I believe, the most complete guide to experience mapping available. New chapters include "Discovery Methods" "Applying mapping in your organization", a glossary and a bibliography. Experience maps can be used to optimize the experience of goods, services, architecture, spaces and interactions or to plan business strategy. They can be used like a concept sketch of a physical object to describe an entirely new service or experience. The service sector makes up nearly 70% of most western economy's GDPs, yet most people are often frustrated by their service experiences. Customers choose products and services that deliver the best experiences. Designing your customer's entire experience is key to differentiating your designs from competitors in increasingly crowded competitive marketplaces. We are moving into a period of development when understanding your customer is the most important factor contributing to business success. 90% of US employment is now in service industries. Mapping builds consensus across your organization with stakeholders, to positively impact your entire organization and your bottom line. I believe that these core strategic tools will become required skills for every working designer in every field of design. My organization, DCC provides on-line classes.

You can review the full list of publications and classes on our web site **www.dcc-edu.org**

WHAT IS EXPERIENCE MAPPING?

An experience map is a representation of your customers' experience in their different interactions, specifying and detailing each component of an experience along a time line. Experience mapping provides insight into the customer experience. It represents the perspectives of the customers and the relevant parts of a service delivering organization that

CONSUMERS ARE SHIFTING THEIR CONSUMPTION FROM GOODS TO EXPERIENCES

Average annual personal consumption expenditure growth 2014 to 2016
Source: McKinsey

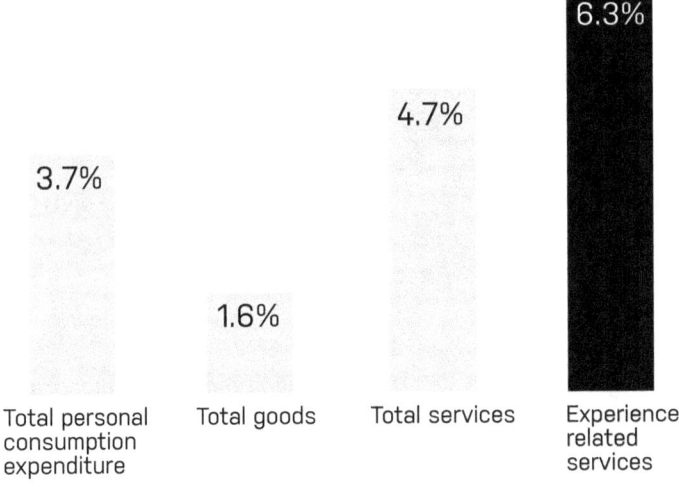

Experiences include membership clubs, sports centers, parks, theaters, events, museums, casino gambling, food service, accommodation, air travel, package tours, and foreign travel by US residents. Bureau of Economic Analysis.

Millennials "aren't spending our money on cars, TVs and watches. We're renting scooters and touring Vietnam, rocking out at music festivals, or hiking Machu Picchu."

Taylor Smith
CEO and co-founder of Blueboard,

contribute to providing the service. Experience maps provide a graphic visualization of the experience. By systematically analysing an experience a service provider can make dramatic improvements to an existing service experience. By obtaining feedback from customers, you can assess and modify the quality of service they receive at each stage of the journey. Experience mapping is a design tool which can be used to develop new innovative services as well as improving existing exp-eriences to address niche markets with specific needs. Through applying this method, designers and organizations can create a holistic user experience by uncovering precisely where to focus efforts to deliver a more compelling and valuable experience. Mapping builds knowledge and consensus across teams and stakeholders, to positively impact your entire organization. By creating a map, you can assess the experience, identify and fix problems, and allocate resources to ensure a consistently high standard.

BENEFITS OF EXPERIENCE MAPPING

Craft superior customer experiences.
- Expand the value that you can deliver as a designer exponentially.
- Identify opportunities to drive strategic innovation for current and future designs.
- Reveal the truth about your designs from the customers perspective.

- Break down the silos between disciplines for the common goal of improving the user experience.
- Define the most effective ways of measuring what matters most to your customers
- Transform organizations of all sizes to be user-centered.
- Understand customers needs and desires across different channels
- Develop better product roadmaps and prioritize design deliverables

"

Organizations that focus on journey optimization perform dramatically better than those that do not.
- *10 to 15% Greater revenue growth*
- *15 to 20% lower cost to serve*
- *20% greater customer satisfaction*
- *20 to 30% more engaged employees"*

Source: McKinsey

THE VALUE OF EXPERIENCE MAPPING
Year over year percentage change
Source: Aberdeen group 2016 n=211

Companies who formally manage customer experience

Companies who do not formally manage customer experience

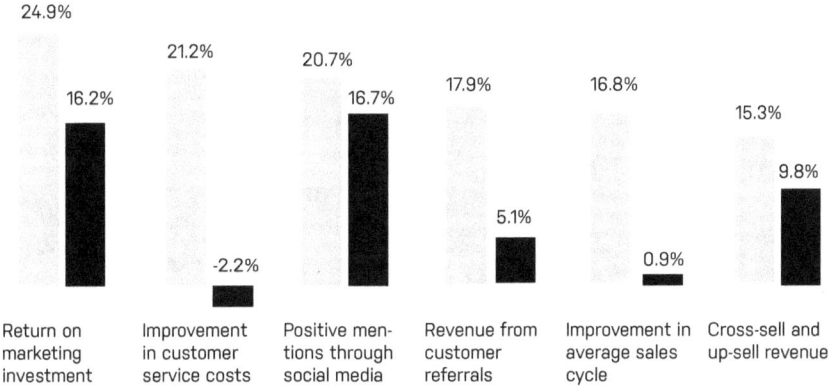

	Return on marketing investment	Improvement in customer service costs	Positive mentions through social media	Revenue from customer referrals	Improvement in average sales cycle	Cross-sell and up-sell revenue
Formally manage	24.9%	21.2%	20.7%	17.9%	16.8%	15.3%
Do not	16.2%	-2.2%	16.7%	5.1%	0.9%	9.8%

MILLENIALS SPEND MORE THAN GENXERS AND BOOMERS ON EXPERIENCES
Spending on experiences
$ reported in average month
Source: McKinsey & Company 2016

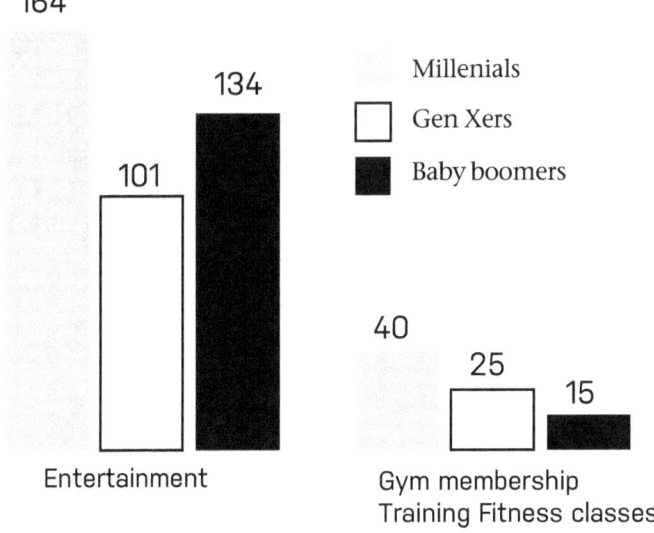

Millenials · Gen Xers · Baby boomers

Entertainment: 164, 101, 134
Gym membership Training Fitness classes: 40, 25, 15

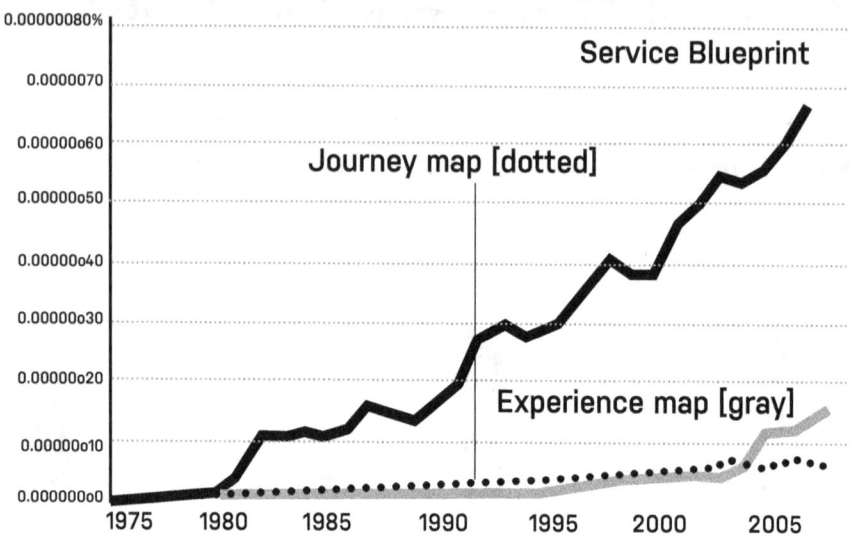

Source: Based on data from Google Ngram viewer

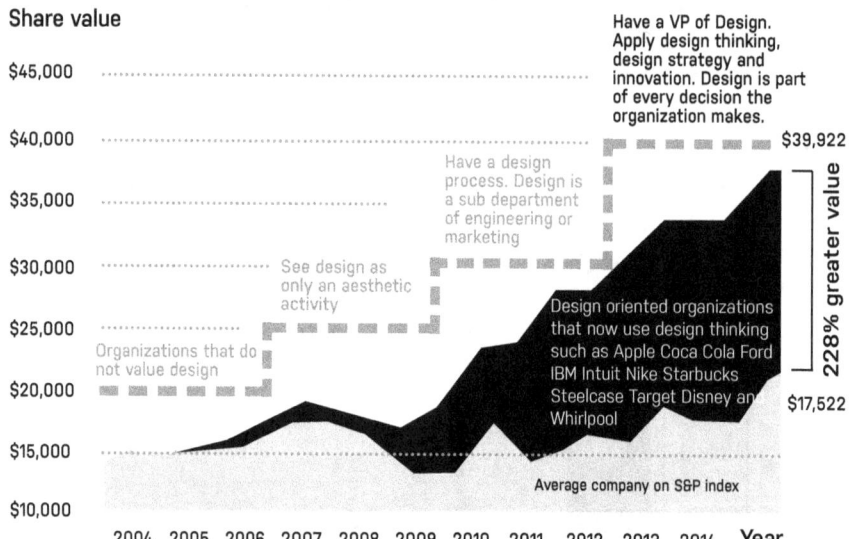

Source: Copyright © Design Thinking Process and Methods 4th Edition, Robert Curedale, 2018 https://dcc-edu.org/product/design-thinking-process-methods-4th-edition Adapted from combining data from studies by DMI Design Index, UK Design Council, Pottsdam University, and Danish Design Center Design Ladder.

01
SERVICE DESIGN

SERVICE DESIGN

Service design is an emerging competence for all designers who are serious about their careers. Service design is about making services desirable, efficient and usable.

We are immersed in services every day. We use the Internet, watch television, travel, shop, drink coffee and eat at restaurants, use government services, and we go to movies.

> ❝ *As services are intangible, difficult to standardize, and co-produced while they are delivered/consumed, the core starting point of the service design approach is to be human-focused. You must engage with the hearts and minds of people if you want to design successful and popular services.*
>
> Dr. Geke van Dijk,
> Strategy Director
> STBY London & Amsterdam

Employment in service industries in the US has grown from around 60% of overall employment in the 1950s to around 90% today. 75% of GDP is generated by services. Over the last 50 years, the United States has evolved from an economy based on creating goods to one based on providing services and service experiences.

The U.S. is now a post-industrial, services-based economy. Between 1995 and 2005, the US economy lost 3 million manufacturing jobs and created 17 million service sector jobs. Service providers and retailers employ about six in seven of the nation's workers. The majority of developed countries' gross national product is already derived from services. And the majority of employees work in services businesses. In 2013, the United States accounted for $662.0 billion, or 14 percent, of global services exports and imported $431.5 billion of services.

> ❝ *Deindustrialisation—the shrinkage of industrial jobs is popularly perceived as a symptom of economic decline. On the contrary, it is a natural stage of economic development. As a country gets richer, it is inevitable that a smaller proportion of workers will be needed in manufacturing. The first reason is that households need only so many cars, fridges or microwaves, so as they become richer they tend to spend a bigger chunk of their income on services, such as holidays,*

health and education, rather than on goods.

Second, it is much easier to automate manufacturing than services, replacing men by machines. Faster productivity growth than in services means that manufacturing needs fewer workers. In turn, as workers move into more productive areas, this gives a boost to overall productivity and hence living standards."

The Economist

Services are transforming all design industries. Service design requires new skills for designers. Services are not tangible and physical and services change over time. Service design puts customers at the center of the design process. Designers who do not have the skills to discover and design for unmet needs of end users are replaced by designers who have those skills.

"

Businesses planned for service are apt to succeed. Businesses planned for profit are apt to fail.

Nicholas Murray Butler

Design is no longer about only the aesthetics or surfaces of things. Today designers create diverse and complex systems of experiences of products, services, spaces and touchpoints – the people, information, products and spaces that customers encounter.

Service design can be used to redesign an existing service to make it better, or it can be used to create a new service. Most companies realize that by designing not just the product, but the system of services, and experiences they can add value and maximize profit.

In this edition are the practical methods, processes, and tools that service designers use.

Learn here how to understand your customers' service journey, how to develop new services and how to prototype and test your ideas for real customers in the most efficient and effective way possible.

"

Traditionally, service design had been characterized by the lack of systematic method for design and control." As a result, new services were usually developed by trial and error: in the absence of a detailed design there was no metric to gauge whether the service was complete, rational, and fulfilled the original need."

G. Lynn Shostack,
Designing Services That Deliver
-Harvard Business Review.

SERVICE DESIGN 15

Service design is a broad field that involves many disciplines, management, technology and an understanding of people.

Service design uses many methods and techniques. During the discovery phase methods are used to understand the unique perspectives of the customers who will be using the services. In the synthesis stage other methods are used to make sense of the initial research and to generate insights which will be explored during the ideation phase of service design.

> *Society is no longer based on mass consumption but on mass participation. New forms of collaboration such as Wikipedia, Facebook, MySpace, and YouTube are paving the way for an age in which people want to be players, rather than mere spectators, in the production process.*
>
> Charles Leadbeater

GROWING USE OF THE TERM SERVICE DESIGN AMONG HALF A TRILLION WORDS IN BOOKS SCANNED BY GOOGLE

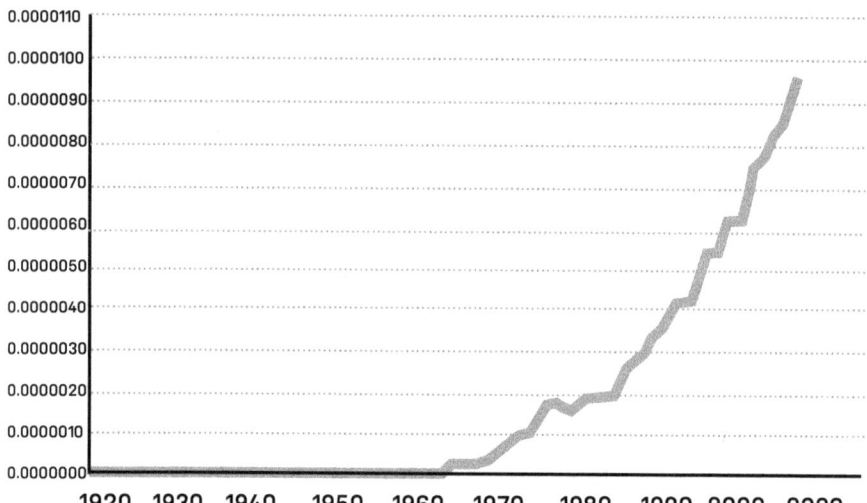

Source: Based on data from Google Ngram viewer

LARGEST US PRIVATE EMPLOYERS

1960

GOODS PRODUCING
GM
Ford
General Electric
US Steel
Esso
Bethlehem Steel
ITT
Westinghouse
General Dynamics
Chrysler
Sperry Rand
International Harvester

SERVICE PROVIDING
Bell System
Sears Roebuck
AP

2010

GOODS PRODUCING
HP
PepsiCo
General Electric

SERVICE PROVIDING
Walmart
Kelly Services
IBM
UPS
McDonald's Corp
Yum
Target
Kroger
Home Depot
Sears
Bank Of America
CVS Pharmacy

Source: New York Times

PRIVATE SECTOR EMPLOYMENT
1948 TO 2010 % OF TOTAL PRIVATE EMPLOYMENT
Source: Bureau of Economic Analysis, National Income and Product Accounts

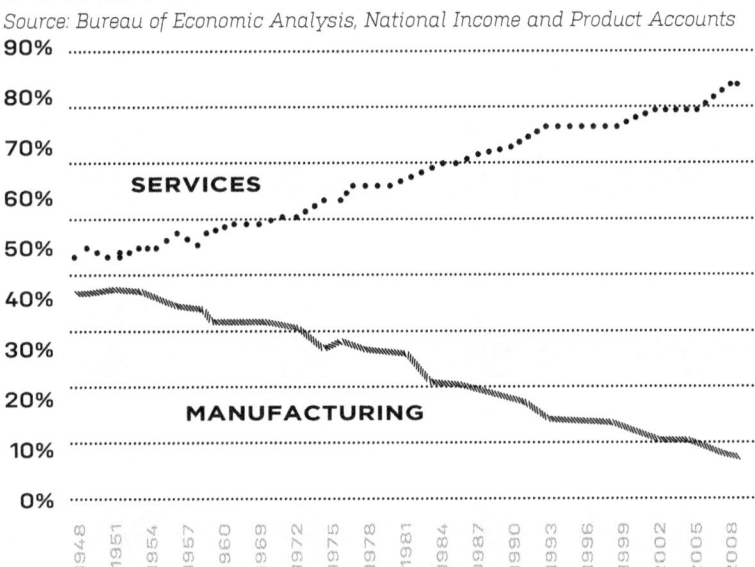

SERVICE DESIGN

THE GROWTH OF SERVICES

WHAT

A.G.B. Fisher proposed a model for economies of primary, secondary, and tertiary industries. Primary production is defined as agriculture, fishing, forestry, hunting, and mining. He concluded that as income rises demand shifts from the primary to secondary and then to tertiary sectors. Sociologist Daniel Bell proposed a model in three general stages. Preindustrial, industrial and post-industrial societies.

PREINDUSTRIAL SOCIETY

The principal activities are agriculture, fishing, forestry, and mining. Technology is simple, and productivity is low. People depend on their bodies to get things done. Success depends on nature, the climate and on soil quality. The social unit is the family and extended household. People seek only enough to feed themselves. Many people are employed in household services.

Before 1900 in the US.
1. More than 80% workforce in Agriculture sector
2. Service occupations mostly were domestic servants and sailors
3. Family relationships and tradition important.
4. Education and innovation are not important
5. Quality of life dependent on nature

INDUSTRIAL SOCIETY

The dominant activities are associated with the production of goods. Economic and social life has become mechanized and more efficient. Productivity is improved. Focus on optimization. Division of labor is further extended. Technological advancements support constant improvement of machines. The workplace is where men, women, materials, and machines are organized for efficient production and distribution of goods. The unit of social life is the individual in a free market society. Quantity of goods possessed by an individual is an indicator of his standard of living

1900 TO 1950
1. Important activity goods production.
2. Quality of life measured by goods.
3. Focus on maximizing the productivity of labor and machines.
4. Extreme division of labor
5. Dehumanizing jobs.

THE EVOLVING FOCUS OF DESIGN PRACTICE

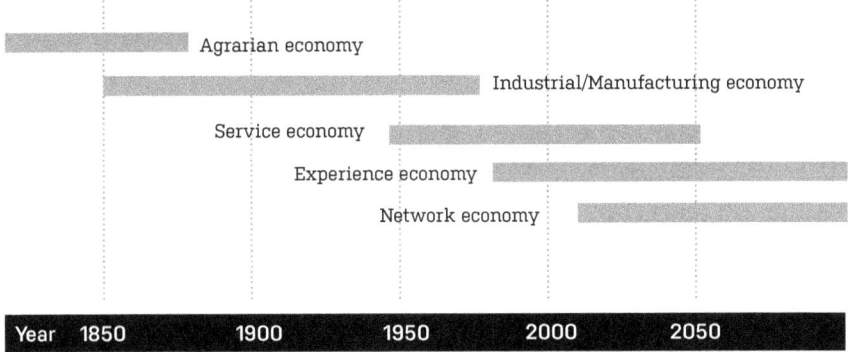

Adapted from a framework proposed by Brand and Rocchi 2011 in a Philips Design document entitled "Rethinking Value in a Changing Landscape".

BELLS STAGES OF ECONOMIC DEVELOPMENT

SOCIETY	PRE-INDUSTRIAL	INDUSTRIAL	POST-INDUSTRIAL
Game	Against Nature	Against fabricated nature	Among Persons
Predominant Activity	Agriculture, Mining	Goods, Production	Services
Use of Human Labor	Raw Muscle Power	Machine tending	Artistic, Creative, Intellectual
Unit of Social Life	Extended Household	Individual	Community
Standard of Living Measure	Subsistence	Quantity of Goods	Quality of life in terms of health, education, recreation
Structure	Routine, Traditional, Authoritative	Bureaucratic, Hierarchical	Interdependent, Global
Technology	Simple hand tools	Machines	Information

This framework was first proposed by sociologist Daniel Bell

6. "Manual workers" outnumber "white collar workers."

Source: . Adapted from: Theories Explaining the Growth of Services

POSTINDUSTRIAL SOCIETY

Activities focused on service production, information and knowledge. Networks of people. The central character of economic life is the professional. Higher education a prerequisite to entry into postindustrial society. The quantity and quality of services are indicators of standard of living. The inadequacy of the market mechanism in meeting service demands leads to the growth of government.

Expansion of services is needed for the development of industry and distribution of goods. Expansion of service industries. The percentage of money devoted to food declines. Increments in income are first spent for durable consumer goods, such as housing, automobiles, and appliances. Further increases in revenue are devoted to services such as education, healthcare, vacations, travel, restaurants, entertainment, and sports.

AFTER 1950

1. Service-producing industries increased from 50% to 80% of GDP in US.
2. Health, education, & recreation measures of quality of life.
3. Service experiences dominate economic value.
4. Workers value based on judgment, creativity & theoretical reasoning
5. Increase in efficiency of agriculture and manufacturing releases labor to services.
6. Workers move from rural locations to cities.
7. A decrease in investment as a percentage of gross domestic product in high-income industrialized countries.
8. A rise in per capita income.
9. Deregulation.
10. Demographic shifts.
11. An increase in international trade.
12. The symbiotic growth of services with manufacturing.
13. Advances in information and telecommunication technologies.
14. People pursue more sophisticated needs (Maslow "hierarchy of needs)

Source: Adapted from Service Management: An Integrated Approach to Supply Chain Management and Operations Cengiz Haksever and Barry Render 2013

WHY SERVICE DESIGN IS ONE OF THE FASTEST-GROWING AREAS OF DESIGN
INDUSTRY % SHARE OF TOTAL EMPLOYMENT

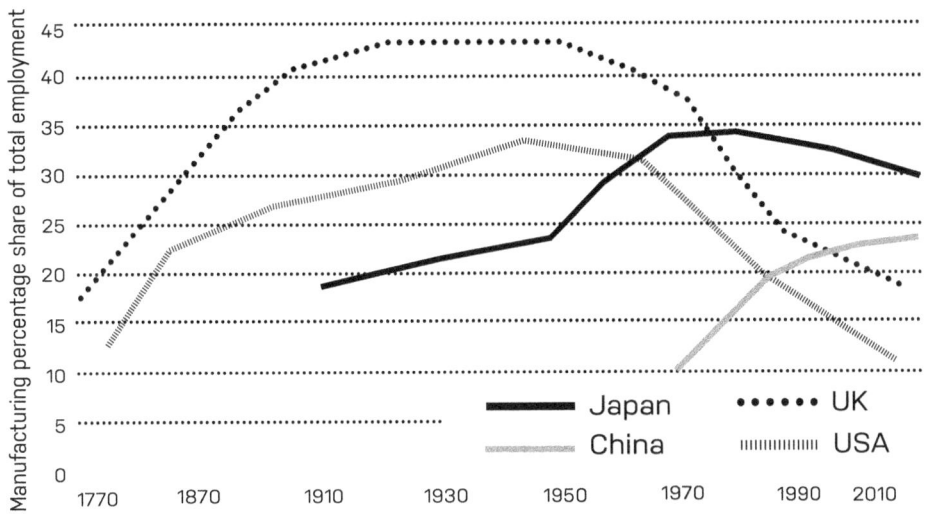

Adapted from "China's Future in the Knowledge Economy" by Peter Sheehan
ANote: scale condensed before 1900

DISTRIBUTION OF US LABOR FORCE
1840 TO 2010 % OF TOTAL WORKFORCE
Source: Bureau of Economic Analysis, National Income and Product Accounts

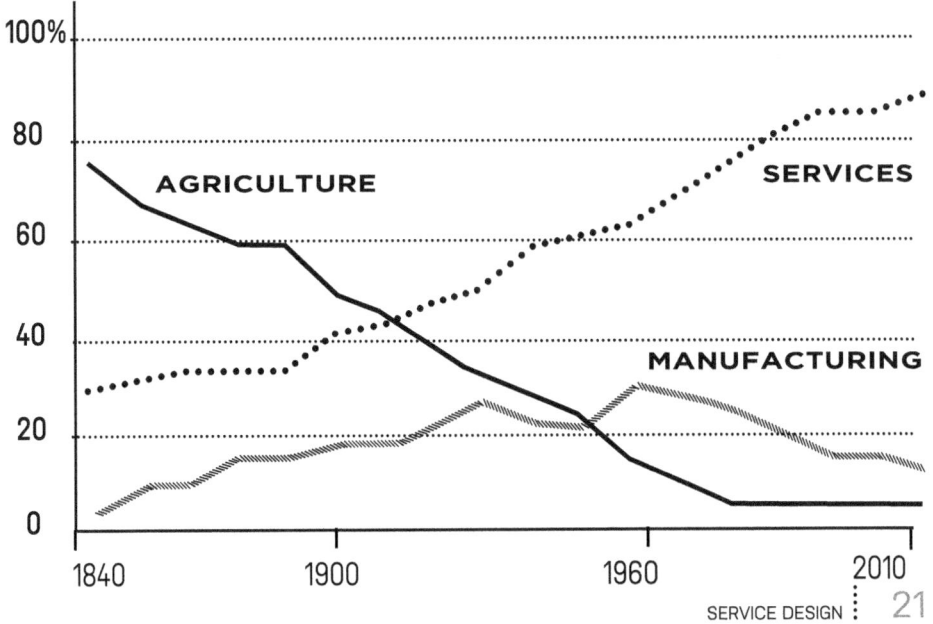

SERVICE DESIGN

SERVITIZATION

WHAT

Servitization is a shift from selling product to selling product-service systems.

The growth of Design Thinking is closely linked to the growing economic importance of service industry. Design Thinking with its emphasis on team collaboration and user experience is the best approach for designing services and product service systems.

A study of 50,000 servitized and non-servitized French firms between 1997 and 2007 concluded that servitized firms are more profitable, employ more workers and have higher total sales than non-servitized firms. "Firms that start selling services increase their profitability by 3.7% to 5.3%, increase their numbers of employees by 30%, and boost their sales of good by 3.6% on average."

Source: Matthieu Crozet & Emmanuel Milet The effect of servitization on manufacturing firm performance 2015 Universite de Geneve

TYPES OF PRODUCT SERVICE SYSTEMS

1. Product Oriented: This is a where the consumer has a tangible product, and services, such as maintenance contracts, are provided.
2. Use Oriented: This is where the service provider owns the product and sells services, such as sharing, pooling, and leasing.
3. Result Oriented: This is a where products are replaced by services, such as, for example, voice-mail.
4. Solution-oriented: For example, selling a promised level of heat transfer instead of radiators.
5. Effect oriented: For example, selling a promised temperature level instead of selling radiators
6. Demand-fulfillment oriented: For example, selling a guaranteed level of thermal comfort for building occupants instead of heaters."

WHY SERVITIZE?

1. Manufacturing firms in developed economies cannot compete on cost.
2. Technology is allowing the development of new services.
3. Competitive opportunities.
4. Installed base. For every new car there are 13 existing. 4 chairs for every person in the

world. 15 aircraft for each new aircraft.
5. Services have a large potential for growing profits. Grows revenue streams Additional revenue from existing customers.
6. On average manufacturers report a growth in services revenue of 5 to 10% per year.

Source Aston Centre For Servitization Research.

7. Better cash flow.
8. Environmental benefits. De-materialization and investment in cleaner technologies.
9. Selling a Solution, in Addition to a Product:
10. Greater Financial Stability:
11. Stronger Customer Retention Rate:
12. Industrial Internet of Things growing in Importance.

Source: What is Servitization and Why Should Manufacturers Care?

STRATEGIC RATIONALE
1. Lock in customers.
2. Lockout competitors.
3. Increase differentiation.
4. Customers want services.

Source: Professor Andy Neely University of Cambridge

CHALLENGES FOR SERVITIZATION
Challenges include:
5. Leadership support
6. investments to develop and implement services and solutions.
7. Mind-set and capabilities of the organisation to selling and delivering services and solutions
8. Defining and creating a clear strategy.
9. Creating organizational infrastructure.
10. Develop capabilities for designing and delivering services.
11. Creating an organizational culture with the values supporting service design and delivery, including customer orientation, flexibility and innovation.
12. Coordinate and align the development of new products. integrated with new services
13. Involve customers in the process.
14. Create the necessary flexibility and adaptability to enable customization.
15. Formulate attractive value propositions through better understanding of customer needs.
16. Ensure that the quality of service provision lives up to customer expectations.
17. Develop trustful relationships
18. Manage the geographical and cultural distances in a globally distributed network of service partners.
19. Lock out competitors.
20. Increase differentiation
21. Customers want services.

Source: Driving Competitiveness Through Servitization A Guide For Practitioners Avlonitis, Frandsen, Hsuan & Karlsson

IMPLEMENTING SERVITIZATION FROM GOODS-CENTERED TO CUSTOMER-CENTERED SOLUTIONS

	Manufacturing Solution	Service Customer-centered Solution
Underlying Business logic	Products	Solutions
Customization	Standard product	Customizable
Integration	Low	High
Scope	Narrow	Wide
Delivery process	Transactional	Relationship
Outcome	Functioning product	Value for customers
Design driven	From manufacturer forward	From customer backward
Physicality	Tangible	Intangible
Output	Goods	An experience
Production	Produced	Co-produced
Consumption	Transferred and used	Consumed as produced
Dimensions	Length breadth height	Experience and time

Source: adapted from Filippo Visintin Aalto University 2012

SERVICE INDUSTRY GROWTH IN CHINA

SERVICES NOW ACCOUNT FOR A HIGHER PERCENTAGE OF GDP THAN MANUFACTURING

In the first 11 months of 2015, China registered 3.9 million new companies, up 19 percent, with more than four-fifths in services, according to the State Administration for Industry and Commerce.

China's service sector now employs more than 300 million people, the largest share of the country's 775 million workers. The fastest growth has been in low-end jobs in retail, restaurants, hotels, and real estate. Over the last five years, education and government jobs, most of which are filled by college graduates, have fallen from a little less than half of total service employment to a third or so. Finance's share has also fallen, says Albert Park, professor of economics at Hong Kong University of Science and Technology. "The higher-skilled sectors—telecoms, information technology, computers, finance, and business services—are still not a large share of the total service industry," he says. "And while some are growing, they aren't growing very quickly."

Source: China Trumpets Its Service Economy - Bloomberg
https://www.bloomberg.com/news/articles/2016-01-28/china-trumpets-its-service-economy

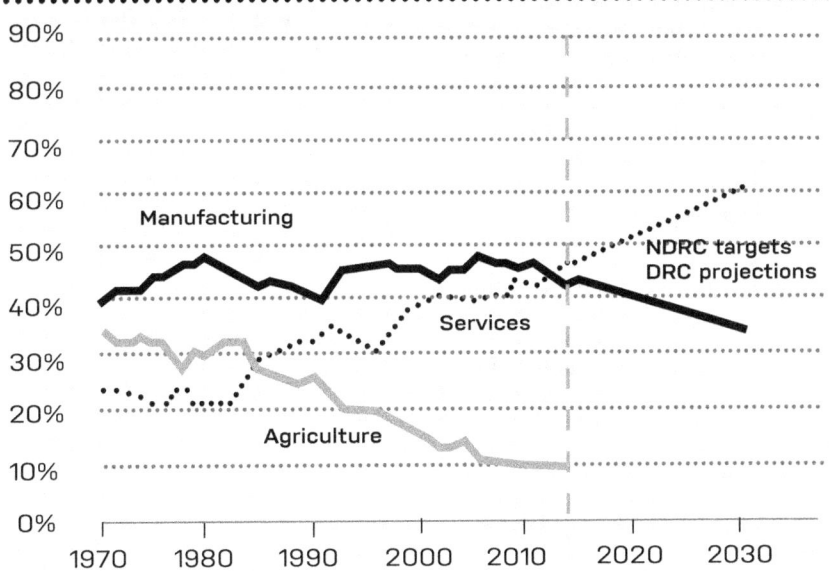

PERCENTAGE OF CHINA'S GDP FROM SERVICES

Source: Adapted from EIA

SERVICE DESIGN

WHY DESIGN SERVICES?

The reasons to design services are varied:

1. To give an organization an understanding of changing market needs and desires.
2. To create more value with existing resources
3. To create more effective services
4. To create more efficient services
5. To create higher quality service experiences
6. To differentiate services from competitors
7. To better align services and brand.
8. To plan future service offerings
9. Costs can be reduced, by integrating the service and products
10. Increasing service revenue.
11. Improved forecasting.
12. Improve customer satisfaction levels.
13. To ensure that new services are consistent with other services.
14. To ensure that technology and management systems are consistent with new services.
15. To ensure that roles responsibilities and skills are able to support new services.

"

Service design is exploring the interconnectedness of people, work-flows, tools, and products to create systems, offerings, interactions, and experiences.

Meredith DeZutter
Service designer at the Center for Innovation at the Mayo Clinic in Rochester, Minnesota.

"

Service Design is not a new specialist design discipline. It is a new multi-disciplinary platform of expertise. Born in design thinking it integrates various fields of expertise.

Moritz

SERVICE DESIGN NETWORK MANIFESTO

In 2004, the Service Design Network was launched by Köln International School of Design, Carnegie Mellon University, Linköpings Universitet, Politecnico di Milano and Domus Academy to create an international network for service design academics and professionals. In the first joint manifest of the network, Service Design and its approach was described in the manifesto "[Service Design] is an emerging discipline and an existing body of knowledge, which can dramatically improve the productivity and quality of services.

Service Design provides a systematic and creative approach to:
1. Meeting service organizations' need to be competitive
2. Meeting customers' rising expectations of choice and quality
3. Making use of the technologies' revolution, that multiplies the possibilities for creating, delivering and consuming services
4. Answering the pressing environmental, social and economic challenges to sustainability
5. Fostering innovative social models and behaviors
6. Sharing knowledge & learning

The Service Design approach is uniquely oriented to service specific design needs and is rooted in the design culture. The Service Designer contributes crucial competencies. The Service Designer can:
1. Visualize, express and choreograph what other people can't see, envisage solutions that do not yet exist
2. Observe and interpret needs and behaviors and transform them into possible service futures express and evaluate, in the language of experiences, the quality of design
3. Service Design aims to create services that are Useful, Usable, Desirable, Efficient & Effective
4. Service Design is a human-centered approach that focuses on customer experience and the quality of service encounter as the key value for success.
5. Service Design is a holistic approach, which considers in an integrated way strategic, system, process and touchpoint design decisions.
6. Service Design is a systematic and iterative process that integrates user-oriented, team-based, interdisciplinary approaches and methods, in ever-learning cycles."

Service Design - Design is Not Just for Products .., https://www.interaction-design.org/literature/article/service-design-design-is-n (accessed June 25, 2016).

THE DESIGN LADDER

Companies often start at stage one then progress to higher levels. At the beginning of the 5-year study, 36% of 1,000 companies were at stage 1 by the end of the study only 15% of companies remained at stage 1. Companies that were using design only as styling were growing slower on average than companies not using design at all.

Stage 4

Design as Strategy

Design is a key strategic means of supporting innovation. These companies have VPs of Design. Design connected to all business decisions. The cross-disciplinary approach of service design helps place an organization at this level of the ladder.

Stage 3

Design as Process

Design is integral to the development process. Design is often a sub-department of marketing or engineering. Companies may have cross-disciplinary teams.

Stage 2

Design as Styling

Design focuses on and aesthetics. Traditional design education can deliver designers whose primary goals are creative and artistic self-fulfillment, fame and awards rather than team business goals, technological innovation, and user needs.

Stage 1

No design

Design plays no role in product and service development

Source: Danish Design Center study of 1,000 companies 2003

THE DESIGN LADDER IN RELATION TO SUCCESS IN EXPORT

	EXPORT IN % OF TURNOVER	
	AVERAGE	NUMBER OF COMPANIES
STEP 4 DESIGN AS INNOVATION	26.34%	131
STEP 3 DESIGN AS PROCESS	22.67%	330
STEP 2 DESIGN AS STYLING	16.48%	125
STEP 1 NON-DESIGN	12.21%	342
TOTAL	18.5%	927

"There are marked differences regarding exports according to the step on the design ladder. The export share of turnover is considerably larger in companies on the highest level than for those companies that do not employ design – and the share rises progressively according to the design-ladder level. The largest increase in export share of turnover is achieved where a systematic approach to design has been adopted, namely, companies that employ professional designers and purchase design externally. The increase in exports is twice the size of companies that employ designers and purchase design externally (33.5%) compared to companies that neither employ designers nor purchase design externally (17.6 %). *Source: "The Economic Effects of Design" 2003 Denmark*

AVERAGE GROWTH IN TURNOVER

Based on study of 1000 companies and their position on the Design Ladder Danish. Design Center study 2003

Stage 4. Service design is a strategic approach to design and so is more likely to support faster organizational growth. **9.0%**

Stage 3. Design is integral to the development process. Companies may have cross-disciplinary teams. **8.9%**

Stage 2. Companies seeing design only as aesthetics in the Danish study. Turnover grew slower than companies not using design at all. **6.5%**

Stage 1. Design plays no role in product service development **7.4%**

0   10   20   30   40   50   60   70   80   90   100

SERVICE DESIGN

STORYTELLING

WHAT

A powerful story can help ensure the success of a new product, service or experience. Storytelling can be an effective method of presenting a point of view. Research can uncover meaningful stories from the end that illustrate needs or desires. These stories can become the basis of new designs or actions and be used to support decisions. Research shows that our attitudes, fears, hopes, and values are strongly influenced by story. Stories can be an effective way of communicating complex ideas and inspiring people to change. Characters are a good way to express human needs and generate empathy from your audience

THE BIG QUESTIONS
1. Who are we presenting to?
2. Why are we presenting to them?
3. How do we want them to respond?

STORY STRUCTURE
A story has a beginning, a middle, and an end. It details events and orders them in a way that creates meaning. Stories speak to accomplishments and inspire action.

NARRATIVE
Relates separate events to a central theme but doesn't seek resolution. In a presentation, the narrative encompasses the past, present, and future. "Where we've come from. Where we are. Where we're headed." The narrative is the overarching emphasis of a presentation. Start with the narrative. Advance the Narrative with Stories. Support stories visually.

Source: Micah Bowers

AN EFFECTIVE STORY
1. Answer in your story: What, why, when, who, where, how?
2. Offer a new vantage point
3. Share emotion
4. Communicate transformations
5. Communicate who you are.
6. Show cause and effect Describe conflicts and resolution.
7. Speak from your experience.
8. Describe how actions created change
9. Omit what is irrelevant.
10. Reveal meaning
11. Share your passion
12. Be honest and real
13. Build trust
14. Show connections
15. Transmits values
16. Share a vision
17. Share knowledge
18. Your story should differentiate you.
19. Meets information needs for your audience
20. Offer a new vantage point
21. Tell real-world stories
22. Evoke the future
23. Share emotion
24. Communicate transformations.
25. Communicate who you are.
26. Describe actions.
27. Show cause and effect
28. Speak from your experience.
29. Describe how actions created change
30. Omit what is irrelevant.
31. Share your passion
32. Be honest and real
33. Build trust
34. Transmit values
35. Share a vision
36. Share knowledge
37. Use humor

38. Engage the audience
39. Craft the story for your audience.
40. Pose a problem and offer a resolution
41. Use striking imagery
42. The audience must be able to act on your story.

PLAN YOUR STORY
Plan what you are going to say and how you are going to say it. Describe the the transformation of your character in one sentence. Start with a dozen bullet points describing what you want to say.

Your story should have
1. Action,
2. Conflict
3. Transformation

What is your character trying to do? What stands in the way? What is the insight of your story? What does your character learn?

> *A character who sees things the way we'd see them gets to a strange place, observes things that interest him (or her), is transformed by what he sees, and fantastic new product or service that we're designing and realize how it can help make their life just that little bit better."*

Chelsea Hostetter

AUDIENCE
Think about the elements – plot, setting, characters, conflict, and resolution in relation to the audience. What is going to resonate with your audience?
include a bit of yourself.

CONTEXT
Think about the context of where your audience are hearing the story and what they are doing there. When you introduce your characters outline the context that surrounds them and what led them to this place.

HOW
How are you going to tell your story? How much backstory will you need to give? Are you going to need any artifacts, such as storyboards?

BE AUTHENTIC
Describe how one of your personas will experience the design.

FOCUS ON WHAT'S IMPORTANT
Focus on what is most important to your audience and how the design will meet their unmet needs.

BE VISUAL
Use photos, video, prototypes, storyboards or sketches to support your story.

Source: Adapted from Chelsea Hostetter, Austin Centre for Design

ASK FOR FEEDBACK FROM YOUR AUDIENCE
Engage your audience. Ask them for feedback.

CHALLENGES
1. A story with too much jargon will lose an audience.
2. Not everyone has the ability to tell vivid stories.
3. Stories are not always generalizable.

HUMAN NEEDS

	BEING (PERSONAL OR COLLECTIVE ATTRIBUTES)	HAVING (INSTITUTIONS, NORMS, TOOLS)
SUBSISTENCE	Physical health, mental health, equilibrium, sense of humor, adaptability	Food., shelter. work
PROTECTION	Care, adaptability, autonomy, equilibrium, solidarity	Insurance systems, savings, social security, health systems, rights, family, work
AFFECTION	Self-esteem, solidarity, respect, tolerance, generosity, receptiveness, passion, determination, sensuality, sense of humor	Friendships, partners, family, partnerships, relationships with nature
UNDERSTANDING	Critical conscience, receptiveness, curiosity, discipline intuition, rationality	Literature, teachers, method, educational and communication policies
PARTICIPATION	Adaptability, receptiveness, solidarity, willingness, determination, respect, passion, sense of humor	Rights, responsibilities, duties, privileges, work
LEISURE	Curiosity, receptiveness, imagination, recklessness, sense of humor, lack of worry, tranquility, sensuality	Games, spectacles, clubs, parties, peace of mind
CREATION	Passion, determination, intuition, imagination, boldness, rationality, autonomy, inventiveness, curiosity	Abilities, skills, methods, work
IDENTITY	Sense of belonging, consistency, differentiation, self-esteem, assertiveness	Symbols, language, religions, habits, customs, reference groups, roles, groups, sexuality, values, norms, historic memory, work
FREEDOM	Autonomy, self-esteem, determination, passion, assertiveness, open-mindedness, boldness, rebelliousness, tolerance	Equal rights

HUMAN NEEDS

	DOING (PERSONAL OR COLLECTIVE ACTIONS)	INTERACTING (SPACES OR ATMOSPHERES)
SUBSISTENCE	Feed, procreate, rest, work.	Living environment, social setting.
PROTECTION	Co-operate. prevent. plan, take care of, cure. help.	Living space, social environment, dwelling.
AFFECTION	Make love, express emotions. share, .take care of. cultivate, appreciate.	Privacy, intimacy, home, Spaces of togetherness.
UNDERSTANDING	Investigate, study, educate, experiment, meditate, interpret.	Settings of formative interaction, schools, and universities academies groups. communities. family.
PARTICIPATION	Become affiliated, cooperate, propose. share, dissent. obey, interact, agree on, express opinions.	Settings of participative Interaction, parties. associations, communities, neighborhoods, family.
LEASURE	Day-dream, brood, dream recall old times, give way to fantasies, remember. relax, have fun, play.	Privacy, intimacy, spaces of closeness, free time, surroundings, landscapes.
CREATION	Work, invent, build, design, compose, interpret.	Productive and feedback settings, workshops, cultural groups, audiences, spaces for expression, temporal freedom.
IDENTITY	Commit oneself, integrate oneself. confront, decide on, get to know oneself, recognize oneself, actualize oneself, grow.	Social rhythms, every day belongs to. maturation stages
FREEDOM	Dissent, choose to be different from, run risks, develop awareness. commit oneself, disobey, meditate	36/ Temporal/special plasticity

Adapted from Matrix of needs and satisfiers. I. Cruz. A. Stahel . M. Max-Neef 2009

BALANCE

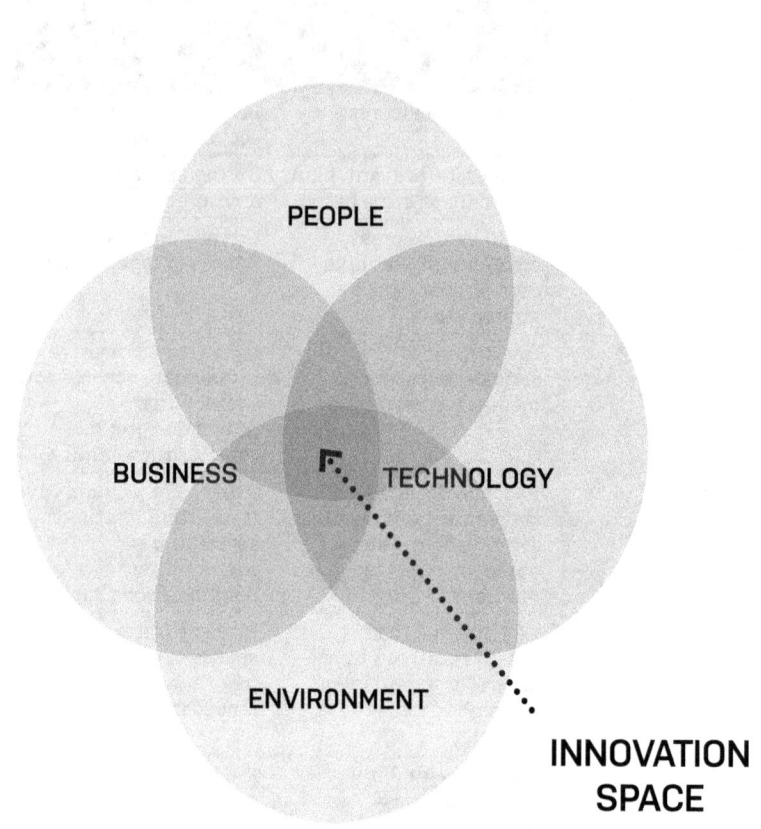

Larry Keeley innovation strategist, devised his triangle as a way of expressing how successful businesses are balanced in the concerns about the desirability, technical feasibility and financial viability of their products and services. To the three factors listed by Keeley, this author would like to add the environment to recognize the role of designers in designing for the environmental challenges we face.

SHOSHIN: THE BEGINNER'S MIND

WHAT

The phrase shoshin means beginner's mind. It refers to having an attitude of full of openness, enthusiasm, and fresh perspectives in learning something new, eagerness, and lack of preconceptions even at an advanced level, like a child.

Shoshin also means "correct truth" and is used to describe a genuine signature on a work of art. It is used to describe something that is perfectly genuine.

WHERE DID IT ORIGINATE?
1. Shoshin is a term from Zen Buddhism and Japanese martial arts.

HOW
1. Withhold judgment. Do not suggest that an idea will not work or that it has negative side-effects. All ideas are potentially good so do not judge them until afterward.
2. Observe and Listen
3. Ask why
4. Be curious
5. Look for new connections

WHY
1. Sometimes expertise can create closed-mindedness.
2. Our assumptions can stand in the way of creating new ideas. A beginner is not aware of biases that can stand in the way of a good new idea.
3. Our experience is an asset but our assumptions may be misconceptions and stereotypes.
4. Innovation often requires looking at a problem in a new way.
5. Beginner's minds can help make breakthroughs
6. Observe and engage users without value judgments.
7. Question your assumptions. Ask why?
8. Be curious and explore.
9. Search for patterns and connections no one else has seen.
10. Be open and listen

Source: http://blog.triode.ca

The older you get as a designer, the more you realize that you just don't know anything. If you can embrace that you don't know, but you know how to go find out, that makes you very effective."

Daniel Burka
Google Ventures

SERVICE DESIGN SPACES

WHAT
An adequate office helps concentrate the energy of the team and build connections between team members.

HOW

PHYSICAL ENVIRONMENT FOR SERVICE DESIGN
1. Space should be flexible.
2. Space should be capable of being personalized.
3. Space should support interaction.
4. Size of working space in a service design office should be adequate in relation to the amount of workers.
5. According to Kelley and Littman (2001) large and empty, as well as, small and cramped offices suppress the creative work
6. All employees have an equal workplace.
7. Each person has an access to an individual, personal working area
8. The space allows project teams to come together for group work within seconds.
9. Space devoted only to the particular team for the whole length of their project.
10. The design team can keep and access all of project related materials
11. Space is customizable.
12. Every employee has to be able to create a personally most suiting and stimulating space (Kelley & Littman 2001, 123–125).
13. Personalization is done through group decisions of furniture setting.
14. Every employee has a say in how the overall office space looks like.
15. Furniture and people are flexible and easily movable to ensure the best setting for each project and team (Brown 2009, 34–35; Kelley & Littman 2001, 123–125).
16. Common areas are designed to increase human interaction.

SPACES FOR CREATIVE WORK HAWORTH RECOMMENDATIONS
1. Lightweight, comfortable, readily movable chairs perhaps on wheels can maximize a relatively small footprint and be arranged in multiple configurations
2. Show your work in progress and let people comment.
3. Surround yourself with the material that your team is working on.
4. Mobile large White-boards 6 ft x 4 ft and pin boards.
5. Mobile boards can have a magnetic White-board on one side and a pin board on

the reverse side.
6. A laptop-sized surface for each attendee
7. Walls can be used for projection, writing, or pinning up information in areas visible to everyone
8. Acoustic privacy should be ensured.
9. Large walls can be used as display spaces.
10. Use work tools that are easily accessible
11. Think of every vertical surface as a potential space for displaying work
12. Use flexible technologies such as wi-fi that allow relocation of services such as Internet and power connections.
13. Have a projector and screen
14. Seating should allow all participants to see one another and read body language
15. Select furniture with wheels that can be easily moved
16. Small tables can be used for breakouts or grouped into a common surface
17. Ample writing and display areas, as well as surfaces for laying things out, support the need for visual cues and reference materials
18. Provide a large area of vertical displays such as walls Whiteboards, pin boards, foam core boards, projection surfaces, that allow users to actively and flexibly interact with the information
19. Build spaces that support different types of collaboration.
20. Consider physical and virtual collaboration.
21. Spaces should be flexible for unplanned collaboration.
22. Provide comfortable group areas for informal interactions and information sharing.
23. The spaces need to be large enough to accommodate all the research materials, visuals, and prototypes in order to keep them visible and accessible all of the time.

Collaborative Spaces - media. haworth.com, http://media.haworth. com/asset/28519/Collaborative%20 Spaces Whitepaper_C2..pdf

TACIT KNOWLEDGE

WHAT
Tacit knowledge is the knowledge that is gained through personal experience. Examples of tacit knowledge are the ability to ride a bicycle or recognizing someone's face. Tacit knowledge is difficult to pass on to another person by writing it down or describing it. Tacit knowledge is a form of intellectual property. Tacit knowledge includes best practices, stories, experience, wisdom, and insights.

WHO FIRST USED THE TERM?
Michael Polanyi 1958

WHY
1. Tacit knowledge is valuable to any organization.

CHALLENGES
1. Mapping tacit knowledge needs immersion in context.
2. A researcher can map behavior and perceptions.

HOW
The methods of capturing tacit knowledge include:
1. Interviews
2. Observation

RESOURCES
Camera
Notepad computer
Digital voice recorder

QUALITATIVE RESEARCH

WHAT
Qualitative or ethnographic research is a core part of the approach of service design. It seeks to understand people in the context of their daily experiences. Uses ethnographic methods including observation and interviews. Aims to understand questions like why and how. Obtains insights about attitudes and emotions. Often uses small sample sizes. Seeks to see the world through the eyes of research subjects. Methods are flexible. Used to develop an initial understanding.

WHO INVENTED IT?
The Royal Statistical Society founded in 1834 pioneered the use of quantitative methods. Early examples of ethnographers include Malinowski 1922, Radcliffe Brown, Margaret Mead, Gregory Bateson and Franz Boas, all of whom studied 'native' populations abroad, and Robert Park and the work of the Chicago school where the focus was on the life and culture of local groups in the city.

CHALLENGES
1. Concerned with validity
2. Subjective
3. Hard to recreate results
4. People may behave differently to the way they say they behave
5. Experiences cannot be generalized.
6. Methods are static. Real-world changes.
7. Structured methods
8. Difficult to control the environment
9. Can be expensive if studying a large number of people.

HOW
1. Define research question
2. Select research subjects and context to study.
3. Collect data
4. Interpret data.
5. Study data for insights
6. Collect more data
7. Analyze data

QUESTIONS TO CONSIDER

PEOPLE

1. What user group does this service or experience target?
2. What problems or needs does our product help with for this group?
3. When and how and where is our product, service or experience used?
4. What features are most important to end users?
5. How should our service or experience look and work?
6. Who should we employ?
7. What external partners do we need?
8. What does the customer need?
9. What does the customer want?
10. How does the customer learn to use this product or service?
11. What is the experience when the customer enters this experience?
12. How does the customer purchase or initiate this experience?
13. How does the customer interact with each touchpoint?
14. How are customers retained?
15. What are the barriers to a customer returning?

What is the process if a customer has an unsatisfactory experience?

16. We will know this assumption is true when we see:
- What market feedback?
- What quantitative measure?
- What qualitative insight?

BUSINESS

1. We will make money by:
2. Our customers will find our service or experience valuable because:
3. We will acquire customers through:
4. It will cost how much to establish these products or services. It will cost how much per month/year to offer these services and maintain our business.
5. Establishing these or services will be funded by:
6. My primary competition of brand and products in the market will be:
7. We will eat them because:
8. Our biggest business risk is:
9. We will reduce this risk by:
10. What could cause our business to fail?

TECHNOLOGY

Why do particular technologies/ materials/ processes/ finishes offer a strategic advantage?

THINKING STYLES

ABDUCTIVE THINKING

Abductive reasoning is the core thinking approach in service design. With abductive reasoning, unlike deductive reasoning, the premises do not guarantee the conclusion. Abductive reasoning can be understood as "inference to the best explanation" Abductive reasoning typically begins with an incomplete set of observations and proceeds to the likeliest possible explanation. Its goal is to explore what could possibly be true. Abductive thinking allows designers to find solutions in ambiguous, changing situations. It is the thinking approach necessary for innovation. Abductive thinking finds solutions by creating prototypes and testing and improving the designs. This mode of thinking wasn't taught in management, science and engineering schools. It doesn't start with clearly defined evidence.

"
A person or organization instilled with that discipline is constantly seeking a fruitful balance between reliability and validity, between art and science, between intuition and analytics, and between exploration and exploitation. The design-thinking organization applies the designer's most crucial tool to the problems of business. That tool is abductive reasoning."

Roger Martin

Charles Sanders Peirce originated the term and argued that no new idea could come from inductive or deductive logic.

1. **Abductive logic**: The logic of what might be.
2. **Deductive logic** reasons from the general to the specific.
3. **Inductive logic** reasons from the specific to the general.

DEDUCTIVE THINKING

The process of reasoning from one or more general statements (premises) to reach a logically certain conclusion. Deductive reasoning is one of the two basic forms of valid reasoning. It begins with a general hypothesis or known fact and creates a specific conclusion from that generalization.

Described by Aristotle 384-322bce, Plato 428-347bce, and Pythagoras 582-500 BCE

INDUCTIVE THINKING

Inductive thinking is a kind of reasoning that constructs or evaluates general propositions that are derived from specific examples. Inductive reasoning contrasts with deductive reasoning, in which specific examples are derived from general propositions. Described by Aristotle 384-322 BCE.

CRITICAL THINKING

"The process of actively and skillfully conceptualizing, applying, analyzing, synthesizing, and evaluating information to reach an answer or conclusion. disciplined thinking that is clear, rational, open-minded, and informed by evidence, willingness to integrate new or revised perspectives into our ways of thinking and acting". Critical thinking is an important element of all professional fields and academic disciplines."

DESIGN THINKING

Design Thinking is not a style of thinking. Design Thinking is a formal method for practical, creative resolution of problems and creation of solutions, with the intent of an improved future result. In this regard it is a form of solution-based, or solution-focused thinking

Source: Deductive, Inductive and Abductive Reasoning - TIP Sheet.

Historically most organizations were managed by divergent or analytical thinkers. Over the last ten years, this has changed.

Silicon Valley didn't think a designer could build and run a company. They were straight up about it. We weren't MBAs, we weren't two PhD students from Stanford."

Brian Chesky
Co-founder of AirBnb
Graduate of the Rhode Island School of Design

Coming up with a way to fix mistakes challenges your creativity and your critical thinking skills and your resourcefulness. Often you end up with something better than what you planned on in the first place."

Mark Frauenfelder

DIVERGENT AND CONVERGENT THINKING

DIVERGENT THINKING

Divergent thinking is a thought process or method used to generate creative ideas by exploring many possible solutions. Divergent thinking occurs in a spontaneous, free-flowing, 'nonlinear' manner.

During the divergent phase of design the designer creates a number of choices. The goal of this approach is to analyze alternative approaches to test for the most stable solution. Divergent thinking is what we do when we do not know the answer when we do not know the next step. Divergent thinking is followed by convergent thinking, in which a designer assesses, judges, and strengthens those options.

A study by J.A. Horne, and a separate study by Ullrich Wagner and his colleagues in Germany have shown that sleep loss can significantly impair creativity.

Left brain people are said to be more rational, analytic, and controlling, while right brain people are said to be more intuitive, creative, emotionally expressive and spontaneous. There is evidence that regions of the right hemisphere have a role in what is called divergent thinking and creative problem-solving.

CONVERGENT THINKING

The psychologist J.P. Guilford first coined the terms convergent thinking and divergent thinking in 1956. The design process is a series of divergent and convergent phases.

This process is systematic and linear. This kind of thinking is particularly appropriate in science, engineering, maths and technology. Convergent thinking is opposite from divergent thinking in which a person generates many unique, design solutions to a design problem.

The design process is a series of divergent and convergent phases. During the divergent phase of design the designer creates a number of choices. The goal of this approach is to analyze alternative approaches to test for the most stable solution. Divergent thinking is what we do when we do not know the answer, when we do not know the next step. Divergent thinking is followed by convergent thinking, in which a designer assesses, judges, and strengthens those options.

On his account, the left brain is specialized for convergent thinking, while the right brain is specialized for divergent thinking.

TRIANGULATION

WHAT

Denzin (1978) defined triangulation as "the combination of methodologies in the study of the same phenomenon".

Triangulation is a powerful technique that facilitates validation of data through cross verification from two or more sources. to see if the different methods give similar findings. The researcher looks for patterns to develop or support an interpretation by comparing the results from two or more different research methods. The researcher looks for patterns of convergence to develop or corroborate an overall interpretation One example of triangulation is to compare observed behavior with the responses of a survey.

The term originates in surveying land where triangulation is used to create a map.

Denzin (1978) and Patton (1999) identify four types of triangulation:

1. Methods triangulation - checking out the consistency of findings generated by different data collection methods.
   - It is common to have qualitative and quantitative data in a study.
   - These elucidate complementary aspects of the same phenomenon.
   - Often the points were these data diverge are of great interest to the qualititive researcher and provide the most insights.
2. Triangulation of sources - examining the consistency of different data sources from within the same method. For example:
   - at different points in time
   - in public vs. private settings
   - comparing people with different viewpoints.
3. Analyst Triangulation - using multiple analysts to review findings or using multiple observers and analysts
   - This can provide a check on selective perception and illuminate blind spots in an interpretive analysis.
   - The goal is not to seek consensus, but to understand multiple ways of seeing the data.
   - Theory/perspective triangulation - using multiple theoretical perspectives to examine and interpret the data. *Source: qualres.org*

PRIMARY RESEARCH

WHAT
Primary research also called as field research involves collecting data first hand created during the time of the study. Primary research methods can include, including questionnaires and interviews and direct observations.

WHO INVENTED IT?
Robert W. Bruere of the Bureau of Industrial Research 1921 may have been the first to use the term.

WHY
You can collect this information yourself. There may be no secondary research available. It may be more reliable than secondary research. It may be more up to date than secondary research.

CHALLENGES
1. May be more expensive than secondary research.
2. Information may become obsolete
3. Large sample can be time-consuming

HOW
Methods such as:
1. Diaries
2. E-mail
3. Interviews
4. News footage
5. Photographs
6. Raw research data
7. Questionnaires
8. Observation

RESOURCES
Camera
Notebook
Pens
Digital Voice recorder
Diaries
E-mail

> *Every problem can be solved as long as you use common sense and apply the right research and techniques. "*
>
> Daymond John

SECONDARY RESEARCH

WHAT
Research data that conveys the opinions and experiences of others. Secondary research is the most widely used method of data collection. Secondary research accesses information that is already gathered from primary research.

WHO INVENTED IT?
Robert W. Bruere of the US Bureau of Industrial Research 1921 may have been the first to use the term secondary research.

WHY
1. Ease of access
2. Low cost
3. May be the only resource, for example, historical documents
4. Only way to examine large scale trends

CHALLENGES
1. Possible bias in sources
2. May be out of date
3. May not be aligned with research goals
4. Lack of consistency of perspective
5. Biases and inaccuracies
6. Data affected by context of its collection

HOW
1. Define goals.
2. Define the context of the problem to be researched.
3. Frame research questions.
4. Develop procedure.
5. Select and retrieve appropriate data.
6. Proceed with analysis and interpretation
7. Compare your findings and interpretations with other relevant studies.
8. Draw conclusions.

RESOURCES
Books
Internet
Online search engines
Magazines
E-books
Bibliographies
Biographical works
Commentaries, criticisms
Dictionaries, Encyclopedias
Histories;
Newspaper articles
Website

Steps in the research process - University of Hong Kong

SERVICE DESIGN

WHY USE MAPPING METHODS?

CRAFT A BETTER USER EXPERIENCE
1. Understand your customer's point of view.
2. Deliver a seamless, useful experience.
3. Bring more humanity to your business.
4. Designing the moments of truth
5. Identify those moments of a user experience that leave a lasting impression both positive or negative.
6. The entire company can focus on the vision of creating an exceptional customer experience.
7. Compare what your customers want with what your competitors are providing.
8. Understanding the ideal experience
9. Reveal the truth through your customer's eyes
10. Understand what customers think about your products and services rather than what you think they think.
11. Identify opportunities
12. When you understand where a customer experience is poor, it is an opportunity to improve your competitiveness and make your business more profitable. Evolve and stay competitive. Adapt to changing customer needs and expectations.
13. Empathize with your customers
14. Lack of understanding your customer's point of view is the number one reason new
15. Products and services fail. More than 50% of new goods and services fail in the market.
16. Get connected to your customers or end users
17. 80% Of service companies believe they offer superior services. Only 8% of their customers agree.
18. Develop more relevant products services and experiences for your customers or end users
19. Balance the needs of stakeholders more efficiently.
20. Diagnose experience problems.

IMPROVE YOUR BUSINESS PERFORMANCE
1. Strategic and tactical innovation.
2. Help all your employees and external stakeholders to contribute to the change process.
3. Improve business systems
4. Ensure systems are efficient,
5. And customer-focused.
6. Take cost & complexity out of the system.
7. Develop a better road map. Decide where you should be going with your business, what products and services you can and should be delivering and when it is best to introduce them. Build

strategic advantage against competitors.
8. Identify duplicated touchpoints and position people and other resources where they are most needed.
9. Prioritize competing deliverables
10. Plan how to allocate resources. Decide what should be the top priorities for your business to grow and generate the best returns on investment. Your decisions are guided by real customer data and feedback.
11. Plan for hiring. Plan strategically and select the best employees and skills for long-term expansion of your business.
12. Bring your whole organization together around the common goal of customer experience.
13. Understand the role that each department plays in a customer-focused strategy. Overcome silo thinking. Help different groups identify common ground.
14. Build and share knowledge. Build a common understanding both internally and externally.
15. Understand competitive positioning.
16. Knowledge of customer behaviors and needs across channels. Customers commonly access a number of different channels when engaging an organization. Understand complex processes across channels.
17. Drive ideation and innovation
18. Decide how to allocate resources to improve best current offerings or to build whole new sets of deliverables based on what customers need and want rather than what your employees think that they want, benchmark your current performance against competitors and help you plan future initiatives.
19. Make intangible services tangible
20. Understand where friction exists between the needs of different market segments
21. Various interested parties commonly have conflicting needs and desires.
22. Tailor your experiences more efficiently to different segment's needs
23. Understand the differences in their expectations and experience.
24. Introduce metrics for what matters most for your customers
25. Plan strategically to achieve long-term organizational goals and to measure progress towards those goals
26. Align your offerings to brand promise
27. Understand where your current business supports or conflicts with your brand promise.
28. Eliminate potential failure points
29. See where your customer experience is most likely to fail and to plan to reduce the

risk and cost of failure.
30. Improve efficiency
31. Break down organizational silos
32. Reduce duplication. Prioritize between competing requirements. Identify cheapest 'cost to serve', and set performance indicators that you can measure.
33. Imagine future product and service experiences
34. Plan and implement future product and service offerings.
35. Holistic thinking
36. Balance the competing needs of your customers, your business, and technology.
37. Improve your whole organization's performance
38. Work towards one goal of the best possible customer experience rather than multiple departmental goals
39. A living strategy
40. Improve and evolve your strategy as your business changes and your customer needs and expectations evolve.
41. Make better decisions
42. Ethnographic methods used by design thinking practitioners reduce the risk of design development by validating designs as they are being designed with end users.

I believe that all brands will become storytellers, editors and publishers, all stores will become magazines, and all media companies will become stores. There will be too many of all of them. The strongest ones, the ones who offer the best customer experience, will survive.

Natalie Massenet
Chair of the British Fashion Council

Making things people want is better than making people want things."

Customers want high-quality food, good service, and good store experience, and most retailers fail to deliver on those."

John Mackey

DESIGN ETHNOGRAPHY

WHAT
Design ethnography is a collection of methods that helps create better more compelling and meaningful design. It helps a designer understand the points of view of people who will use the designs. Ethnographers study and interpret culture, through fieldwork.

WHO INVENTED IT?
Bronisław Malinowski 1922

WHY
1. To inform the design and innovation processes rather than basing your designs on intuition.
2. To ensure that your design solutions resonate with the people that you are designing for.
3. Ethnography helps designers see beyond their preconceptions.

CHALLENGES
1. People may behave differently when they are in groups or alone.
2. Researchers need to be aware of the potential impacts of the research on the people and animals they study.

HOW
There are many different ethnographic techniques. Some of the general guidelines are:
3. Listen.
4. Observe.
5. Be empathetic and honest.
6. Do research in context, in the environments that the people you are studying live or work.
7. Influence your subject's behavior as little as possible with your presence.
8. Beware of bias.
9. Take photos and notes.
10. Have clear goals related to understanding and prediction.
11. Study representative people.

RESOURCES
Notepad computer
Pens
Post-it-notes
Video camera
Camera
Voice recorder
White-board
Dry-erase pens.

Source: Publication bias: raising awareness of a potential problem

SOME DISRUPTIVE TRENDS THAT NEED NEW DESIGN APPROACHES

The methods described in this book are a more effective approach than traditional applying traditional design skills like sketching when working with design problems that involve these types of complex, ill-defined and sometimes ambiguous global trends.

1. Being human in a digital world.
2. Entrepreneurship.
3. Focus on regional/ local characteristics
4. Growth of Asian markets
5. Information society
6. Internet of things. Connected devices.
7. Less predictable world.
8. Looking at the creative community holistically to tackle larger societal issues.
9. Massive data sets.
10. Move from transaction to experience society.
11. Multidisciplinary collaboration
12. Outsourcing.
13. Storytelling.
14. Tiny moments of value rather than big wow delight.
15. Urgency for innovation
16. Wearables.
17. a never- ending cycle of decisions and choices.
18. Design automation.
19. Service design in the public sector.
20. Data + Design
21. Brands will become less branded.
22. Design as a discipline becomes more accepted in the business world. Elevation of design.
23. Design Research is expanding to use intelligent tools such as machine learning.
24. T-shape designers. Designers are specialist in one area, while generalists in related fields.
25. Design metrics.
26. The war for talent. Growing challenges in talent recruitment.
27. Digital experiences have democratized luxury and elevated our standard of living.
28. Digital trust.
29. Continuing education. Education doesn't happen in college only, people get trained all their life.
30. Networking. "Everything is networked now," says Pinterest co-founder Evan Sharp, whom I interviewed for my project on designer founders. "All of culture, all of communications, it all is going through networks."
31. Artificial intelligence.
32. Machine learning.
33. Fortune 500 Design firm acquisitions.
34. Digital design.
35. Advertising and marketing budgets will be diverted to design.
36. Wisdom of crowds. Many individuals provide content and make decisions rather

than a few experts.
37. Mobile technology becomes an integrated part of communication.
38. Health monitoring. Consumers are now routinely using wearable health monitoring devices.
39. Telework. More employees enjoy flexibility in working hours and locations.
40. Design focus moves from styling to human-centered design.
41. Neuroscience and Design Research. Now when we test prototypes, we can measure behavior, cognition, emotional reactions, physiological markers, and brain activity.
42. Transit culture. People live and work in many cultures.
43. Social networking. People share interests and activities in online communities.
44. The personalization of content, products, and services.
45. Digital security.
46. Luxury
47. Service Economy. Service industry now employs 90% of Americans.
48. Smaller organizations. Small organizations and startups have the opportunity to enter the market and compete with large organizations.
49. Wellbeing.
50. The strategic contribution of design is expected.
51. Brands that focus on customer experience.
52. Active Listening.
53. App integration.
54. Micro co-creation
55. Growth of user experience design.
56. User generated content & open sharing People provide information and share their information on line.
57. Virtual reality.
58. Privacy by design

> *Design today is no longer about designing objects, visuals or spaces; it is about designing systems, strategies and experiences."*

Gjoko Muratovski
Professor in design and innovation. Tongji University, Shanghai

> *We need to invent a new and radical form of collaboration that blurs the boundaries between creators and consumers. It's not about "us versus them" or even "us on behalf of them." For the design thinker, it has to be "us with them."*

Tim Brown IDEO

SEGMENTATION

WHAT

Market segmentation involves subdividing a market into a number of groups where the people in each group have some commonality, or similarity. Members of a market segment share something in common. Segmentation is done to provide deign solutions that work for a group of people without the expense of developing a different solution for each person. There are many ways to segment a market. The best way to segment customers depends on your goals. For example if you are entering a new global market one way is to segment your customers by where they live.

GEOGRAPHIC SEGMENTATION

This is one of the more common methods of market segmentation. For example, a company selling products in Europe may segment their customers by the country that they live in. In Europe regional differences in customer preferences exist. You may decide to segment you customers by those who live in a city and those who live in a rural location.

DISTRIBUTION SEGMENTATION

Experience maps and Service blueprints help designers understand a market where most people access multiple channels when purchasing or using a product or service

PRICE SEGMENTATION

Another common way of segmenting a market is by income. Different price-points for a product or service may appeal to people with different incomes. Mass market car companies like ford have models that appeal to people with lower incomes and luxury models that appeal to customers with higher incomes.

DEMOGRAPHIC SEGMENTATION

Demographic segmentation is possibly the most commonly used type of segmentation. There are large number of demographic factors such as gender, age, type of employment and education that are often used for segmentation. Some products and brands are targeted mainly at men. Most people over the age of 40 require glasses to read.

TIME SEGMENTATION

Some products are sold at a particular time of day or year. For example surfboards are sold in summer.

PSYCHOGRAPHIC OR LIFESTYLE SEGMENTATION

Psychographic or lifestyle segmentation, is based on, values, behaviors, emotions, perceptions, beliefs, and interests. For example some customers prefer luxury products. Some customers may follow a particular sporting team.

Markets segments should be large enough to justify creating targeted products and services. Four to six market segments is often a manageable number. Targeting too many segments is sometimes unsuccessful. Products usually do not appeal to everyone.

Consider the income potential of each segment carefully when defining segments.
When defining segments consider:
1. Can you measure the segment?.
2. Is the segment big enough to make a profit?
3. Is the segment changing or evolving?
4. Can you reach the segment?
5. Is there one factor that unites everyone in the segment?
6. Do you have enough data to understand the segment?

PERSONAS

WHAT

"A persona is a archetypal character that is meant to represent a group of users in a role who share common goals, attitudes and behaviors when interacting with a particular product or service personas are user models that are presented as specific individual humans. They are not actual people, but are synthesized directly from observations of real people." *(Cooper)*

WHO INVENTED IT?
Alan Cooper 1998

WHY
1. Helps create empathy for users and reduces self reference.
2. Use as tool to analyze and gain insight into users.
3. Help in gaining buy-in from stakeholders.
4. Personas are user models, characters with a purpose who will represent your target users throughout the design process from brainstorming ideas to designing ideal user experience journey.
5. Personas support storytelling, foster user understanding and evolve design. Stories help communicate information in a compelling manner and evoke emotions and action.

HOW
1. Inaccurate personas can lead to a false understandings of the end users. Personas need to be created using data from real users.
2. Collect data through observation, interviews, ethnography.
3. Segment the users or customers
4. Create the Personas
5. Avoid Stereotypes
6. Each persona should be different. Avoid fringe characteristics. Personas should each have three to four life goals which are personal aspirations,
7. Personas are given a name, and photograph.
8. Design personas can be followed by building customer journeys.

RESOURCES
Raw data on users from interviews or other research
Images of people similar to segmented customers.
Computer
Graphics software

ORIGIN OF PERSONAS

The Inmates Are Running the Asylum, written by Alan Cooper published in 1998, introduced the use of personas as a design tool. Alan Cooper describes his first application of the persona technique:

"In 1995 I was working with the three founders of Sagent Technologies, pioneers in the field of what is now called "Business Intelligence" software. It was almost impossible for those brilliant, logical programmers to conceive of a single use of their product when it was obviously capable of so many uses. In frustration I demanded to be introduced to their customers.

The users fell into three distinct groups, clearly differentiated by their goals, tasks, and skill levels. Had I been creating the software myself, I would have role-played those users as I had with Ruby and Super Project, but in this case I had to describe those user models to the Sagent team. So I created Chuck, Cynthia, and Rob. These three were the first true, Goal-Directed, personas. At the next group meeting, I presented my designs from the points of view of Chuck, Cynthia, and Rob instead of from my own. The results were dramatic. While there was still resistance to this unfamiliar method, the programmers could clearly see the sense in my designs because they could identify with these hypothetical archetypes. The product was so successful that it defined a new product segment. The company was a success, too, going public four years later.
Over the next few years, we developed and perfected the technique.

Many of my predecessors have employed ethnographic user research and created persona-like constructs to aid their designing. Product marketing professionals have also been using persona-like entities for many years to define demographic segments. But personas are unique and uniquely effective."

TYPES OF PERSONAS

PRIMARY
The users who are the main focus of the product or service.

SECONDARY
Secondary users may use the product but are not the primary focus.

STAKEHOLDERS
Stakeholders are people who may be affected by the products or services. A patient may be the primary persona but stakeholders may be doctors, nurses, hospital workers, medical insurance company employees, or relatives of the patient.

Usually persona are not created for each stakeholder. There may be conflicts between the needs of different stakeholders that should be considered.

EXCLUSIONARY
Someone we're not designing for. It is useful to consider non users when defining personas.

BIOGRAPHICAL INFORMATION

NAME
Give each persona a name that may be representative of the user group.

PHOTO
Choose a photograph which represents someone like the persona that you have constructed.

COUNTRY/ REGION
Where within the country does the persona live?

CITY/METROPOLITAN SIZE
9. Under 5,000,
10. 5,000-10,000,
11. 10,000 -20.000
12. 20,000-50,000,
13. 50,000- 250,000,
14. 250,000-500,000,
15. 500,000-1 million,
16. 1 million-4 million,
17. More than 4 million

URBAN OR RURAL?
Do they live in the city or in the country?

DEMOGRAPHIC

AGE
Give the persona a precise age. Segments often give age as a range:
1. Under 6
2. 6-11
3. 12-20
4. 20-35
5. 35-50

6. 50-65
7. Over 65

GENDER
Male or female?

FAMILY SIZE
1. 1-2
2. 3-4
3. More than 5

SINGLE OR MARRIED?
Single married or divorced?

LIFE STAGE
1. Child
2. Teenager
3. Young
4. Middle aged
5. Elderly

INCOME
1. Under $10,000;
2. $10,000-20,000,
3. $20,000-30,000,
4. $30,000-50,000,
5. $50,000-100,000,
6. $100,000-150,000
7. Over 150.000

HOUSING
Renter or owner?
Type of dwelling?

OCCUPATION
1. Sales
2. Office worker
3. Nurse
4. Waiter
5. Administration
6. Building
7. Professional
8. Other

EDUCATION
1. Grade school
2. High school
3. College
4. Post Graduate

ETHNICITY
Consider with nationality

NATIONALITY
Many different groups are represented with nationality.

PSYCHOGRAPHIC

SELF-IMAGE
Outgoing, leader, shy

BELIEFS
Focus on those beliefs that may be most relevant to your product or service.

ATTITUDES
Favorable and unfavorable attitudes relevant to the product or service.

TECH STATUS
1. Innovator
2. Early adopter
3. Fast followers
4. Early mainstream
5. Late mainstream
6. Lagger

INTERESTS
1. Music
2. Sport
3. Food
4. Others

MEDIA
5. Websites

6. TV shows
7. Magazines
8. Other

WEB

TENURE
How long has the persona been using the web?

TIME ONLINE
Hours per week or month

TYPE OF USAGE
1. Email
2. Social networking
3. News
4. Other

BANDWIDTH
How fast is their connection?

INTERNET DEVICE
1. Desk
2. Tablet
3. Phone
4. Other

BROWSER
Type of browser

Sources:"Principles of Marketing" 8th Edition, Phillip Kotler and Gary Armstrong, "The People Who Make Organization Go – Or Stop," Rob Cross and Laurence Prusak, Havard Business Review, June Persona Creation and Usage Toolkit, George Olsen 2004

PROBLEM STATEMENT

CREATING A PROBLEM STATEMENT
A problem statement includes three elements:
1. user
2. need
3. insight

User xxxx needs xxxx because xxxx

1. What is the need?
2. Who has the need?
3. Why is there a needs?

1. Create a number of problem statements based on different user groups and different needs.
2. Compare the problem statements.
3. Use the problem statement during the ideation phase. Don't try to solve all problems.

EMPATHY

WHAT

Empathy is defined as 'standing in someone else's shoes' or 'seeing through someone else's eyes'. It is The ability to identify and understand another's situation, feelings, and motives. In design it may be defined as: identify with others and, adopting his or her perspective. It is different to sympathy. Empathy does not necessarily imply compassion. Empathy is a respectful understanding of other people's point of view.

WHO INVENTED IT?

The English word was coined in 1909 by E.B. Titchener in an attempt to translate the German word "Einfühlungsvermögen". It was later re-translated into the German language as "Empathie".

WHY

1. Empathy is a core skill for designers to design successfully for other people.
2. Empathy is needed for business success and for designs to be accepted and used by those people we are designing for.
3. Empathy builds trust.

CHALLENGES

1. Increasing use of teams.
2. The rapid pace of globalization.
3. Global need to retain talent.

HOW

1. Put yourself in contact and the context of people who you are designing for.
2. Ask questions and listen to the answers.
3. Read between the lines.
4. Observe.
5. Don't interrupt.
6. Listen.
7. Ask clarifying questions.
8. Restating what you think you heard.
9. Recognize that people are individuals.
10. Notice body language. Most communication is non-verbal
11. Withhold judgment when you hear views different to your own.
12. Take a personal interest in people.

EXPERIENCE DESIGN

WHAT
Experience design is the practice of designing products, processes, services, events, and environments with a focus placed on the quality of the user experience. Experience design is concerned with moments of engagement, or touchpoints, between people and brand. Experience design requires a cross-disciplinary approach.

Source: On Point Creative, http://opcatl.com/ (accessed July 03, 2016)

WHO INVENTED IT?
Donald Norman 1990s

WHY
A user experience can be more valuable than an individual product or service.

CHALLENGES
1. Research methods are necessary to understand another person's experiences
2. Observations can be subjective.

HOW
1. Experience evaluation. Methods include:
2. Diary Methods.
3. Experience sampling method.
4. Day reconstruction method.
5. Laddering interviews.

RESOURCES
Cameras
Video cameras
Notepad computer
Digital voice recorder
Cell phones
Tablets

What we know about the destination resort business is clearly established. But it's all about one thing, and one thing only. All of the razzmatazz and jazz we hear about facilities and everything else doesn't amount to a hill of beans. It's customer experience that determines the longevity and endurance of these enterprises.

Steve Wynn

HUMAN NEEDS

The greatest single cause of failure of design projects according to many studies is a lack of understanding of the what is most important to the customer or end user

This really comes down to a lack of identification of what are unmet user needs. Unmet needs represent market opportunities. customers struggle to get a job done.

Identifying and addressing those unmet needs is the key to success.

Many managers do not have a process for identifying what is most important to their customers. Knowing which customer needs to address in priority order is a key requirement of the innovation process.

> *Post-modernism is dead because it didn't address human needs.*

David Guterson

> *"One of the oldest human needs is having someone to wonder where you are when you don't come home at night. "*

Margaret Mead

> *Human needs are a powerful source of explanation of human behavior and social interaction. All individuals have needs that they strive to satisfy, either by using the system, 'acting on the fringes.' or acting as a reformist or revolutionary. Given this condition, social systems must be responsive to individual needs, or be subject to instability and forced change."*

Preface," in The Power of Human Needs in World Society, ed. Roger A. Coate and Jerel A. Rosati, ix. Boulder, CO: Lynne Rienner Publishers.

> *"The work of an advertising agency is warmly and immediately human. It deals with human needs, wants, dreams and hopes. Its 'product' cannot be turned out on an assembly line."*

Leo Burnett

HUMAN NEEDS

PHYSICAL SUSTENANCE
1. Air
2. Food
3. Health
4. Movement
5. Physical Safety
6. Rest / sleep
7. Shelter
8. Touch
9. Water

SECURITY
1. Consistency
2. Order/Structure
3. Peace
4. Peace of mind
5. Protection
6. Safety
7. Stability
8. Trusting

LEISURE/RELAXATION
1. Humour
2. Joy
3. Play
4. Pleasure

AFFECTION
1. Appreciation
2. Attention
3. Closeness
4. Companionship
5. Harmony
6. Intimacy
7. Love
8. Nurturing
9. Sexual Expression
10. Support
11. Tenderness
12. Warmth

UNDERSTANDING
1. Awareness
2. Clarity
3. Discovery
4. Learning

> *Our real goal, then, is not so much fulfilling manifest needs by creating a speedier printer or a more ergonomic keyboard; that's the job of designers. It is helping people to articulate the latent needs they may not even know they have, and this is the challenge of design thinkers."*
>
> Tim Brown
> IDEO

> *The most secure source of new ideas that have true competitive advantage, and hence, higher margins, is customers' unarticulated needs."*
>
> Jeanne Liedtka
> Darden School of the University of Virginia

DOWNLOAD A FREE PDF COPY OF THIS PERSONA TEMPLATE WITH TEXT BOXES THAT YOU CAN FILL FROM OUR SITE WWW.DCC-EDU.ORG

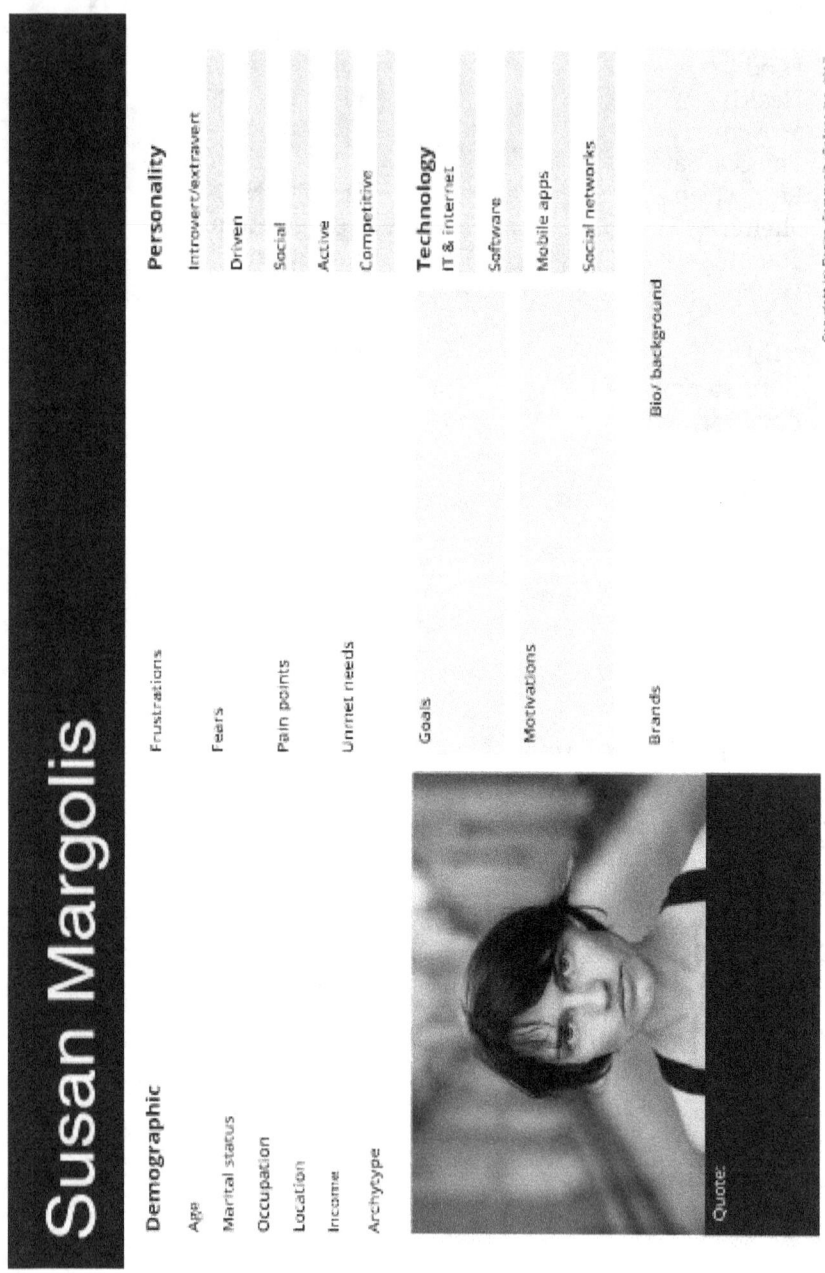

AUTONOMY
1. Choice
2. Ease
3. Independence
4. Power
5. Self-responsibility
6. Space
7. Spontaneity

MEANING
1. Aliveness
2. Challenge
3. Contribution
4. Creativity
5. Effectiveness
6. Exploration
7. Integration
8. Purpose

MATTERING
1. Acceptance
2. Care
3. Compassion
4. Consideration
5. Empathy
6. Kindness
7. Mutual Recognition
8. Respect
9. To be heard, seen
10. To be known, understood
11. To be trusted
12. Understanding others

COMMUNITY
1. Belonging
2. Communication
3. Cooperation
4. Equality
5. Inclusion

1. Mutuality
2. Participation
3. Partnership
4. Self-expression
5. Sharing

SENSE OF SELF
1. Authenticity
2. Competence
3. Creativity
4. Dignity
5. Growth
6. Healing
7. Honesty
8. Integrity
9. Self-acceptance
10. Self-care
11. Self-knowledge
12. Self-realization
13. Mattering to myself

TRANSCENDENCE
1. Beauty
2. Celebration of life
3. Communion
4. Faith
5. Flow
6. Hope
7. Inspiration
8. Mourning
9. Peace (internal)
10. Presence

Sources: Marshall Rosenberg, Manfred Max-Neef, Miki and Arnina Kashtan

PERSONAS

WHAT

"A persona is a archetypal character that is meant to represent a group of users in a role who share common goals, attitudes and behaviors when interacting with a particular product or service personas are user models that are presented as specific individual humans. They are not actual people, but are synthesized directly from observations of real people."*(Cooper)*

WHO INVENTED IT?
Alan Cooper 1998

WHY
1. Helps create empathy for users and reduces self reference.
2. Use as tool to analyze and gain insight into users.
3. Help in gaining buy-in from stakeholders.
4. Personas are user models, characters with a purpose who will represent your target users throughout the design process from brainstorming ideas to designing ideal user experience journey.
5. Personas support storytelling, foster user understanding and evolve design. Stories help communicate information in a compelling manner and evoke emotions and action.

HOW
1. Inaccurate personas can lead to a false understandings of the end users. Personas need to be created using data from real users.
2. Collect data through observation, interviews, ethnography.
3. Segment the users or customers
4. Create the Personas
5. Avoid Stereotypes
6. Each persona should be different. Avoid fringe characteristics. Personas should each have three to four life goals which are personal aspirations,
7. Personas are given a name, and photograph.
8. Design personas can be followed by building customer journeys.

RESOURCES
Raw data on users from interviews or other research
Images of people similar to segmented customers.
Computer
Graphics software

ORIGIN OF PERSONAS

The Inmates Are Running the Asylum, written by Alan Cooper published in 1998, introduced the use of personas as a design tool. Alan Cooper describes his first application of the persona technique:

PERSONA TEMPLATE

PHOTO OF PERSONA   PERSONA NAME

image of persona

DEMOGRAPHICS
Age
Occupation
Location

Income
Gender
Education

CHARACTERISTIC

demograhic factors

GOALS

What does this person want to achieve

MOTIVATIONS
Incentives
Fear
Growth

Achievement
Power
Social

FRUSTRATIONS

What experiences does this person wish to avoid?

QUOTE

Characteristic quote

BRANDS

What brands doe

CHARACTERIST

sliders show relevant factors

····**X**········ ········
EXTROVERT

·······**X**········ ·······**X**·······
TRAVEL   LUXURY GOODS

····**X**········ ····**X**········
TECHNICAL SAVVY   SPORTS

·········**X**······· ··········**X**····
SOCIAL NETWORKING   MOBILE APPS

SERVICE DESIGN

"In 1995 I was working with the three founders of Sagent Technologies, pioneers in the field of what is now called "Business Intelligence" software. It was almost impossible for those brilliant, logical programmers to conceive of a single use of their product when it was obviously capable of so many uses. In frustration I demanded to be introduced to their customers.

The users fell into three distinct groups, clearly differentiated by their goals, tasks, and skill levels. Had I been creating the software myself, I would have role-played those users as I had with Ruby and Super Project, but in this case I had to describe those user models to the Sagent team. So I created Chuck, Cynthia, and Rob. These three were the first true, Goal-Directed, personas.

At the next group meeting, I presented my designs from the points of view of Chuck, Cynthia, and Rob instead of from my own. The results were dramatic. While there was still resistance to this unfamiliar method, the programmers could clearly see the sense in my designs because they could identify with these hypothetical archetypes. The product was so successful that it defined a new product segment. The company was a success, too, going public four years later. Over the next few years, we developed and perfected the technique.

Many of my predecessors have employed ethnographic user research and created persona-like constructs to aid their designing. Product marketing professionals have also been using persona-like entities for many years to define demographic segments. But personas are unique and uniquely effective."

TYPES OF PERSONAS

PRIMARY PERSONAS
The users who are the main focus of the product or service.

SECONDARY PERSONAS
Secondary users may use the product but are not the primary focus.

STAKEHOLDERS
Stakeholders are people who may be affected by the products or services. A patient may be the primary persona but stakeholders may be doctors, nurses, hospital workers, medical insurance company employees, or relatives of the patient.

Usually persona are not created for each stakeholder. There may be conflicts between the needs of different stakeholders that should be considered.

EXCLUSIONARY PERSONAS
Someone we're not designing for. It is useful to consider non users when defining personas.

BIOGRAPHICAL INFORMATION

NAME
Give each persona a name that may be representative of the user group.

PHOTO
Choose a photograph which represents someone like the persona that you have constructed.

COUNTRY/ REGION
Where within the country does the persona live?

CITY/METROPOLITAN SIZE
9. Under 5,000,
10. 5,000-10,000,
11. 10,000 -20.000
12. 20,000-50,000,
13. 50,000- 250,000,
14. 250,000-500,000,
15. 500,000-1 million,
16. 1 million-4 million,
17. More than 4 million

URBAN OR RURAL?
Do they live in the city or in the country?

DEMOGRAPHIC

AGE
Give the persona a precise age. Segments often give age as a range:
1. Under 6
2. 6-11
3. 12-20
4. 20-35
5. 35-50
6. 50-65
7. Over 65

GENDER
Male or female?

FAMILY SIZE
1. 1-2
2. 3-4
3. More than 5

SINGLE OR MARRIED?
Single married or divorced?

LIFE STAGE
1. Child
2. Teenager
3. Young
4. Middle aged
5. Elderly

INCOME
1. Under $10,000;
2. $10,000-20,000,
3. $20,000-30,000,
4. $30,000-50,000,
5. $50,000-100,000,
6. $100,000-150,000
7. Over 150.000

HOUSING
Renter or owner?
Type of dwelling?

OCCUPATION
1. Sales
2. Office worker
3. Nurse
4. Waiter
5. Administration
6. Building
7. Professional
8. Other

EDUCATION
1. Grade school
2. High school
3. College
4. Post Graduate

ETHNICITY
Consider with nationality

NATIONALITY
Many different groups are represented with nationality.

PSYCHOGRAPHIC

SELF-IMAGE
Outgoing, leader, shy

BELIEFS
Focus on those beliefs that may be most relevant to your product or service.

ATTITUDES
Favorable and unfavorable attitudes relevant to the product or service.

TECH STATUS
1. Innovator
2. Early adopter
3. Fast followers
4. Early mainstream
5. Late mainstream
6. Lagger

INTERESTS
1. Music
2. Sport
3. Food
4. Others

MEDIA
5. Websites
6. TV shows
7. Magazines
8. Other

WEB

TENURE
How long has the persona been using the web?

TIME ONLINE
Hours per week or month

TYPE OF USAGE
1. Email
2. Social networking
3. News
4. Other

BANDWIDTH
How fast is their connection?

INTERNET DEVICE
1. Desk
2. Tablet
3. Phone
4. Other

BROWSER
Type of browser

Sources:"Principles of Marketing" 8th Edition, Phillip Kotler and Gary Armstrong, "The People Who Make Organization Go – Or Stop," Rob Cross and Laurence Prusak, Havard Business Review, June Persona Creation and Usage Toolkit, George Olsen 2004

APPLYING MAPPING METHODS IN YOUR ORGANIZATION

APPLYING DESIGN THINKING IN YOUR ORGANIZATION

Here is some advice to help you introduce design thinking into your organization.

FIRST LEARN ABOUT DESIGN THINKING
Arrange for several leaders in your organization representing the main cross-functional departments to do a substantial course in design thinking together.

GIVE EVERYONE A VOICE
Invite everyone to a series of meetings to discuss the introduction of design thinking in your organization.

LEAVE YOUR OFFICE AND EXPERIENCE YOUR CUSTOMER'S WORLD
Listen to your customers to understand what their problems are. Don't solve the wrong problem because you are remote from your customers.

COLLABORATE
Define the goals together as a team with everyone's input.

WHEN YOU HAVE A PRELIMINARY DESIGN GET FEEDBACK FROM CUSTOMERS
Share the designs as widely as possible with internal and external stakeholders and invite their feedback.

LEARN BY FAILING AND TRYING AGAIN
It is important to understand that if you are trying new things not every design idea will be successful. Use the methods in this book to minimize the cost of inevitable failures during prototyping and experimentation.

INVITE ALL DEPARTMENTS AND EXTERNAL STAKEHOLDERS TO YOUR WORKSHOPS
You should have one team composed of stakeholders with different perspectives.

CHOOSE THE TEAM MEMBERS IN YOUR GROUPS CAREFULLY
Four to eight people is an optimum groups size. If you have a larger group break it into smaller groups. Consider diversity and personalities when forming groups. Don't put several people with strong personalities into the same group. Create space for discussion where people feel safe.

START WITH A MANAGEABLE DESIGN PROBLEM
Run several small-scale design thinking exercises before taking on a larger project.

> *Because we invested in building innovation skills into our employee base, we are not only a design-thinking company, we're a design-driven company. Meaning, we're going from creating a culture of design thinking to building a practice of design doing, where we relentlessly focus on nailing the end-to-end customer experience. This means that before anything gets built, the whole team engineers, designers, marketers, product managers are interfacing with the customers to ensure they understand the problem well, and together, they design the best solution.*

Suzanne Pellican,
Vice President Of Experience Design at Intuit

EMPATHY IS NOT THE SAME AS HUMAN FACTORS
Design thinking tools consider not just usability issues but also people's emotions, attitudes, and values.

THINK HOLISTICALLY
Analytical thinkers can sometimes focus on the small details rather than the bigger issues. The process of design thinking will allow you to consider both. Think about design problems systematically, products, services, and experiences. How are these things connected?

LOOK FOR UNMET NEEDS
Consider and involve the customer at every stage.

BUILD UP YOUR SOLUTIONS
Prototype early and learn and build up the solution by asking questions.

CONSIDER THE CUSTOMER JOURNEY NOT JUST THE DESTINATION
The customer journey consists of a series of micro-experiences. Design thinking tools allow you to consider and optimize each of these moments to build a better overall experience.

BUILD A WAR ROOM
Place all your research and all your ideas on a wall where everyone in tour team can see it and think about and discuss what may be relevant and connected. Keep one space dedicated to your project for the entire project. Pick a large space with natural light.

GIVE PEOPLE DEFINED TIMES FOR EACH ACTIVITY
Don't give them too much time. 30-minutes to generate ideas, 15 minutes for discussion, 20-minutes to make a fast prototype. Keep the activities focused and moving. Have clear goals with each team activity.

MODERATING GROUPS

If you have the resources have two people moderate. The moderator can facilitate the group discussion while the assistant moderator takes notes and looks after the video camera. Moderating a team activity successfully is a skill which is partly a talent and partly developed through experience.

ROLES

1. **Facilitator.** The person who moderates the group.
2. **Recorder.** The person who captures the discussion
3. **Data Analyst.** The person who analyses the notes or recordings of the group discussion
4. **Report Writer.** The person who writes executive summary of the discussions.
5. **Scheduler.** The person who schedules the meetings.
6. **Manager of Logistics.** The person who manages the room and other logistics.

ASSISTANT MODERATOR

1. Manages the equipment and refreshments
2. Arranges the room
3. Manages video camera and other recording equipment
4. Welcome participants as they arrive
5. Has good listening skills
6. Has good observation skills
7. Has good writing skills
8. Acts as an observer, not as a participant
9. Can remain impartial
10. Take notes throughout the discussion
11. Notes should include observation of non-verbal behavior
12. Notes should include themes, follow-up questions, body language, confusion, nonverbal communication, facial expressions, gestures, signs of agreement, disagreement, frustration, and participant concerns, head nods, physical excitement, eye contact between participants, or other clues that would indicate level of support, or interest.
13. Notes follow-up questions that could be asked
14. The assistant moderator does not get involved in the group discussion.
15. Assistant should be a "fly on the wall" and only observe the discussion.
16. Should not influence the discussion by their presence.
17. Provides participant seating arrangement
18. Operate recording equipment
19. Do not participate in the discussion
20. Ask questions when invited
21. Give an oral summary
22. Debrief with moderator
23. Give feedback on analysis and reports
24. Can Handle logistics & refreshments
25. Collects signed informed

consent (if required)
26. Takes careful notes
27. Does not participate in discussion
28. Can recap major themes at end of discussion (used before wrap-up question)
29. Monitors recording equipment
30. Liaison between moderator and observers/clients
31. Debriefs with moderator after session
32. Assist with analysis and reports
33. Not required, but can be useful in some situations
34. Balance out strengths/weaknesses in moderator
35. Use to match moderator (without being obvious)
36. Switch leading discussion (good for long or intense discussions)
37. Support leader by keeping on track, recapping major themes, etc.

MODERATOR

Select the moderator carefully.
1. Someone who is culturally like the people participating.
2. Manages the process of the discussion rather than the content.
3. The moderator should have empathy with the group but also have authority.
4. Does not need to be an expert on the discussion topic but needs to show skill in managing discussion.
5. Should not share views,
6. Probes the discussion points to reveal the underlying reasons.
7. Should 'Warm up' the group to help participants feel at ease,
8. Should develop rapport with the participants.
9. Needs to stay focused.
10. Should ensure that all participants are involved in the discussion.
11. Spends the minimum time necessary speaking.
12. Should not show bias.
13. Directs the discussion in real time
14. Follows the question guide.
15. Have an assistant to take notes and manage equipment and time.
16. The moderator should have good listening skills.
17. Use an experienced moderator.
18. A person able to create and manage a friendly and participatory environment.
19. Use pauses and probes
20. Probes:
    - "Can you explain further?"
    - "Could you give an example?"
21. Manage participants
    - Verbal and nonverbal communication
    - Short responses
    - Experts
    - Dominant talkers
    - Shy participants
    - Ramblers
22. The moderator should remain neutral and not show extremes of emotion such as surprise or anger during the conversation.

23. The moderator should be diplomatic.
24. The moderator prevents some participants from dominating the conversation.
25. Can clearly summarize and articulate the views expressed.
26. Do not let the discussion stray into areas that are emotionally charged.

GROUP BEHAVIOR

CONSTRUCTIVE GROUP BEHAVIORS
1. Collaboration. The members of the group are interested and listen to the views of other participants.
2. Clarifies points. Asks questions in order to understand ambiguous ideas.
3. Inspires the group with relevant examples.
4. Harmony. Works to build group cohesion
5. Takes risks. Sticks their neck out to achieve the goals.
6. Reviews the process so they properly understand the goals, agenda, schedule and other points.

DESTRUCTIVE GROUP BEHAVIORS
1. Dominates the conversation with one opinion.
2. Wants to move on before the discussion is complete.
3. Does not participate in the discussion.
4. Discounts or ridicules other opinions.
5. Loses focus on the topic or goals.
6. Blocks unfamiliar ideas.
7. Self-Appointed Experts. Thank them for their knowledge and redirect question to the rest of the group
8. If one participant tries to dominate the session, the moderator should invite each person to speak in turn.
9. Shy Participants. Respect someone's right to be quiet, but do give them a chance to share their ideas
10. Ramblers. Intervene, politely summarize and refocus. Use nonverbal cues; redirect.
11. Side Talking/Side Conversation. Remind the group or individuals about the ground rules

INTERVENTION
A good moderator will intervene in the discussion when necessary Establish the ground rules in the introduction. This gives common expectations so that the team members can help manage people who exhibit destructive behavior. Listen to each person's ideas. Ask questions to clarify points or reveal bias.

1. Break a large group into smaller groups of 4 people.
2. Remind the group of the task.
3. Take a break and speak to a disruptive participant about the goals.
4. Break the problem into

smaller parts.
5. Define a way to make decisions.
6. List the areas of agreement.

TIME MANAGEMENT
It is important that time is planned and managed well so that all the topics can be covered.

KEEP THE INTERVIEW ON TRACK
One of the important skills for a moderator is to steer the conversation back to the topic if it strays and to move on from question to question.

USE THE INTERVIEW GUIDE
Write in prompts to remind you to check the time at several points during the discussion.

DO NOT RUSH THE DISCUSSION
Interrupt as little as possible and not rush them.
1. Have good listening skills
2. Have good observation skills
3. Have good speaking skills
4. Can foster open and honest dialogue among diverse groups and individuals
5. Can remain impartial (i.e., do not give her/his opinions about topics, because
6. This can influence what people say)
7. Can encourage participation when someone is reluctant to speak up
8. Can manage participants who dominate the conversation
9. Are sensitive to gender and cultural issues
10. Are sensitive to differences in power among and within groups.

MODERATOR SKILLS
BUILDING RAPPORT
1. Building rapport is important.
2. Show the participants that you are a person who is prepared and willing to listen to them with interest.
3. Let the participants know that you are there to learn from them.
4. It is important to present yourself as someone facilitating rather than as a friend.
5. Balance rapport and professionalism.

LISTENING TO INTERVIEW AND DISCUSSION PARTICIPANTS
The guidelines for conducting interviews and discussions are closely connected to building rapport. These guidelines include communicating to the participants that you are listening to them as well as these strategies: neutrality, silence, and guidance.
6. Show participants that you are listening.
7. Stay neutral.
8. You want to gather information that is as honest as possible.
9. Silence is acceptable. Asking clarifying questions. Guidance includes giving
10. Monitor time carefully.

TEAMS

History demonstrates that great projects and products are often the result of great teams.

Start with a clear goal and a serious deadline.
A hot group is infused with purpose and personality.
If you distrust the power of teamwork, consider this fact. Even the most legendary individual inventor is often a team in disguise. In six scant years, for example, Thomas Edison generated an astounding four hundred patents. producing: innovations in the telegraph. telephone phonograph, and lightbulb- with the help of a fourteen-man team. As Francis Jehl, Edison's longtime assistant, explained, "Edison is in reality a collective noun and means the work of many men." The same is often true of the lone genius within a company. We've found that loners are so caught up in their idea that they are reluctant to let it go, much less allow it to be experimented with and improved upon.

The right kinds of specializations are important, but specialization is not the only quality required. To make a Design Thinking project successful, we need T-shaped people. T-shaped people have a depth of knowledge and experience in their own fields but they can also reach out and connect with others horizontally and create meaningful collaborations.

WORKING WITH TEAMS

1. The team should have a common vision. Write that vision and display it prominently in the workspace. Refer back to the vision statement when decisions are being made to ensure that they are consistent with the vision.
2. Adopt and work with common values and rules such as the brainstorming rules.
3. Share common precesses.
4. Work together in one space.
5. Promote an atmosphere of trust and acceptance where people feel safe to put forward their ideas.
6. Encorage two way communication with feedback.

DIVERSITY

Each team member brings their unique perspective and expertise to the team, widening the range of possible outcomes. If you want a breakthrough idea, you're more likely to get it with a diverse team. Diverse teams see the same problem from many angles. They have a better understanding of any given situation and generate more ideas, making them more effective problem solvers. While it takes effort to harness and align such different perspectives, it's at the intersection of our differences that our most meaningful breakthroughs emerge.

Cross-disciplinary teams will provide you with the best results. Teams may consist of people unfamiliar with each other, with external members brought on board either as specialists or facilitators depending on the availability of skills.

Identity
1. Age and ability
2. Gender identity
3. Race and ethnicity

Experience
1. Cultural upbringing
2. Geography
3. Language

Expertise
1. Education
2. Organization
3. Discipline

Source:IBM

The right kinds of specializations are important, but specialization is not the only quality required. To make a Design Thinking project successful, we need T-shaped people. T-shaped people have a depth of knowledge and experience in their own fields but they can also reach out and connect with others horizontally and create meaningful collaborations.

A Design Thinking team should ideally be a cross/multi-disciplinary team consisting of a mix of specializations, including specialists associated with problem areas contributing but not dominating the journey. While specialists may have vast knowledge on a technical level, they are working towards solutions targeted towards non-specialists in many cases and require outside perspectives in addition to what they already know.

EMPOWERMENT

Teams should be equipped with the expertise and independence to deliver outcomes without relying on others for decisions or technical support.

Grant them the authority to handle day-to-day activities on the team and hold them accountable for achieving their assigned outcome.

FACILITATION

1. Start with a clear goal and a serious deadline
2. Explain the five stages of the Design Thinking Process.
3. Provide your team members with printed out models of the Design Thinking process and modes to help them understand and recognize the benefits of the Design Thinking work process.
4. Explain how Design Thinking builds a third way – combining the analytical and information-driven approach of science with the holistic, empathic and creative ways of thinking in ethnography and design.
5. Explain that there are lots of proven methods
6. Knowing the background and underlying structure will help your team members to

feel safer as they know that there's a solid background
7. Bring together a diverse team with different thinking styles and specializations.
8. Develop an innovative team culture, which embraces inclusiveness, collaboration, and co-creation.
9. Level the playing field to allow for a diverse set of perspectives to influence the process.
10. Ensure the right person is in charge.
11. Break the ice with some creative exercises to loosen things up.

> *One must still have chaos in oneself to be able to give birth to a dancing star."*
> Friedrich Nietzsche

CONFLICT

> *Diversity invites conflict— and conflict is a wellspring of creativity. Harnessing this creativity requires us to listen to understand, not just argue, with those who may disagree. When you listening to understand, you uncover brand new ideas together and contribute to a more open and collaborative culture."*
>
> *"Empathy: first with each other. Then with our users."*
>
> IBM

1. Instinct often leads us to avoid conflict and seek out those who think alike.
2. At minimum, critical team conversations should include representatives from every discipline affected. It would be unwise for engineering to make timeline decision without engaging offering management in a conversation, or for product designers to make brand decisions without consulting the marketing team.
3. This kind of radical collaboration requires a foundation of trust, respect, and shared ownership across the team.

> *Edison is, in reality, a collective noun and means the work of many men."*
>
> Francis Jehl
> Edison's assistant

> *Which skills and mindsets do team players need for a design project?*

1. Openness: smell, touch, taste, observe, listen, ask, hear, feel...
2. Able to find the right questions.

78 APPLYING DESIGN THINKING IN YOUR ORGANIZATION

3. *Able to suspend your judgment and look beyond the obvious.*
4. *Able to understand different points of view,*
5. *See the big picture and create common grounds.*
6. *Able to imagine and build solutions haven't seen before.*
7. *Able to create cheap experiments in order to learn faster."*

D Osterwalder,
Anna Ploskonos

COLLECTIVE INTELLIGENCE

Collective intelligence is a type of shared intelligence that emerges from the collaboration of many people and is expressed in consensus decision-making.

Collective intelligence requires four conditions to exist.
1. Openness Sharing ideas, experiences and perspectives
2. Peering people are free to share and build on each other's ideas freely.
3. Sharing knowledge, experiences ideas.
4. Acting globally

CROSS POLLINATION

Use cross-disciplinary teams. Share ideas and observations with people outside your organization. Travel can help your design team get exposed to new ways of looking at a problem. Read outside your field. Talk to people in different industries.

CROSS-DISCIPLINARY COLLABORATION

Depending on the design challenge, design teams can engage anthropologists, engineers, educators, doctors, lawyers, scientists, etc. in the innovative problem-solving process. Everyone can contribute. The Design Thinking process involves many stakeholders in working together. The designer is a member of the orchestra. The customer is involved throughout the design process and works with the design team to communicate their needs and desires and to help generate design solutions that are relevant to them.

The process is one of co-creation and the designer is a listener and a facilitator. Everyone adds value to the design.
Design thinking is not just for professional designers. Everyone can contribute. Many schools are now teaching Design Thinking to children as an approach that can be applied to life.

STYLES OF FEEDBACK

TRADITIONAL ENVIRONMENT	DESIGN THINKING APPROACH
Criticism passes judgment	Critique poses questions
Criticism finds fault	Critique uncovers opportunity
Criticism is personal	Critique is objective
Criticism is vague	Critique is concrete
Criticism tears down	Critique builds up
Criticism is ego-centric	Critique is altruistic
Criticism is adversarial	Critique is cooperative
Criticism belittles the designer	Critique improves the design

Source Writing Alone, Writing Together; A Guide for Writers and Writing Groups by Judy Reeves

BREAKING DOWN SILOS

Many organizations struggle to break down the barriers that prevent them from innovating. One of those barriers is the silo mentality where departments do not share information or effectively collaborate. Culture, language, and time zone differences compound the effects of organizational silos. Activities are uncoordinated and duplicative.

In organizations with silos teams work against each other. Breaking down silos starts the people you are hiring. Overcoming organizational silos requires supportive departmental structures, processes, reward mechanisms, reporting structures, furniture selection and office layouts. Siloed teams struggle to solve problems.

In siloed organizations employees follow vertical career paths, staying within one functional group or department.

CREATE ONE ORGANIZATIONAL VISION.

Align leaders to ensure that the leadership team agrees to a common unified vision for the organization. A unified leadership team will build trust in one vision.

WORK TOWARDS ACHIEVING A COMMON GOAL.

First identify existing multiple tactical goals and objectives. Build one unified vision and ensure that all employees are aware of this objective and understand how they can make an impact individually.

CREATE CROSS-FUNCTIONAL TEAMS.
Create clear roles and responsibilities.

INCENTIVIZE.
To motivate team members use common interests, individual investment in growth, shared voice, and positive words of encouragement. Create joint incentives. Request joint deliverables and metrics. Ensure that reviews and bonuses tie everyone to one strategic vision.

JOINT GOVERNANCE FORUM
Create a body with representatives from every department to meet together regularly to debate challenges, issues, and trade-offs, to support your common vision.

METRICS
Managers should establish a time frame to complete the common goal, benchmarks for success and delegate specific tasks and objectives to members of the team.

CO-LOCATE
Global teams have limited time together and complex communication issues. Co-locate teams where possible.
Since the need for Keep teams in the same physical location and have multidisciplinary teams rather than having all the engineers in one room and all the marketing people in another room or building.

CO-LEADERS
Appoint two leaders for "two in a box" style leadership. This will build improved accountability and collaboration.

> *Design thinking is, then, always linked to an improved future. Unlike critical thinking, which is a process of analysis and is associated with the 'breaking down' of ideas, design thinking is a creative process based around the 'building up' of ideas. There are no judgments in design thinking. This eliminates the fear of failure and encourages maximum input and participation. Wild ideas are welcome, since these often lead to the most creative solutions. Everyone is a designer, and design thinking is a way to apply design methodologies to any of life's situations.*
>
> Herbert Simon

INNOVATION DIAGNOSTIC

WHAT

An innovation diagnostic is an evaluation of an organization's innovation capabilities. It reviews practices by stakeholders which may help or hinder innovation. An innovation diagnostic is the first step in preparing and implementing a strategy to create an organizational culture that supports innovation. Before you start to research your audience. Do a diagnostic of your organization to find out how you can remove obstacles to innovation. Do an exercise to help get your team up to speed working.

WHY

1. It helps organizations develop sustainable competitive advantage
2. Helps identify innovation opportunities
3. Helps develop innovation strategy.
4. Evaluate structural weaknesses in an organization that may be limiting that organization's ability to innovate.

HOW

An innovation diagnostic reviews organizational and stakeholder practices using both qualitative and quantitative methods including
1. The design and development process
2. Strategic practices and planning
3. The ability of an organization to monitor and respond to relevant trends.
4. Technologies
5. Organizational flexibility
6. Ability to innovate repeatedly and consistently

SELF-QUESTIONNAIRE

Answer these questions and score yourself to understand to what degree your organization OR your client's organization supports innovation.

DOES MANAGEMENT COMMUNICATE THE NEED FOR INNOVATION?

1. There is no innovation in our organization
2. Innovation is not a high priority
3. Our managers sometimes talk about innovation
4. Our managers discuss innovation but not why it is needed
5. Managers regularly state the compelling need for

innovation

WHAT IS YOUR ORGANIZATIONAL STRATEGY?
1. We make low-cost goods or services
2. Efficient operations
3. We are a customer focused organization
4. Fast Follower
5. Market leaders

IS THE BUSINESS THAT YOU ARE IN UNDERSTOOD BY EMPLOYEES?
1. We are not sure
2. We may get different answers from different managers
3. The definition changes in
4. We have some clarity
5. We are very clear about what business we are in

IS YOUR ORGANIZATION INNOVATIVE?
1. No
2. Probably not
3. We would like to be
4. There is some innovation
5. We are clearly an innovative organization

HOW DOES YOUR COMPANY INNOVATE?
1. We react to market forces without innovation
2. There is little innovation
3. We do some incremental innovation
4. We do mainly incremental innovation but would like to do some breakthrough innovation
5. We manage a portfolio of incremental and more substantial innovation and manage risks

DOES YOUR MANAGEMENT SUPPORT INNOVATION?
1. No
2. No resources are allocated to innovation
3. Some resources are allocated
4. We have some resources and some involvement from managers in innovation
5. We have clearly defined resources allocated and senior management is actively involved in planning and managing innovation

DO YOU HAVE CROSS-DISCIPLINARY DESIGN TEAMS?
1. Never
2. Rarely
3. Sometimes
4. Usually
5. Always

DO YOU USE OUTSIDE EXPERTS TO ASSIST IN YOUR INNOVATION PROCESS?
1. Never
2. Rarely
3. Sometimes
4. Usually
5. Always

HOW OFTEN DOES YOUR ORGANIZATION ENGAGE CUSTOMERS TO IDENTIFY THEIR UNMET NEEDS?
1. Never
2. Rarely

3. Sometimes
4. Usually
5. Always

HOW WOULD YOU DEFINE THE RISK TOLERANCE AT YOUR COMPANY?
1. We don't take any risks
2. We rarely take risks
3. Sometimes we take substantial risks
4. We manage our risk portfolio actively and take big risks when appropriate.

HOW ARE NEW IDEAS RECEIVED IN YOUR ORGANIZATION?
1. We fire people with new ideas
2. We rarely adopt new ideas
3. We sometimes adopt new ideas but they are mostly not considered
4. We regularly consider new ideas
5. We actively generate and adopt new ideas

Add up the numbers of each answer that you selected and calculate a total for all the questions.

> ❝
> *Everything is now subject to innovation, not just physical objects, but also political systems, economic policy, ways in which medical research is conducted, and even complete "user experiences."*
>
> Laura Weiss,
> IDEO

HOW WELL DID YOU SCORE?

SCORE 0 TO 15

Small changes, low investment, low risk and low return. Changing the color of a product. Every company is capable of gaining this score.

SCORE 15 TO 25

You are integrating new features into existing products and services to build differentiated versions of the same new product to sell to various demographic groups. These new features require what can be considered a medium level of investment and risk. Advancement of existing products, medium investment, and risk, medium payoff.

SCORE 25 TO 35
INNOVATIVE ORGANIZATION

The second level is the beginning of large financial and product risk, but it is also where the rewards are potentially larger. This level also requires that the business devote resources to monitoring progress and actively assessing risk throughout the development process. Evolutionary products, large investment, medium risk, some payoff.

SCORE 35 TO 45
HIGHLY INNOVATIVE ORGANIZATION

Your company has the innovation skills to change people's lives. Companies in this category have the highest level of risks you are creating products or services that are new and original. Revolutionary products and services, large investment, big risks high payoff

CHAPTER SUMMARY

INTRODUCING DESIGN THINKING AT YOUR ORGANIZATION

1. First learn about design thinking
2. Give everyone a voice
3. Leave your office and immerse yourself in your customer's world.
4. Collaborate.
5. When you have a preliminary design get feedback from customers.
6. Do not punish failure.
7. Invite all departments and external stakeholders to your workshops.
8. Choose the team members in your groups carefully.
9. Start with a manageable design problem.
10. Empathy is not the same as human factors.
11. Think holistically.
12. Look for unmet needs.
13. Build up your solutions.
14. Consider the customer journey not just the destination.
15. Build a war room.
16. Give people defined times for each activity.

MODERATING ROLES

1. Facilitator. The person who moderates the group.
2. Recorder. The person who captures the discussion
3. Data Analyst – the person who analyses the notes or recordings of the group discussion
4. Report Writer. The person who writes executive summary of the discussions.
5. Scheduler. The person who schedules the meetings.
6. Manager of Logistics. The person who manages the room and other logistics.
7. Assistant moderator. The person who schedules the meetings.

REVIEW QUESTIONS

1. What should you do before you introduce design thinking to your organization?
2. How should you deal with failures on the project?
3. What should you look for from customers as part of the design thinking process?
4. What is a war room?
5. What are four roles when moderating groups?
6. What does an assistant moderator do?
7. What are four things you should consider when selecting a moderator?
8. What are four constructive group behaviors?
9. What are four destructive group behaviors?
10. How can a moderator build rapport with the group?
11. What is an innovation diagnostic?
12. When could you use an innovation diagnostic?

POOR UNDERSTANDING OF THE CUSTOMER'S PERSPECTIVE IS THE BIGGEST REASON FOR NEW PRODUCT AND SERVICE FAILURE

Source of data: Stage-gate.com

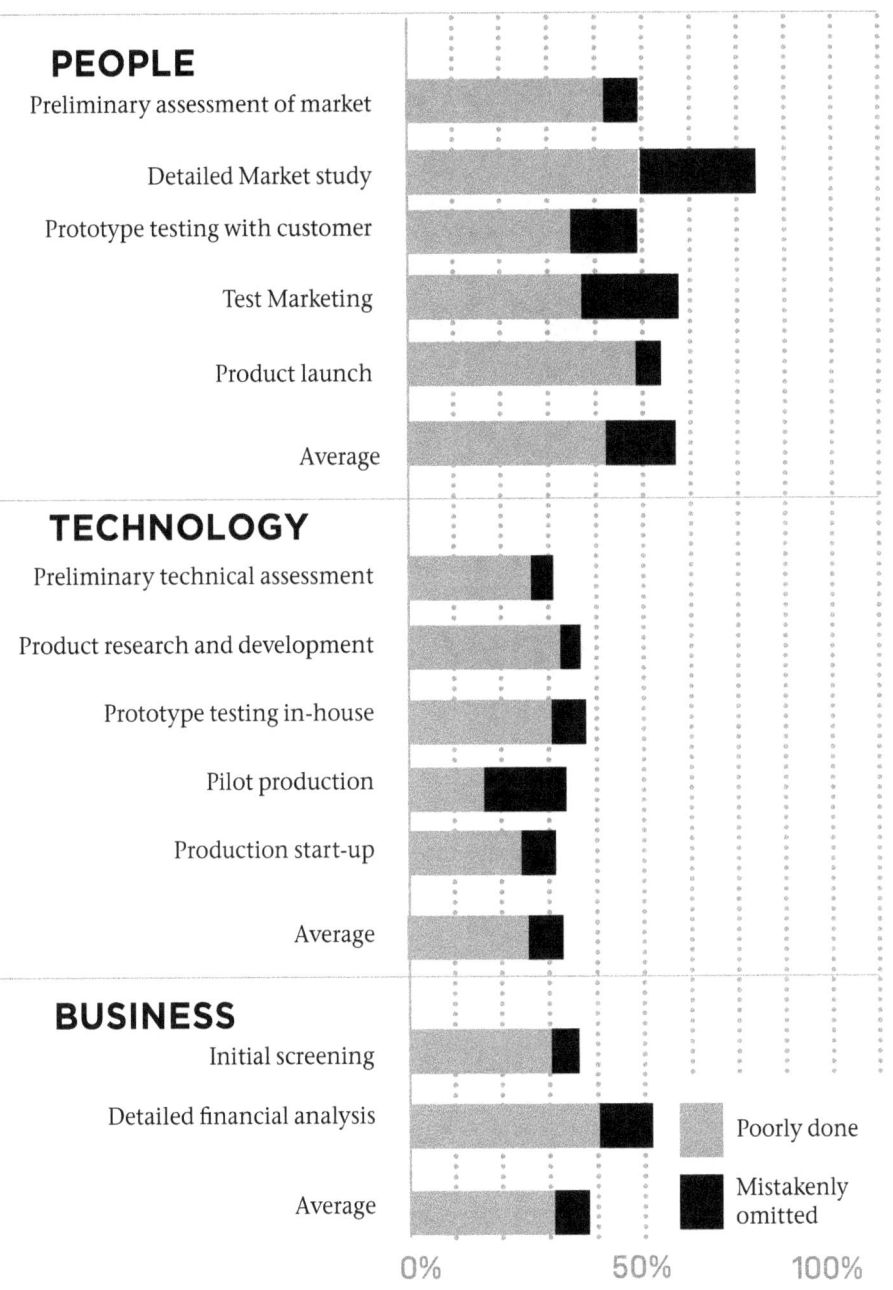

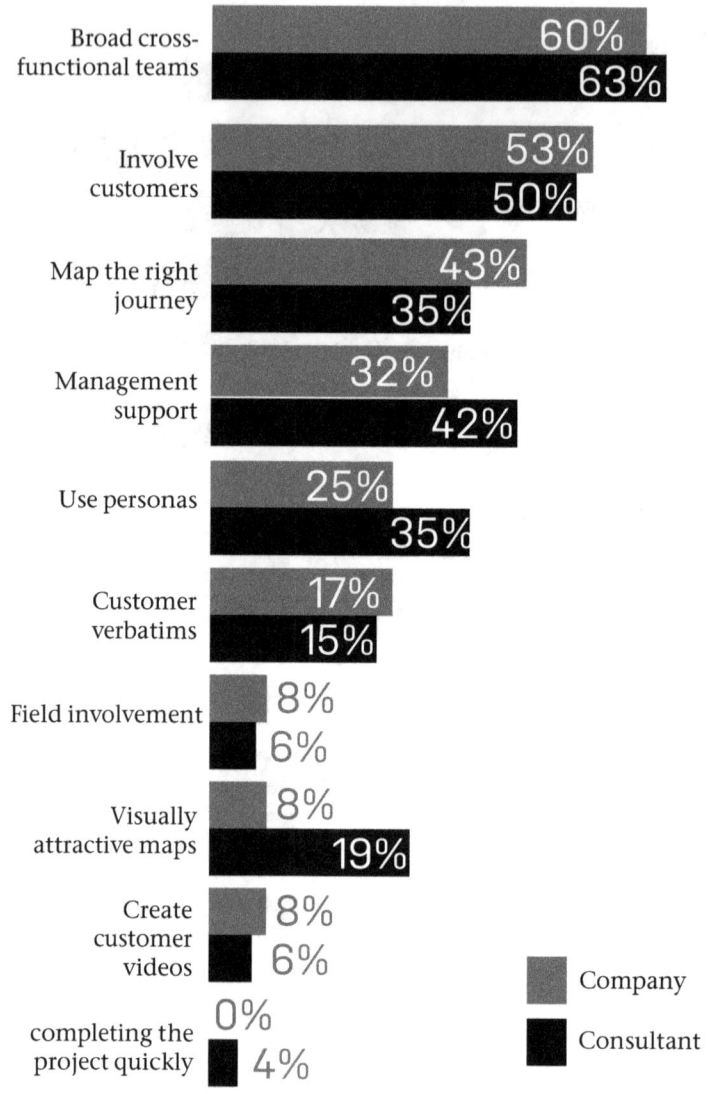

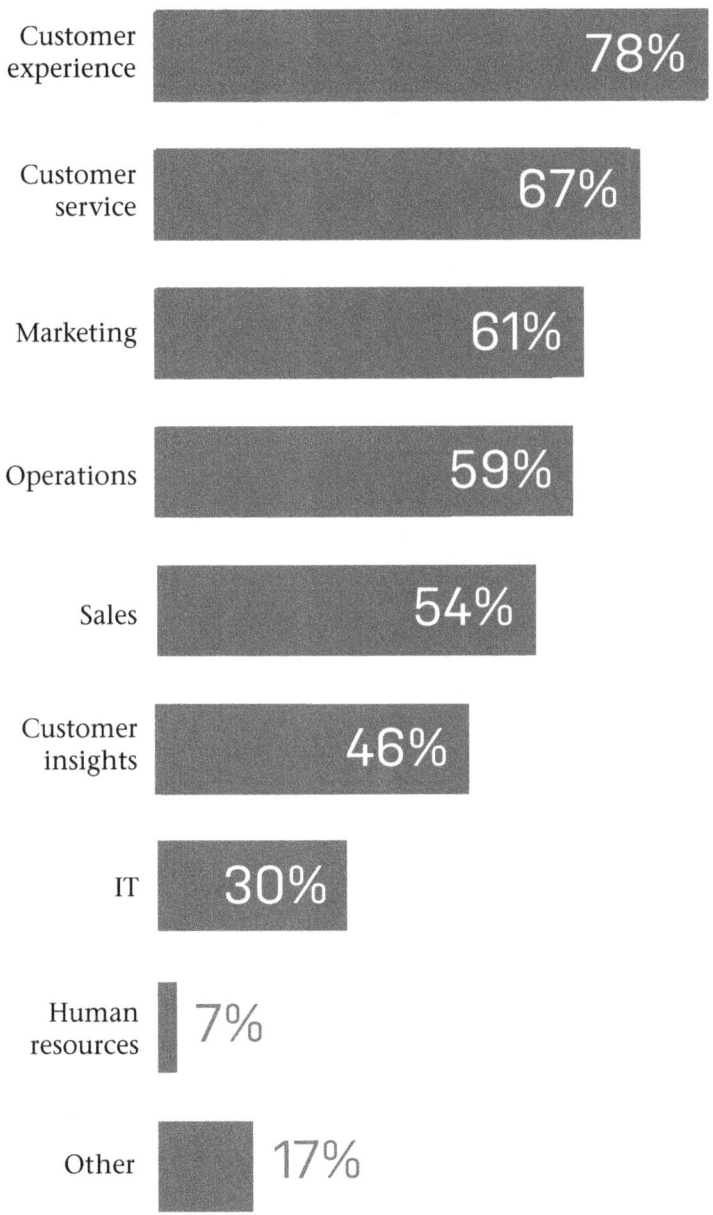

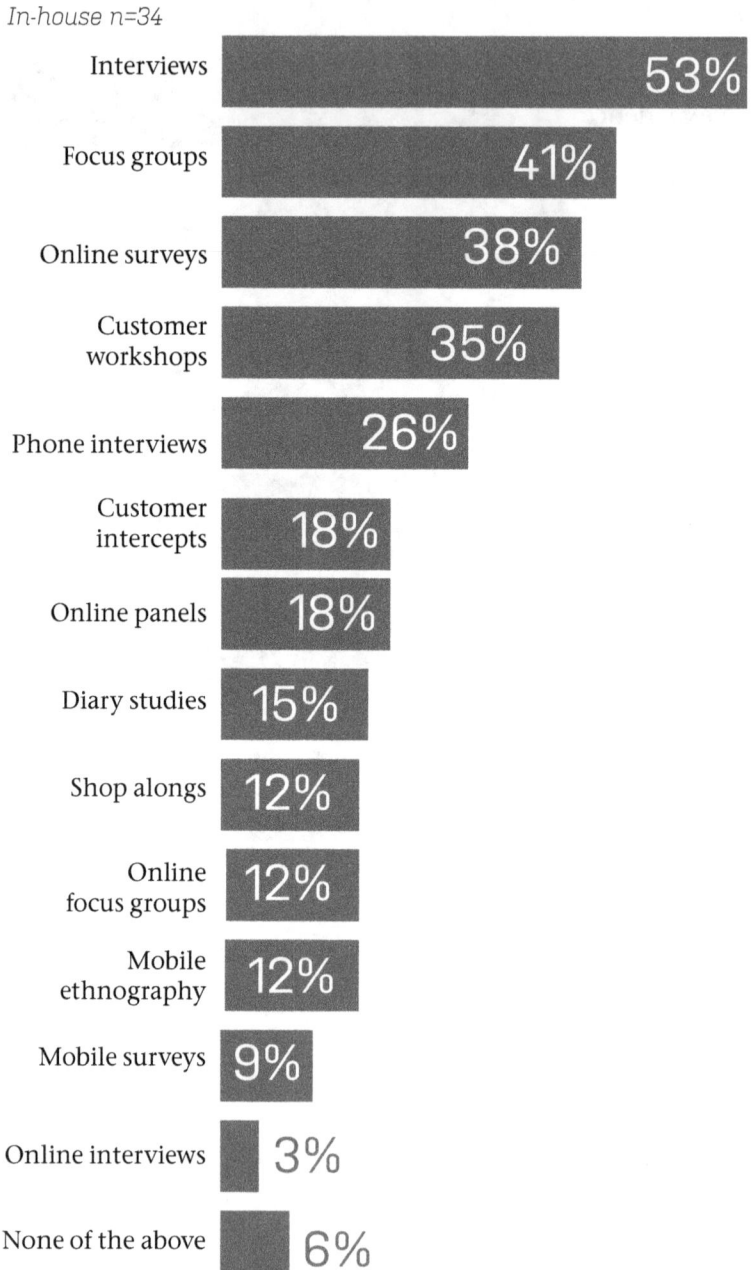

WHAT TYPE OF JOURNEY DID YOU LAST MAP?

In-house n=57

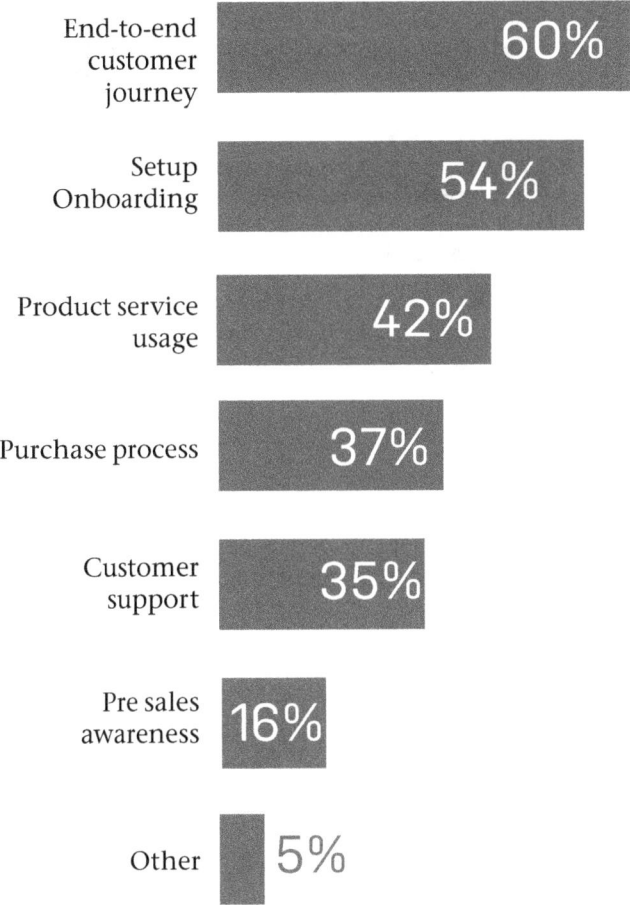

- End-to-end customer journey: 60%
- Setup Onboarding: 54%
- Product service usage: 42%
- Purchase process: 37%
- Customer support: 35%
- Pre sales awareness: 16%
- Other: 5%

Source of data: 2016 Survey of 134 CX professionals by The Customer Experience Professionals Association and Heart of the Customer

WHO SPONSORED YOUR MOST RECENT MAPPING PROJECT?

In-house n=53

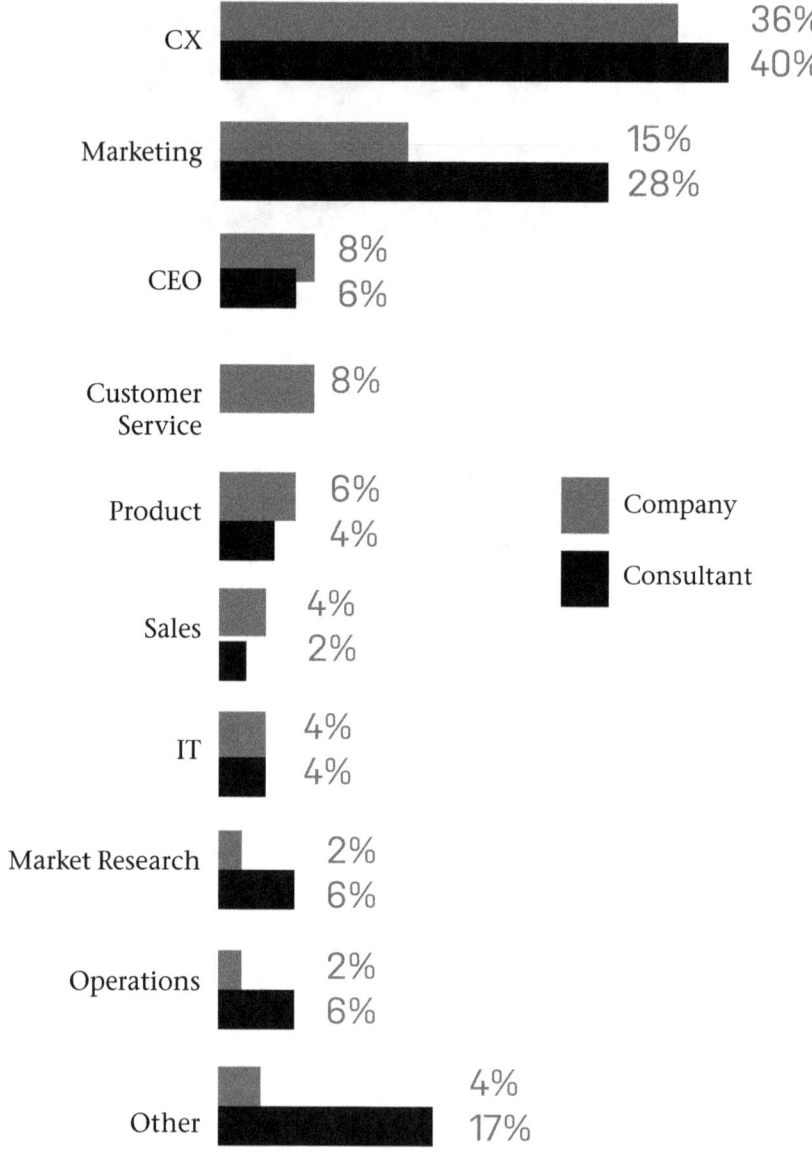

Source of data: 2016 Survey of 134 CX professionals by The Customer Experience Professionals Association and Heart of the Customer

WHICH RESEARCH METHOD WAS MOST EFFECTIVE FOR JOURNEY MAPPING?

In-house n=32

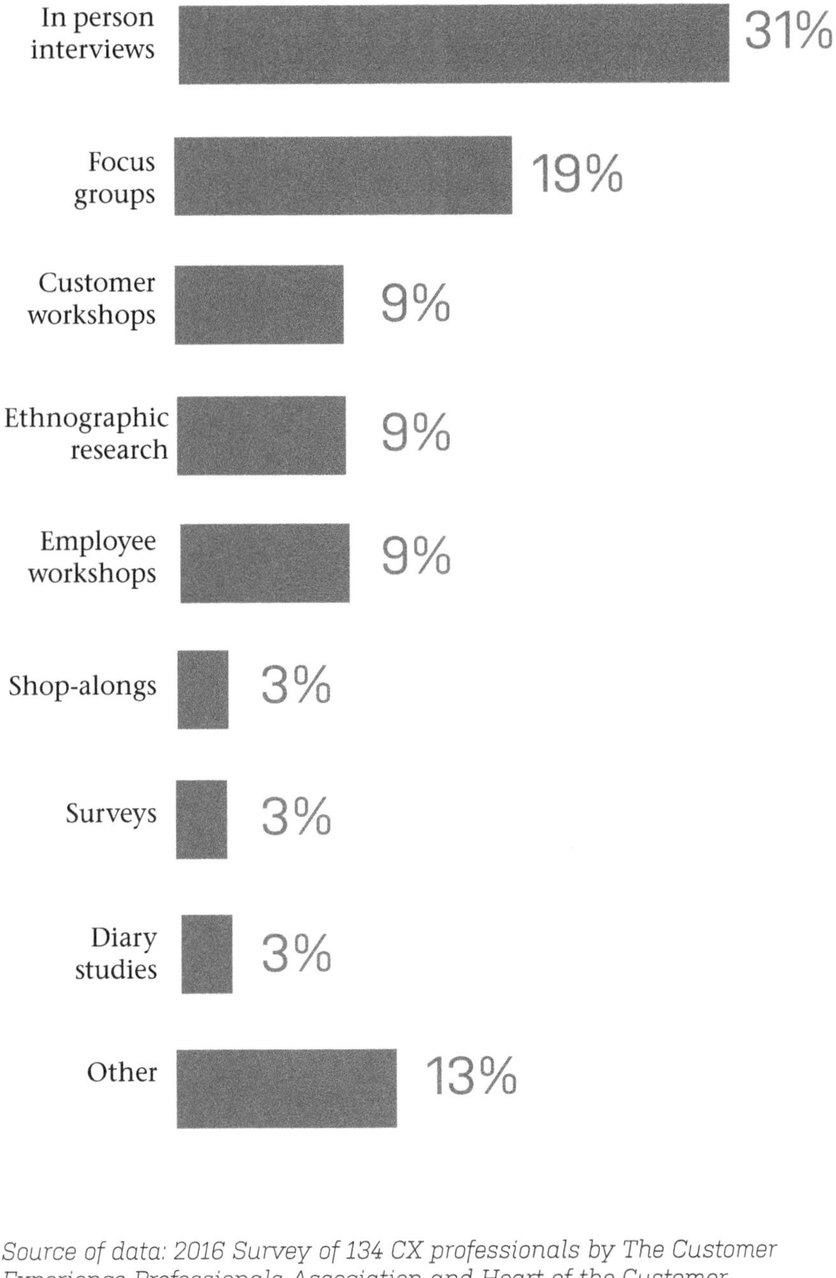

Method	%
In person interviews	31%
Focus groups	19%
Customer workshops	9%
Ethnographic research	9%
Employee workshops	9%
Shop-alongs	3%
Surveys	3%
Diary studies	3%
Other	13%

Source of data: 2016 Survey of 134 CX professionals by The Customer Experience Professionals Association and Heart of the Customer

WHICH SOFTWARE TOOLS HAVE YOU USED TO CREATE JOURNEY MAPS?

In-house n=56 Consultants n=50

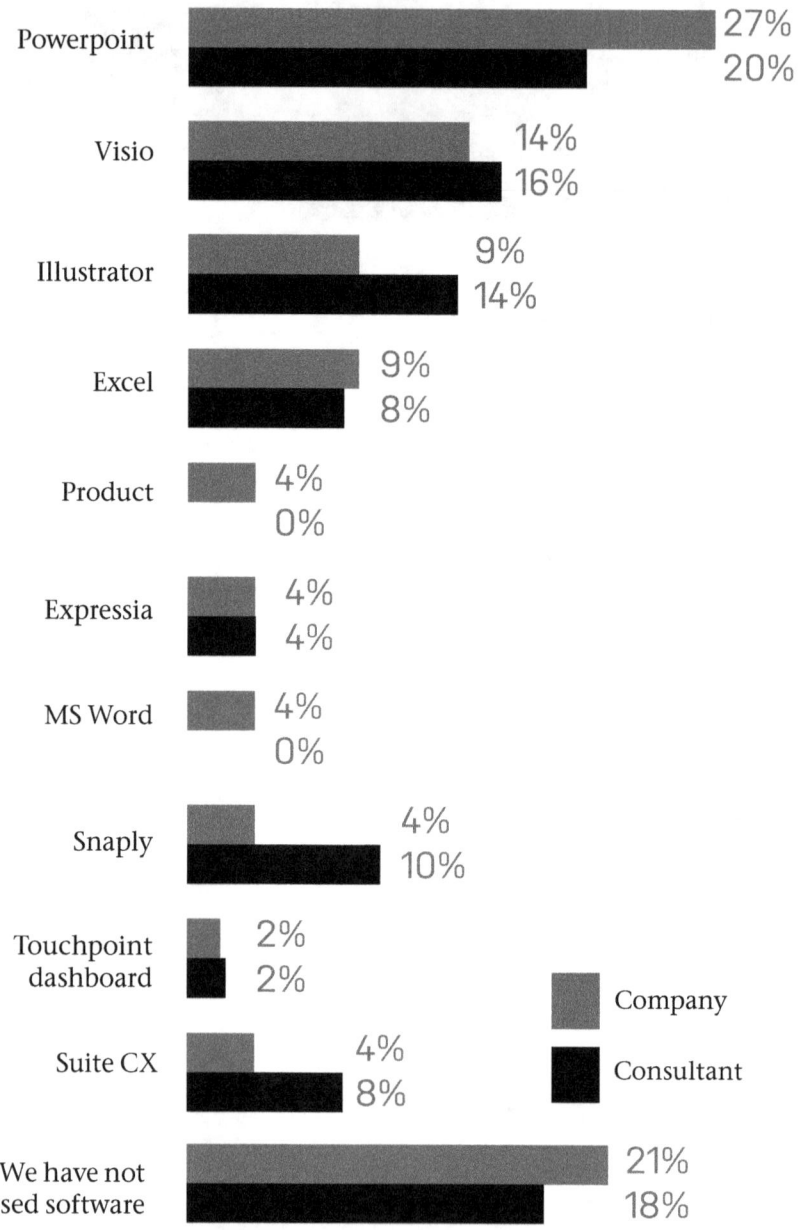

Source of data: 2016 Survey of 134 CX professionals by The Customer Experience Professionals Association and Heart of the Customer

WHICH METHODS DID YOU USE TO RESEARCH YOUR CUSTOMERS?

In-house n=34 Consultants n=43

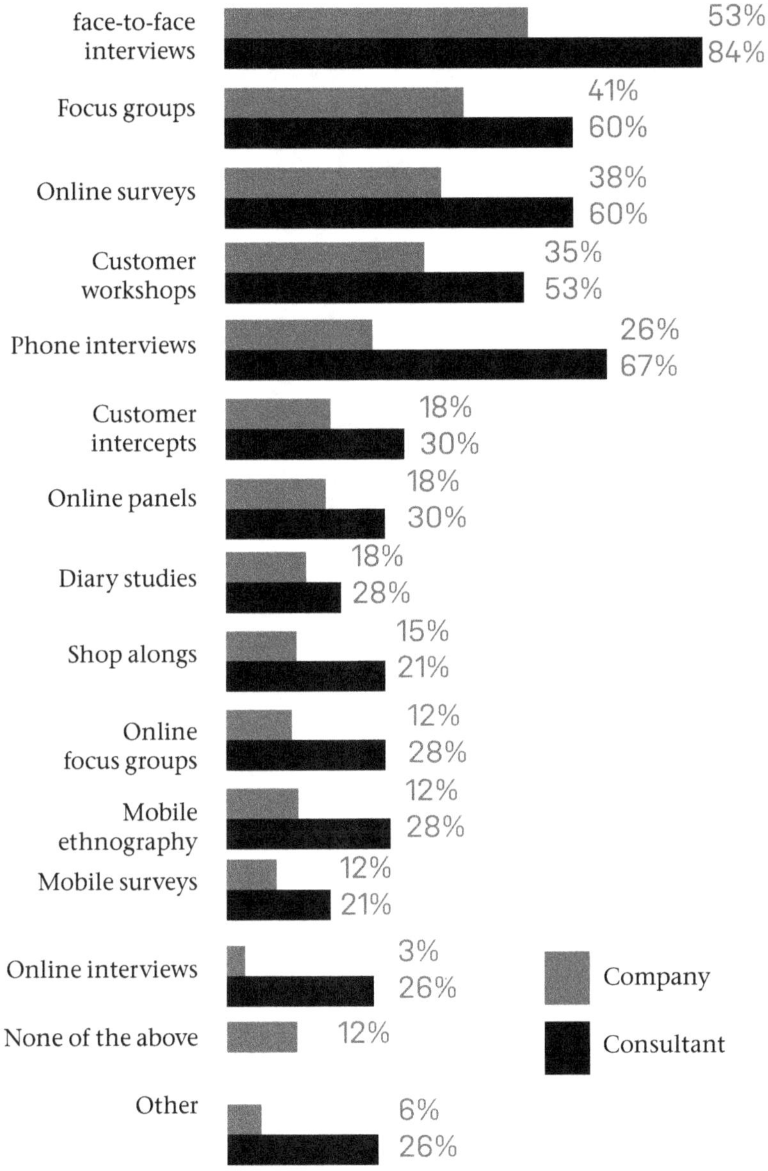

Method	Company	Consultant
face-to-face interviews	53%	84%
Focus groups	41%	60%
Online surveys	38%	60%
Customer workshops	35%	53%
Phone interviews	26%	67%
Customer intercepts	18%	30%
Online panels	18%	30%
Diary studies	18%	28%
Shop alongs	15%	21%
Online focus groups	12%	28%
Mobile ethnography	12%	28%
Mobile surveys	12%	21%
Online interviews	3%	26%
None of the above	12%	
Other	6%	26%

Source of data: 2016 Survey of 134 CX professionals by The Customer Experience Professionals Association and Heart of the Customer

DESIGN PROCESS OVERVIEW

DESIGN PROCESS OVERVIEW

PLANNING
What are our goals?
1. Meet with key stakeholders to set vision and intent.
2. Assemble a diverse team
3. Explore scenarios of user experience.
4. Document stakeholders performance requirements
5. Define the group of people or user segment that you are designing for. What are their gender, age, and income range? Where do they live? What is their culture?
6. Define your scope and constraints
7. Identify a needs that you are addressing. Identify a problem that you are solving.
8. Identify opportunities.
9. Consider project risks
10. What are the main hurdles that your team will need to overcome?
11. What information do you not have that will be necessary for a successful design?
12. Create a budget and plan.
13. Create tasks and deliverables.
14. Create a schedule.

DISCOVER EMPATHIZE
What does the research tell us?
15. Identify what you know and what you need to know.
16. Document a research plan
17. Benchmark competitive products.
18. Explore the context of use
19. Understand the risks.
20. Observe and interview individuals, groups, experts.
21. Develop design strategy.
22. Undertake qualitative, quantitative, primary and secondary research.
23. Talk to vendors.

SYNTHESIZE
What have we learned?
24. Review the research.
25. Make sense out of the research.
26. Develop insights.
27. Cluster insights.
28. Create a hierarchy.

HAVE A UNIQUE POINT OF VIEW
What is the design brief?

IDEATE
How is this for as a starting point?
29. Brainstorm
30. Define the most promising ideas.
31. Refine the ideas.
32. Establish key differentiation of your ideas.

DESIGN PROCESS

| PLAN | WARM UP | DISCOVER/ RESEARCH/ EMPATHIZE | SYNTHESIS/ POINT OF VIEW |

ACTIVITIES

PLAN
Define project goals and opportunities and end users.

The goal is to understand the value of the proposed design project and some basic objectives.

WARM UP
Some fast exercises to get the team up to speed and working productively with each other.

DISCOVER
Develop a deep understanding of your customers or end users through engaging them and using ethnographic research methods. Identify stakeholder needs.

SYNTHESIS POV
Make sense from your research. What are the insights? What is connected? What are the unmet needs? What is the opportunity? Define the problem that you will solve.

METHODS

Innovation Diagnostic
Smart goals
Blue ocean
Goal grid
Reframing matrix
Warming up
Wwwwwh
Interviews
Observation
Focus groups
Day in the life
Perceptual maps

Desert island
Milestones
Common Ground
Hobby
Barney
Difficult experience
Observe
Compliment
Free association
Zombie cats

Research plan
Observation
Focus Groups
Day in the life
Diary studies
Benchmarking
Competitors Analysis
Camera journals
Empathy tools
Web analytics
Stakeholder interviews

Affinity diagrams
5 Whys
Mind Maps
Personas
Perceptual Maps
Empathy Maps
Experience Maps
Service blueprints

OUTPUT

| PROJECT PLAN | PRODUCTIVE TEAM | RESEARCH DATA/NEEDS FINDING | UNIQUE INSIGHTS/ POINT OF VIEW |

MAKING CHOICES — MAKING CHOICES — CREATING CHOICES — MAKING CHOICES

DIVERGENT OR CONVERGENT

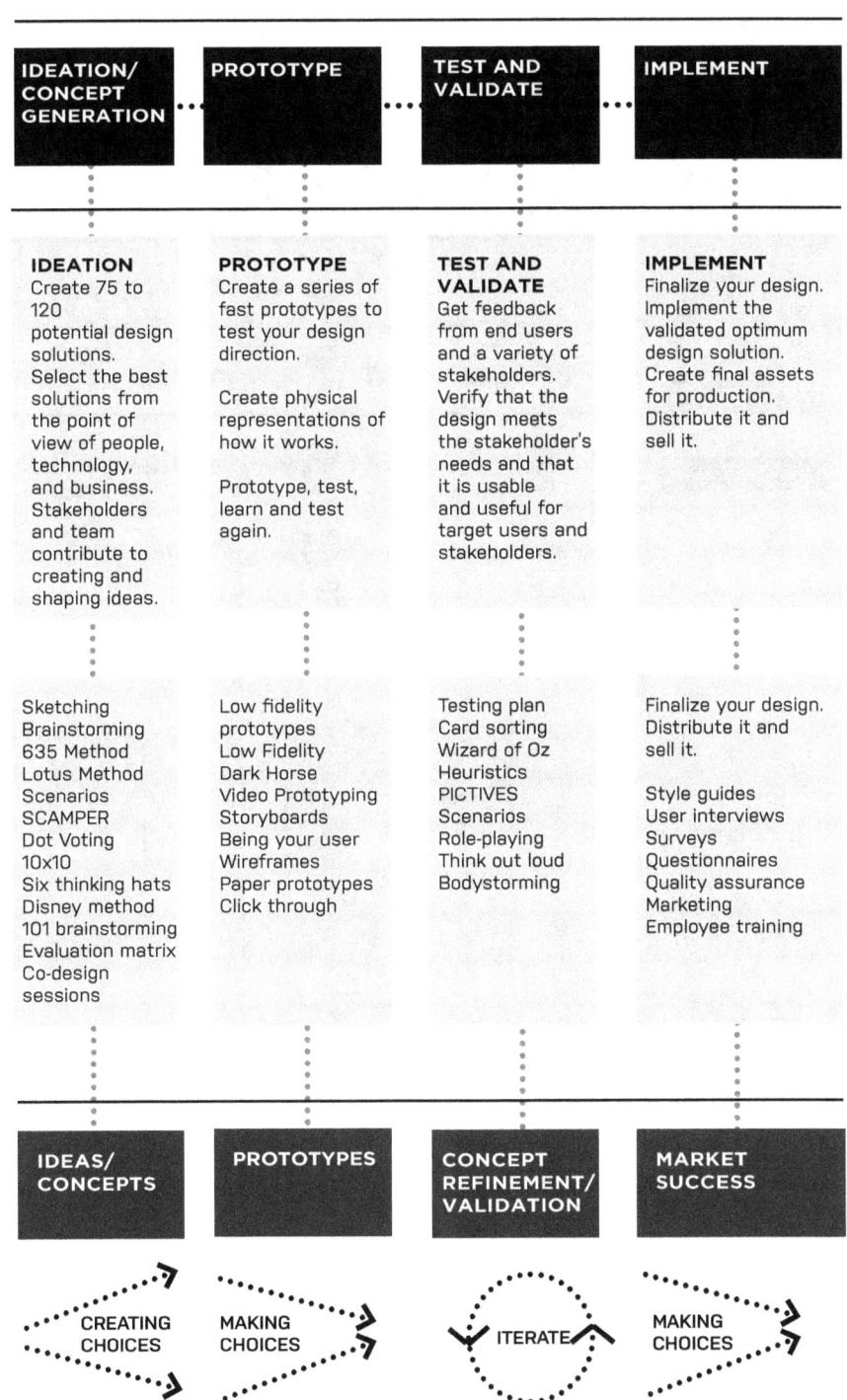

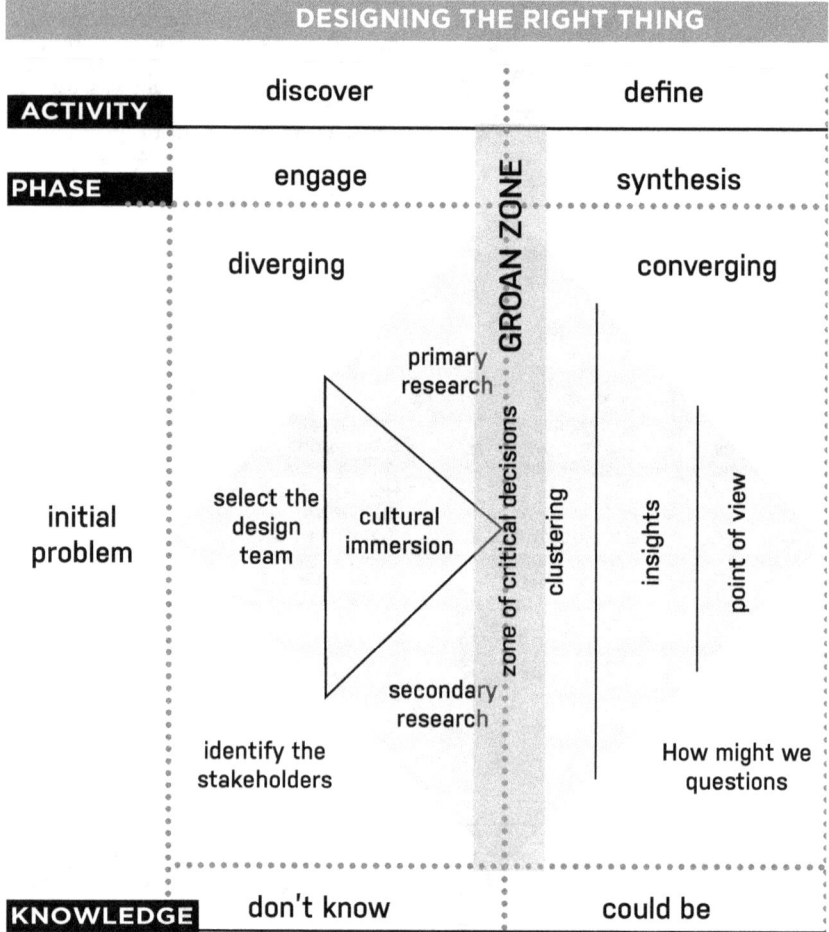

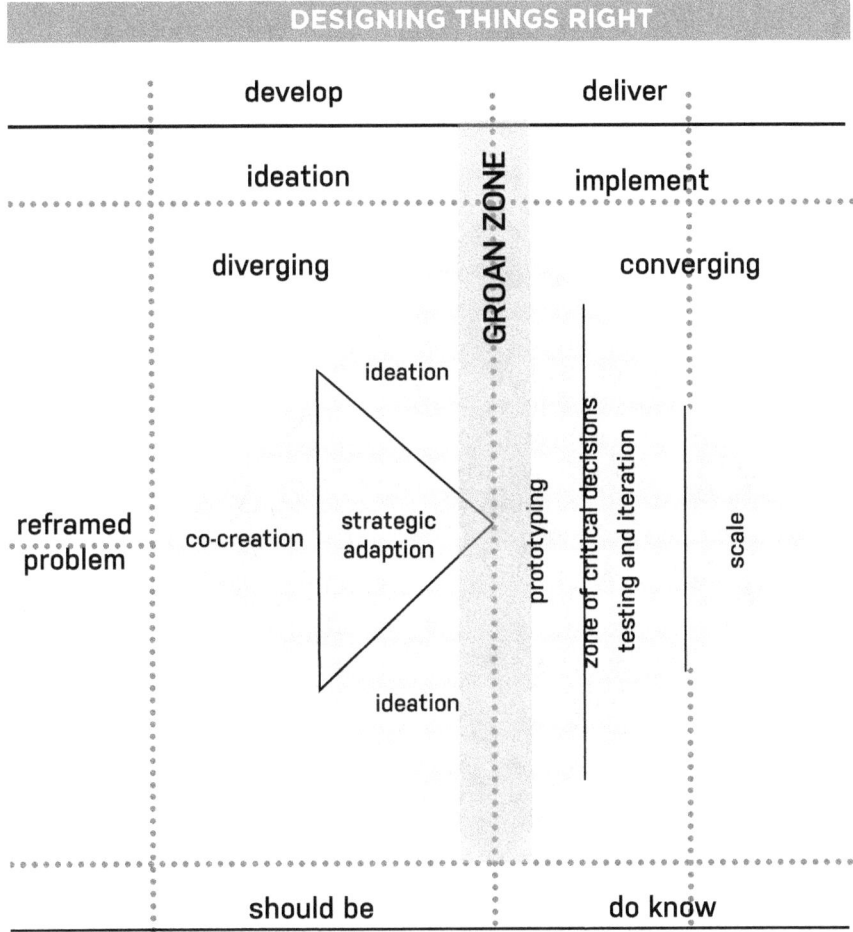

THE GROAN ZONE

WHAT

The groan zone is the place between place between a Divergent state, where many ideas are considered to the convergent state where one direction is found and refined. The groan zone is the transition from to the divergent phase. It is the most difficult and probably the most valuable phase of a design project.

During this phase the different team members will argue their points of view and from discussion and often some conflict a shared understanding will prevail. The groan zone is a necessary part of resolving different perspectives and choosing amongst possible directions.

Challenging problems demand that we push beyond familiar options into new territory in order to solve them. But leaving the familiar behind is uncomfortable and sometimes unpleasant. Solutions reached in the groan zone through a certain level of conflict can be enduring and better solutions.

WHO

This model is described in the Facilitator's Guide to Participatory Decision-Making by Sam Kaner et al (Jossey-Bass, 2nd ed 2007) and further developed by the Art of Hosting community

CHALLENGES

1. Luckner and Nadler (1997) argued that, 'Through involvement in experiences that are beyond one's comfort zone, individuals are forced to move into an area that feels uncomfortable and unfamiliar, the groan zone.
2. Groups experience confusion and frustration as part of their decision-making process. It describes the phase during which members of the group may be insensitive, defensive, ill-tempered, and headstrong and during which they struggle to "understand a wide range of foreign or opposing ideas" (Kaner, 2014, p.19).
3. Disagreement is a divergent state we differ on how to resolve a conflict or solve a problem. Agreement is a convergent state we come together on a resolution or solution.
4. The group experiences feelings close to despair and has a very hard time finding their way forwards in the process.
5. By overcoming these anxious feelings and thoughts of self-doubt while simultaneously sampling success, individuals

move from the groan zone to the growth zone'
6. 'Experience has shown that learning occurs when people are in their stretch zone. Intellectual development and personal growth do not occur if there is no disequilibrium in a person's current thinking or feeling' "Panicucci (2007) (p. 39)
7. Struggling to understand foreign or opposing ideas is not a pleasant experience. Group members can be repetitious, insensitive, defensive, short-tempered!
8. It's uncomfortable there, so we want to hurry through or past it.
9. Tricky, unknown territory brings out the human messiness of conflict, but hurrying through leaves important work undone.
10. It can feel hopeless there.
11. Cultures can avoid conflict due to a preference for interpersonal harmony but this may work against the best ideas rising to the top.

HOW
1. Being in the Groan Zone does NOT mean your group is dysfunctional or that you have reached an impasse. Nor does it mean you are 'failing' as a facilitator. Acknowledge the Groan Zone's existence.
2. It's a usual part of the design process Explain to the team that your are now in the Groan Zone and explain what the groan zone is.

3. Break big issues into smaller parts. Create a list of issues and work through them.
4. Take breaks.
5. Deepen your knowledge of and skill with problem solving strategies and tactics
6. Manage conflict.
7. Staying in the Groan Zone long enough to find innovative solutions.
8. Recognize unproductive comments like "we tried that before."
9. The effort to understand one another's perspectives and build a shared framework of understanding is the defining work of the groan zone.

"

Being in the Groan Zone does NOT mean your group is dysfunctional or that you have reached an impasse. Nor does it mean you are 'failing' as a facilitator."

Sam Kaner
Participatory Decision-Making

DESIGN PROCESS OVERVIEW 103

PROTOTYPE TEST ITERATE
How could we make it better?
33. Make your favored ideas physical.
34. Create low-fidelity prototypes from inexpensive available materials.
35. Develop question guides.
36. Develop test plan.
37. Test prototypes with stakeholders.
38. Get feedback from people.
39. Refine the prototypes.
40. Test again.
41. Build in the feedback.
42. Refine again.
43. Continue iteration until design works.
44. When you are confident that your idea works make a prototype that looks and works like a production product.

IMPLEMENT AND DELIVER
Let's make it. Let's sell it.
45. Create your proposed production design.
46. Test and evaluate.
47. Review objectives.
48. Manufacture your first samples.
49. Review first production samples and refine.
50. Launch.
51. Obtain user feedback.
52. Conduct field studies.
53. Define the vision for the next product or service.

CHAPTER SUMMARY

The stages of the design thinking process are:

1. Planning
2. Discovery
3. Synthesis
4. Point of view
5. Ideate
6. Prototype and test
7. Implement and deliver.

REVIEW QUESTIONS

1. What are the stages of the design thinking process?
2. Describe the activities in each stage of the design thinking process.
3. What are four methods that can be used in the discovery phase?
4. What are four methods that can be used in the Synthesis phase?
5. What are four methods that can be used in ideation?
6. What are four prototyping methods used in design thinking?
7. What is iteration?
8. What phase of the process is idea brainstorming usually done?
9. What are four things you do during the planning phase?
10. During which phase do you benchmark competitors?
11. What institution developed the double diamond process model?

DISCOVERY

DISCOVERY PHASE

WHAT

One of the most important considerations when building a service blueprint is that you use real information relevant to your customers or end users. Organizations very often choose not to connect with their customers to understand their customer's real experience. The methods in this chapter are good methods to collect data to ensure the success of your blueprinting effort.

Studies show that greatest single reason for the failure of new products and services is a lack of empathy within the design team of the perspectives of the stakeholders. Over 75% of new product initiatives fail in the market.

During this phase we investigate our users unmet needs and develop a deep understanding of the way they think, what they feel, the behaviors they engage in and the values they hold through engaging them observing and listening to them explain their point of view, their problems, and their underlying needs.

In order to create a design effectively, we need to understand the context that surrounds the end users. We use a variety of research techniques to investigate the user needs and the design context.

By the end of this phase, we will have an overview of user needs, existing services, and their effectiveness and have a foundation to explore many possible design directions. We will investigate the business requirements of the design. We explore user unmet needs through.

1. Workshops
2. Interviews
3. Observation
4. Focus groups
5. Affinity diagrams
6. Discovery methods

DISCOVER
1. Who your users are.
2. Your users' needs and how you're not meeting them.
3. The people you need on your team.
4. What the stakeholder journey or experience looks like.

When you talk, you are only repeating what you know, but when you listen then you learn something new."

Dalai Lama

HOW?
1. Develop empathy for your stakeholders.
2. Develop and implement a research plan.
3. Assume a beginner's mindset.

4. Carry out user research
5. Imagine yourself in that person's situation.
6. Adopt a beginner's way of thinking. Withhold judgment and preconceived bias.
7. Identify gaps in knowledge.
8. Set aside your beliefs, concerns and personal agenda and try to see things from the stakeholders' points point of view.
9. Question everything. Be curious.
10. Listen.
11. Talk to users to uncover underlying needs.
12. Immerse yourself in your customer's reality.
13. Walk in your user's shoes.
14. Look for your end user's workarounds for their problems.
15. Learn what the stakeholder would do.
16. Immerse yourself in the problem. Walk in your user's shoes, observe what's not being said.
17. Capture your learnings.

OUTPUTS
Outputs of this phase could include:
1. A list of user needs
2. A list of user unmet needs
3. A hierarchy of user needs
4. A plan for the resources required to complete the project.
5. the ability to scope and plan an alpha
6. a decision to progress to next phase
7. Perhaps a low fidelity prototype or several low fidelity prototypes.
8. Four to six personas is an optimum number to cover an organization's customer segments.
9. A list of the most important stakeholders both internally in your organization and externally.
10. A benchmarking of existing or competitive services and a SWOT analysis of these services.
11. A definition of the target audience.

Adapted from Discovery phase Government Service Design Manual, https://www.gov.uk/service-manual/phases/discovery (accessed July 06, 2016).

THE DISCOVERY PROCESS

ASSEMBLE YOUR TEAM
You will need different skills and the team roles and team size may evolve during the different development phases.

Select a diverse cross-disciplinary group of people. Have different disciplines, different genders, ages, cultures, represented for the most successful results. Have some T shaped people. These are people who have more than one area of experience or training such as design and management. They will help your team collaborate productively.

MULTIDISCIPLINARY TEAM
A multidisciplinary team helps you to:
1. Build your service
2. Keep improving it based on user needs
3. Make decisions quickly

TEAM SKILLS
1. Analyze user needs, including accessibility and assisted digital needs, and turn these into user stories
2. Create user stories and prioritize them
3. Manage and report to stakeholders and manage dependencies on other teams
4. Procure services from third parties, if needed

5. Test with real users
6. Find ways of accrediting and handling data

DEFINE YOUR TARGET AUDIENCE

Creating a projected user models will keep the development team rooted to realistic user requirements and minimizes user frustration with the real product. Having a deep understanding of users can help development team better understand the wants & needs of the targeted customers. This will help the development team relate better to the target user. Understanding user tasks helps in developing design solutions that will ensure that the user expectations are met & avoid design errors and customer frustration. Use research methods such as interviewing, observation, empathy maps and user experience maps to better understand your audience. Market segmentation is basically the division of market into smaller segments. It helps identify potential customers and target them.

TYPES OF SEGMENTATION
1. Behavior segmentation.
2. Benefit segmentation.
3. Psychographic segmentation.
4. Geographic segmentation.
5. Demographic segmentation.

SEGMENTATION QUESTIONS
1. What is your target group's goals emotions, experiences, needs and desires?
2. Information collected from just a few people is unlikely to be representative of the whole range of users.
3. What are the user tasks and activities?
4. How will the user use the product or service to perform a task?
5. What is the context of the user?
6. Where are they? What surrounds them physically and virtually or culturally?
7. How large is your user group?

When defining your target audience consider:
1. Age
2. Gender
3. Occupation
4. Industry
5. Travel
6. Citizenship status
7. Marital state
8. Income
9. Culture
10. Language
11. Religion
12. Location
13. Education
14. Nationality
15. Mobility
16. Migration
17. Mental state
18. Abilities
19. Disabilities
20. Health

SHARE WHAT YOU KNOW
1. In the project kick-off meeting ask every team member to introduce themselves and to describe in 3 minutes what experience they have that may be relevant to the project.
2. The moderator can list areas of knowledge on a whiteboard.
3.

IDENTIFY WHAT YOU NEED TO KNOW

Arrange a project kick-off meeting. Invite your team and important stakeholders. On a whiteboard or flip chart create two lists. Ask each person to introduce themselves and describe what they know or have experienced that may be useful for implementing the project. Brainstorm with your group the areas that are unknown and how that information may be obtained. Formulate a research plan and assign responsibilities, tasks, and deliverables with dates.

UNCOVER NEEDS
1. "What causes the problem?"
2. "What are the impacts of the problem?"
3. "What are possible solutions?"
4. Probe about workarounds How do people adapt their environment to solve problems that they have?
5. Ask what their single biggest obstacle is to achieve what they are trying to achieve How can you help them?
6. Ask what's changing in their world What are the trends?
7. Observe people
8. Can you see problems they have that they perhaps do not even recognize are problems?
9. Ask other stakeholders

DEFINE YOUR GOALS
A goal is the intent or intents of the design process.

1. Write a detailed description of the design problem.
2. Define a list of needs that are connected to the design problem.
3. Make a list of obstacles that need to be overcome to solve the design problem.
4. Make a list of constraints that apply to the problem.
5. Rewrite the problem statement to articulate the above requirements.

There is one very important future perspective he [Jonathan Ive] offers though around the increasing complexity and interrelatedness of products and how this requires more effective multidisciplinary working practice to create these products. He explains how they've designed Apple's new donut-like 'Ring' HQ to enable them to create more fully multi-disciplinary design teams, where industrial designers, sound engineers, hardware and software guys, UX people, electronics engineers etc, can all work together throughout the process.

2017 Soundcloud Interview
Sir Jonathan Ive
Apple VP of Design

ANTHROPUMP

DISCOVERY PHASE 109

SHOP-ALONGS

WHAT
In-store interviews, uncover thoughts, influences, and motivations when consumers are shopping. This research method can be used to investigate the effectiveness of design of packaging, placement, customer experience, and in-aisle marketing. A researcher accompanies a consumer while they browse and shop for items, asking questions as they shop. The interviewer meets the recruited shopper at the door or recruits participants at the door. Shop-alongs are used for collecting real-time, in the moment, and point-of-purchase feedback. A shop-along can be designed for both qualitative or quantitative research. Fifty to one hundred shop-alongs can be used for qualitative analysis. Ten shop-alongs at a local store, could be used for qualitative analysis.

WHEN
Shop-alongs are used In-Store to assess:
1. The purchase decision hierarchy
2. The triggers of the need or desire for the product
3. The behaviors that take place in the store and in the aisle
4. The role of in-store sampling, displays, signage, multi-media promotional efforts, customer service, etc.

WHERE
Retail stores and grocery stores are popular locations for shop-alongs. Locations where a customer may spend 30 minutes naturally shopping are preffered over locations wherea shopper may usually spend just a few minutes such as a gas station.

HOW
All shop-along projects work a little differently. Each one has their own unique set of circumstances which drive the process and outcomes. However, like many market research projects, they follow a similar process. The process typically involves a kickoff meeting, set up, fieldwork, and then analysis and reporting.

1. Kickoff Meeting
A shop-along starts with a kickoff meeting between the client and the researcher. At this meeting the goals and steps are defined The researcher will then recruit the participants and create the shop-along interview guide design.

2. Recruitment
The demographics and segmentation of the research subjects are defined. This can range to include gender, age, incomes, types of products purchased, stores preferred or many other factors.

3. Choosing Locations
Next the store locations to study are defined.

4. Begin Recruit
The researcher will use a recruitment firm on line panel, or social media to recruit participants to a particular store at a date and time for a 30-minute shop-along. Sometimes researchers recruit at the door as

participants walk into the store. Participants are screened to ensure they meet the demographic profile and see if they qualify to participate for the shop-along.

5. Guide Design
The guide contains the script used by the interviewer when they conduct the shop-along. The guide is written to achieve the goals of the shop-along. A good quality guide is important for the success of the research.

6. Conduct the Shop-along
Researchers follow the field guide and record data for each participant and work to promote a natural shopping experience. The interviewer should drop back at non critical times.

7. Analysis and Reporting
Review the data from the shop-longs. Recorded data is transcribed. Comments are broken down. The data is clustered and a hierarchy of importance is determined. The report concludes with a list of insights, conclusions and recommendations.

WHAT
This method involves the research videotaping one or more participant's activities. The videos are replayed to the participants, and they are asked to explain their behavior.

WHO
Rick Robinson, John Cain, E- Lab Inc.,

WHY
1. Used for collecting data before concept and for evaluating prototypes after concept phases of projects.

CHALLENGES
1. Best conducted by someone who has practice observing human interactions in a space.

HOW
1. People are first captured on video while interacting with products.
2. The participants are then asked to watch the tapes while researchers question them about what they see, how they felt, etc. Research subjects analyze their actions and experiences.
3. The company invites people who have been captured on video to watch their tapes as researchers pose questions about what's happening.
4. Create videotapes and examines these follow-up sessions, analyzing research subjects analyzing themselves.

BEHAVIORAL MAP

WHAT
Behavioral mapping is a method used to record and analyze human activities in a location. This method is used to document what participants are doing and time spent at locations and traveling. Behavioral maps can be created based on a person or space.

WHO
Ernest Becker 1962

WHY
1. This method helps develop an understanding of space layouts, interactions, experiences, and behaviors.
2. Helps understand way-finding.
3. Helps optimize the use of space.
4. A limitation of this method is that motivations remain unknown.
5. Use when you want to develop more efficient or effective use of space in retail environments, exhibits, architecture and interior design.

HOW
1. Identify the users.
2. Ask what is the purpose of the space?
3. Consider what behaviors are meaningful.
4. Consider different personas.
5. Participants can be asked to map their use of a space on a floor plan and can be asked to reveal their motivations.
6. Can use shadowing or video ethnographic techniques.
7. Create behavioral map.

8. Analyze behavioral map
9. Reorganize space based on insights.

RESOURCES
A map of the space.
Video camera
Digital still camera
Notebook
Pens

BENCHMARKING

WHAT
Benchmarking is a method for organizations to compare their products, services or customer experiences with other industry products, services and experiences to identify the best practices.

WHO
Robert Camp Xerox, 1989 Benchmarking: the search for industry best practices that lead to superior performance.

WHY
1. A tool to identify, and implement the best practices.
2. The practice of measuring your performance against best competitors.

CHALLENGES
1. Can be expensive
2. Organizations often think their companies were performing above the average for the industry when they are not.

HOW
1. Identify what your objective.
2. Identify potential partners
3. Identify similar industries and organizations.
4. Identify organizations that are leaders.
5. Identify data sources
6. Identify the products or organizations to be benchmarked
7. Select the benchmarking factors to measure.
8. Undertake benchmarking
9. Research the "best practice" organizations
10. Analyze the outcomes
11. Target future performance
12. Adjust goal
13. Modify your own product or service to conform with best practices identified in the benchmarking process.

RESOURCES
Post-it-notes
Pens
Dry-erase markers
White-board
Paper

BENEFITS MAP

WHAT
The benefits map is a simple tool that helps your team decide what will give you the best return on investment for time invested.

WHY
1. Aids communication and discussion within the organization.
2. It is human nature to do tasks which are not most urgent first.
3. To gain competitive advantage,
4. Helps build competitive strategy
5. Helps build communication

strategy
6. Helps manage time effectively

CHALLENGES
Can be subjective

HOW
1. Moderator draws axes on whiteboard or flip chart.
2. Worthwhile activity at the start of a project.
3. Map individual tasks.
4. Interpret the map.
5. Create strategy.
6. Tasks which have high benefit with low investment may be given priority.

BOUNDARY SHIFTING

WHAT
Boundary shifting involves identifying features or ideas outside the boundary of the system related to the defined problem and applying to them to the problem being addressed.

WHY
It is fast and inexpensive.

HOW
1. Define the problem.
2. Research outside systems that may have related ideas or problems to the defined problem.
3. Identify ideas or solutions outside the problem system.
4. Apply the outside idea or solution to the problem being addressed.

RESOURCES
1. Pen
2. Paper
3. White-board
4. Dry-erase markers

CAMERA JOURNAL

WHAT
The research subjects record their activities with a camera and notes. The researcher reviews the images and discusses them with the participants.

WHY
1. Helps develop empathy for the participants.
2. Participants are involved in the research process.
3. Helps establish rapport with participants.
4. May reveal aspects of life that are seldom seen by outsiders.

CHALLENGES
1. Should obtain informed consent.
2. Be sensitive to vulnerable people.
3. May be a relatively expensive research method.
4. May be time-consuming.
5. Best used with other methods.
6. Technology may be unreliable.
7. The method may be unpredictable'.
8. Has to be carefully analyzed

HOW
1. Define subject of study
2. Define participants
3. Gather data images and insight statements.
4. Analyze data.
5. Identify insights
6. Rank insights
7. Produce criteria for concept generation from insights.

8. Generate concepts to meet needs of users.

RESOURCES
Cameras
Voice recorder
Video camera
Notepad computer
Pens

OPEN CARD SORT

WHAT
This is a method for discovering the relationships of a list of items. Participants are asked to arrange individual, unsorted items into groups. For an open card sort, the user defines the groups rather than the researcher.

CARD SORTING IS APPLIED WHEN:
9. When there is a large number of items.
10. The items are similar and difficult to organize into categories.
11. Users may have different perceptions related to organizing the items.

WHO
Jastrow 1886
Nielsen & Sano 1995

WHY
1. It is a simple method using index cards,
2. Used to provide insights for interface design.

CHALLENGES
1. Ask participants to fill out a second card if they feel it belongs in two groups.
2. There are a number of online card sorting tools available.

HOW
1. Recruit between 5 and 15 participants representative of your user group.
2. Provide a small deck of cards.
3. Provide clear instructions. Ask your participants to arrange the cards in ways that make sense to them. One hundred cards take about 1 hour to sort.
4. The user sorts labeled cards into groups by that they define themselves.
5. The user can generate more card labels.
6. If users do not understand a card ask them to exclude it. Ask participants for their rationale for any dual placements of cards.
7. Analyze the piles of cards and create a list of insights derived from the card sort.
8. Analyze the data.

CLOSED CARD SORT

WHAT
This is a method for understanding the relationships of a number of pieces of data. Participants asked to arrange individual, unsorted items into groups. A closed sort involves the cards being sorted into groups where the group headings may be defined by the researcher.

Card sorting is applied when:
1. When there is a large number of pieces of data.
2. The individual pieces of data are similar.
3. Participants have different perceptions of the data.

WHO
Jastrow 1886
Nielsen & Sano 1995

WHY
1. It is a simple method using index cards,
2. Used to provide insights for interface design.

HOW
1. Recruit 15 to 20 participants representative of your user group.
2. Provide a deck of cards using words and or images relevant to your concept.
3. Provide clear instructions. Ask your participants to arrange the cards in ways that make sense to them. 100 cards takes about 1 hour to sort.
4. The user sorts labeled cards into groups by under header cards defined by the researcher.
5. The user can generate more card labels.
6. If users do not understand a card ask them to exclude it. Ask participants for their rationale for any dual placements of cards.
7. Discuss why the cards are placed in a particular pile yields insight into user perceptions.
8. Analyze the data. Create a hierarchy for the information
9. Use postcards or post-it notes.

RESOURCES
Post cards
Pens
Post-it-notes
Laptop computer
A table

CONVERSATION CARDS

WHAT
Cards used for initiating conversation in a contextual interview and to help subjects explore.

WHO
Originator unknown. Google Ngram indicates the term first appeared around 1801 in England for a collection of "Moral and Religious Anecdotes particularly adapted for the entertainment and instruction of young persons, and to support instead of destroying serious conversation."

WHY
1. Questions are the springboard for conversations.
2. Can be used to initiate sensitive conversations.

CHALLENGES
1. How will data from the cards be used?
2. How will cards be evaluated?
3. How many cards are necessary to be representative?
4. What are potential problems relating card engagement
5. Use one unit of information per question.

HOW
1. Decide on the goals for research.
2. Formulate about 10 questions related to topic
3. Create the cards.
4. Recruit the subjects.
5. Undertake pre-interview with sample subject to test.
6. Use release form if required.

7. Carry light equipment.
8. Record answers verbatim.
9. Communicate the purpose and length of the interview.
10. Select location. It should not be too noisy or have other distracting influences
11. Work through the cards.
12. Video or record the sessions for later review.
13. Analyze
14. Create Insights

RESOURCES
Conversation Cards.
Notebook
Video Camera
Pens
Interview plan or structure
Questions, tasks and discussion items

Interview cards

CULTURAL INVENTORY

WHAT
It is a survey focused on the cultural assets of a location or organization.

WHO
Julian Haynes Steward may have been the first to use the term in 1947.

WHY
1. Can be used in strategic planning
2. Can be used to solve problems.

CHALLENGES
Requires time and resources

HOW
1. Create your team
2. Collect existing research
3. Review existing research and identify gaps
4. Host a meeting of stakeholders
5. Promote the meeting
6. Ask open-ended questions about the culture and heritage
7. Set a time limit of 2 hours for the meeting.
8. Plan the collection phase
9. Compile inventory. This can be in the form of a website
10. Distribute the inventory and obtain feedback.

RESOURCES
Diary
Notebooks
Pens
Post-it notes
Voice recorder
Postcards
Digital Camera

CULTURAL PROBES

WHAT
A cultural probe is a method of collecting information about people, their context, and their culture. The aim of this method is to record events, behaviors, and interactions in their context. This method involves the participants to record and collect the data themselves.

WHO
Bill Gaver Royal College of Art London 1969

WHY
1. This is a useful method when the participants that are being

studied are hard to reach for example if they are traveling.
2. It is a useful technique if the activities being studied take place over an extended period or at irregular intervals.
3. The information collected can be used to build personas.

CHALLENGES
It is important with this method to select the participants carefully and give them support during the study.

HOW
1. Define the objective of your study.
2. Recruit your participants.
3. Brief the participants.
4. Supply participants with kit. The items in the kit are selected to collect the type of information you want to gather and can include items such as notebooks, diary, camera, voice recorder or postcards.
5. You can use an affinity diagram to analyze the data collected.

DAY EXPERIENCE METHOD

WHAT
The method requires participants to record answers to questions during a day. The person's mobile phone is used to prompt them The participants use a notebook, a camera or a voice recorder to answer your questions. The interviews are followed by a focus group.

WHO
Intille 2003

WHY
1. The participants are co-researchers.
2. Reduces the influence of the researcher on the participant when compared to methods such as interviews or direct observation.

CHALLENGES
1. Cost of devices.
2. This method should be used with other methods.

HOW
1. Conduct a preliminary survey to focus the method on preferred questions.
2. Recruit participants.
3. The experience sampling takes place over one day.
4. The participants are asked to provide answers to questions at irregular intervals when promoted by a SMS message via the participant's mobile phone.
5. The interval can be 60 to 90-minutes.
6. The participant can record the activity with a camera, notebook or voice recorder.
7. Soon after the day organize a focus group with the participants.
8. The participants describe their day using the recorded material.

RESOURCES
Mobile phone
Automated SMS messaging
Notebook
Camera
Software

Day Experience Resource Kit Matthew Riddle, http://www.matthewriddle.com/papers/Day_Experience_Resource_Kit.pdf (accessed July 06, 2016).

DAY IN THE LIFE

WHAT
A study in which the designer observes the participant in the location and context of their usual activities, observing and recording events to understand the activities from the participant's point of view. Mapping a 'Day in the Life' as a storyboard can provide a focus for discussion.

WHO
Alex Bavelas 1944

WHY
1. This method informs the design process by observation of real activities and behaviors.
2. This method provides insights with relatively little cost and time.

CHALLENGES
1. Choose the participants carefully
2. Document everything. Something that seems insignificant may become significant later.

HOW
1. Define activities to study
2. Recruit participants
3. Prepare
4. Observe subjects in context.
5. Capture data,
6. Create storyboard with text and timeline.
7. Analyze data
8. Create insights.
9. Identify issues
10. Identify needs
11. Add new/more requirements to concept development

DOT VOTING

WHAT
Dot voting is a way of efficiently selecting from a large number of ideas the preferred ideas to carry forward in the design process.

WHY
It is a method of selecting a favored idea by collective rather than individual judgment. It is a fast method that allows a design to progress. It leverages the strengths of diverse team member viewpoints and experiences.

CHALLENGES
1. The assessment is subjective.
2. Groupthink
3. Not enough good ideas
4. Inhibition
5. Lack of critical thinking

RESOURCES
Large wall
Adhesive dots

HOW
1. Gather your team of between four and twelve participants.
2. Brainstorm ideas, for example, ask each team member to generate between ten and thirty ideas as sketches.
3. Each idea should be presented on one post-it-note or page.
4. Each designer should quickly explain each idea to the group before the group votes.
5. Spread the ideas on a wall or table.
6. Ask the team to vote on their two

or three favorite ideas and total the votes. You can use sticky dots or colored pins to indicate a vote or a moderator can tally the scores.
7. Rearrange the ideas ranked from most dots to least.
8. Refine the preferred ideas.

DIARY STUDY

WHAT
This method involves participants recording particular events, feelings or interactions, in a diary supplied by the researcher. User Diaries help provide insight into behavior. Participants record their behavior and thoughts. Diaries can uncover behaviour that may not be articulated in an interview or readily visible to outsiders.

WHO
Gordon Allport, may have been the first to describe diary studies in 1942.

WHY
1. Can capture data that is difficult to capture using other methods.
2. Useful when you wish to gather information and minimize your influence on research subjects.
3. When the process or event you're exploring takes place over a long period.

CHALLENGES
1. Process can be expensive and time-consuming.
2. Needs participant monitoring.
3. It is difficult to get materials back.

HOW
1. A diary can be kept over a period of one week or longer.
2. Define focus for the study.
3. Recruit participants carefully.
4. Decide method: preprinted, diary notebook or online.
5. Prepare diary packs. Can be preprinted sheets or blank twenty-page notebooks with prepared questions or online web-based diary.
6. Brief participants.
7. Distribute diaries directly or by mail.
8. Conduct study. Keep in touch with participants.
9. Conduct debrief interview.
10. Look for insights.

RESOURCES
Diary
Preprinted diary sheets
Online diary
Pens
Disposable cameras
Digital camera
Self-addressed envelopes

BIASES

We all have unconscious biases. These biases can reduce the effectiveness of our decision-making in design thinking. Understanding our own biases can help us overcome them. Understanding the biases of others can help us improve the user experience and help us better understand team dynamics and diversity.

COGNITIVE DISSONANCE

Cognitive dissonance is the stress experienced by a person who simultaneously holds contradictory beliefs, ideas, or values.

Leon Festinger proposed in 1957 that people strive for internal psychological consistency. A person is motivated to reduce the cognitive inconsistency by changing parts of the cognition to justify the behavior, by adding new parts, or by avoiding contradictory information that are likely to increase the cognitive dissonance.

FALSE CAUSALITY

A bias that involves concluding that since one event followed another in time, the first must have caused the second. False causality is jumping to a conclusion of a causal relationship without supporting evidence.

ACTION BIAS

When faced with an ambiguous problem we sometimes prefer to do something, if it is counterproductive, even when doing nothing is the best course of action.

AMBIGUITY BIAS

If an outcome is risky and unknown, there is a tendency to stick to what is already known and stay with what you've done previously.

STRATEGIC MISREPRESENTATION

This is understating the costs and overstating the likely benefits in order to get a project approved.

GROUPTHINK

Group-think is a type of bias that occurs within a group in which the desire for harmony in the group results in dysfunctional decision-making. Group members try to minimize conflict and reach a consensus decision without critical evaluation, and by isolating themselves from other points of view.

INNOVATION BIAS

Novelty and 'newness' are seen as good, regardless of potential negative impacts.

ANCHORING BIAS

This type of bias involves being influenced by information that is already known or that has just been shown.

STATUS-QUO BIAS

This bias involves favoring a current situation or status quo and maintaining it.. This bias makes us reduce risk and prefer what is familiar and can stand in the way of innovation.

FRAMING BIAS

Being influenced by the way in which information is presented rather than the information itself. People react to a particular choice in different ways depending on how it is presented. An audience tends to avoid risk when a positive frame is presented but seek risks when a negative frame is presented.

CONFLICTS OF INTEREST
A conflict of interest is when a person or organization has conflicting financial, personal or other interests which could corrupt and lead to improper actions.

FUNDING BIAS
Funding bias refers to the tendency of a study to support the interests of the financial sponsor.
Source: Jono Hey

FUNCTIONAL FIXEDNESS
Functional fixedness limits a person to using an object only in the way it's traditionally used.

NARRATIVE FALLACY
Our brains love stories. Narrative. When something is framed as a story, it's memorable, convincing, and easy to understand. It is easy to draw false conclusions.

SURVIVOR BIAS
"Survivorship bias refers to our tendency to focus on the winners in a particular area and try to learn from them while completely forgetting about the losers who are employing the same strategy."

THE IKEA EFFECT
The IKEA effect is a cognitive bias in which consumers place a disproportionately high value on products they partially created.

RESEARCH PLAN

WHAT
The research plan gives a design team and stakeholders the opportunity to discuss proposed research, stating its importance, why and how it will be conducted and costs. It is best to keep it as short and concise as possible.

WHY
A well-structured research plan

1. A communication tool.
2. Provides a clear focus.
3. Creates team alignment
4. Provides a forum to ask questions.
5. Creates an expectation of knowledge gained.
6. Will improve your final design.

HOW
Sections to include
1. Executive summary
2. Problem statement
3. State concisely the goals of the proposed research.
4. Why is the work important
5. What has already been done
6. User profile
7. Stakeholders and their needs
8. Methodology
9. Research questions [5]
10. Number of participants
11. Length of session
12. Where will the research take place?
13. Roles and responsibilities
14. Test artifacts
15. Participant incentive
16. Scenarios
17. Evaluation methods
18. Test environment and equipment
19. Project timeline

20. Deliverables
21. Where supporting information can be found

Sample research activities
1. Preparation for a single project: ten hours
2. Recruiting and scheduling: two to three hours per person
3. Contextual inquiry/task analysis: five hours per person
4. Focus groups: three hours per group
5. Usability tests: three hours per participant
6. Analyzing contextual inquiry/task analysis: five hours per person
7. Analyzing focus group results: four hours per group
8. Analyzing usability tests: two hours per person
9. Preparing a report for email delivery: twelve hours
10. Preparing a one-hour presentation: six hours

Sample timeline
Pilot Testing date: November 25th, 2017 6PM-7PM Pilot User

Testing date:
November 30th, 2017

8AM - 9AM Setup testing area
9AM - 10AM Participant 1
10:15AM - 11:15 Participant 2
11:15AM - 12:30 Lunch
12:30PM - 1:30 Participant 3
1:45PM - 2:45 Participant 4
3:00PM - 4:00PM Participant 5
4:15PM - 5:15
Debriefing and wrap-up
Presentation to Client:
December 14th 6:00PM-8:00PM
Formal Report Submitted: April 28th

SAMPLE ONE-PAGE RESEARCH PLAN
Title
ABC Laptop Data-Entry Usability Test
By John Smith-Doe, Usability

Stakeholders
Wanda Answer (PM),
Sam Doe (Lead Engineer)

Background
Since January 2009, when the ABC laptop was introduced to the world, particularly after its market release, journalists, bloggers, industry experts, other stakeholders and customers have privately and publicly expressed negative opinions about the ABC laptop's keyboard. These views suggest that the keyboard is hard to use and that it imposes a poor experience on customers. Some have claimed this as the main reason why the ABC laptop will not succeed among business users. Over the years, several improvements have been made to keyboard design to no avail.

Goals
Identify the strengths and weaknesses of data entry on the ABC laptop, and provide opportunities for improvement.

Research Questions
1. How do people enter data on the ABC laptop?
2. What is the learning curve of new ABC laptop users when they enter data?
3. What are the most common errors users make when entering data?

Methodology
A usability study will be held in our lab with 20 participants. Each participant session will last 60-minutes and will include a

short briefing, an interview, a task performance with an ABC laptop and a debriefing. Among the tasks: enter an email subject heading, compose a long email, check news updates on Washington Post's's website, create a calendar event and more.

Participants
These are the primary characteristics of the study participants:
- Business user
- Age 22 to 55,
- Never used an ABC Phone,
- Expressed interest in learning more about or purchasing an ABC laptop,
- Uses the Web at least 10 hours a week.
- [Link to a draft screener]

Schedule
Recruiting: begins October 12
Study day: October 22
Results delivery: November 2

Attachments
Script

Source: Adapted from smashingmagazine.com

EMOTION CARDS

WHAT

Emotion cards are a field method of analyzing and quantifying people's emotional response to a design. The method classifies emotions into sets of emotions which each can be associated with a specific recognizable facial expression.

The emotion card tool consists of sixteen cartoon-like faces, half male, and half female, each representing distinct emotions. Each face describes a combination of two emotion dimensions, pleasure, and arousal. Based on these dimensions, the emotion cards can be divided into four quadrants: Calm-Pleasant, Calm-Unpleasant, Excited-Pleasant, and Excited-Unpleasant.

WHO
Bradley 1994

WHY
1. It is an inexpensive method.
2. The results are easy to analyze.
3. Emotional responses are subtle and difficult to measure.
4. Emotion cards is a cross-cultural tool.
5. Facial emotions are typically universally recognized

CHALLENGES
1. Emotions of male and female faces are interpreted differently.
2. Sometimes users want to mark more than one picture to express a more complex emotional response.

HOW
1. Decide the goal of the study.
2. Recruit the participants.
3. Brief the participants.
4. When each interaction is complete the researcher asks the participant to select one of a number of cards that shows facial expressions that they associate with the interaction.

RESOURCES
Emotion cards
Notebook
Pens
Video camera
Release forms
Interview plan or structure
Questions, tasks and discussion items
Emotion cards

FIVE WHYS

WHAT

Five whys is an iterative question method used to discover the underlying cause of a problem. For every effect, there is a root cause. The primary goal of the technique is to determine the underlying cause of a problem by repeating the question "Why?"

WHO INVENTED IT

The technique was originally developed by Sachichi Toyoda Sakichi Toyoda was a Japanese inventor and industrialist. He was born in Kosai, Shizuoka. The son of a poor carpenter, Toyoda is referred to as the "King of Japanese Inventors". He was the founder of the Toyota Motor company. The method is still an important part of Toyota training, culture and success.

Sakichi Toyoda - Wikipedia, the free encyclopedia, https://en.wikipedia.org/wiki/Sakichi_Toyoda (accessed July 06, 2016).

WHY
When we fix the root cause the problem does not reoccur

HOW
1. Five whys could be taken further to a sixth, seventh, or higher level, but five is generally sufficient to get to a root cause.
2. Gather a team and develop the problem statement in agreement
3. Establish the time and place that the problem is occurring
4. Ask the first "why" of the team: why is this problem taking place?
5. Ask four more successive "whys," repeating the process

DESCRIPTIVE QUESTION MATRIX

Spradley, J. 1980. Participant observation. New York Holt, Rinehart & Winston

	SPACE	OBJECT	ACT	ACTIVITY
SPACE The physical place or places	Can you describe in detail all the places?	What are all the ways space is organized by objects?	What are all the ways that space are organized by actions?	What are all the ways space is organized by activities?
OBJECT The physical things that are present	Where are objects located?	Can you describe in detail all the objects?	What are all the ways objects are used in acts?	What are all the ways objects are used in activities?
ACT Single actions that people do	What are all the places acts occur?	What are all the ways acts incorporate objects?	Can you describe in detail all the acts?	What are all the ways that acts are involved in activities?
ACTIVITY A set of related acts people do	What are all the places activities occur?	What are all the ways activities incorporate objects?	What are all the ways activities incorporate acts?	Can you describe in detail all the activities?
EVENT A set of related activities that people carry out	What are all the places events occur?	What are all the ways events incorporate objects?	What are all the ways events incorporate acts?	What are all the ways events incorporate activities?
TIME The sequencing that takes place over time	Where do time periods occur?	What are all the ways time affects objects?	How do acts fall into time periods?	How do activities fall into time periods?
ACTOR The people involved	Where do actors place themselves?	What are all the ways actors use objects?	How are actors involved in acts?	How are actors involved in activities?
GOAL The things people are trying to accomplish	Where are goals sought and achieved?	What are all the ways goals involve use of objects?	What are all the ways goals involve acts?	What activities are goal seeking or linked to goals?
FEELINGS The emotions felt and expressed	Where do the various feeling states occur?	What feelings lead to the use of what objects?	What are all the ways feelings affect acts?	What are all the ways feelings affect activities?

DESCRIPTIVE QUESTION MATRIX

Spradley, J. 1980. Participant observation. New York Holt, Rinehart & Winston

EVENT	TIME	ACTOR	GOAL	FEELINGS
What are all the ways space is organized by events?	What spatial changes occur over time?	What are all the ways space is used by actors?	What are all the ways space is related to goals?	What places are associated with feelings?
What are all the ways objects are used in events?	What are all the ways objects are used in activities?	What are all the ways objects are used by actors?	How are objects used in seeking goals?	What are all the ways objects evoke feelings?
What are all the ways that acts are involved in events?	How do acts vary at different times?	What are all the ways acts incorporate actors?	What are all the ways acts involve goals?	How do acts involve feelings?
What are all the ways that activities are involved in events?	How do activities vary at different times?	What are all the ways activities incorporate actors?	What are all the ways activities involve goals?	How do activities involve feelings?
Can you describe in detail all the events?	How do events occur over time? Is there an order of events?	What are all the ways events incorporate actors?	What are all the ways events involve goals?	How do events involve feelings?
How do events fall into time periods?	Can you describe in detail all the time periods?	When are all the times actors are "on stage"?	How are goals related to time periods?	When are feelings evoked?
How are actors involved in events?	How do actors change over time or at different times?	Can you describe in detail all the actors?	Which actors are linked to which goals?	What are the feelings experienced by actors?
What are all the ways goals involve events?	Which goals are scheduled for which times?	How do the various goals affect the various actors?	Can you describe in detail all the goals?	What are all the ways goals evoke feelings?
What are all the ways feelings affect events?	How are feelings related to various time periods?	What are all the ways feelings involve actors?	What are the ways feelings influence goals?	Can you describe in detail all the feelings?

ACTIVITY MAP

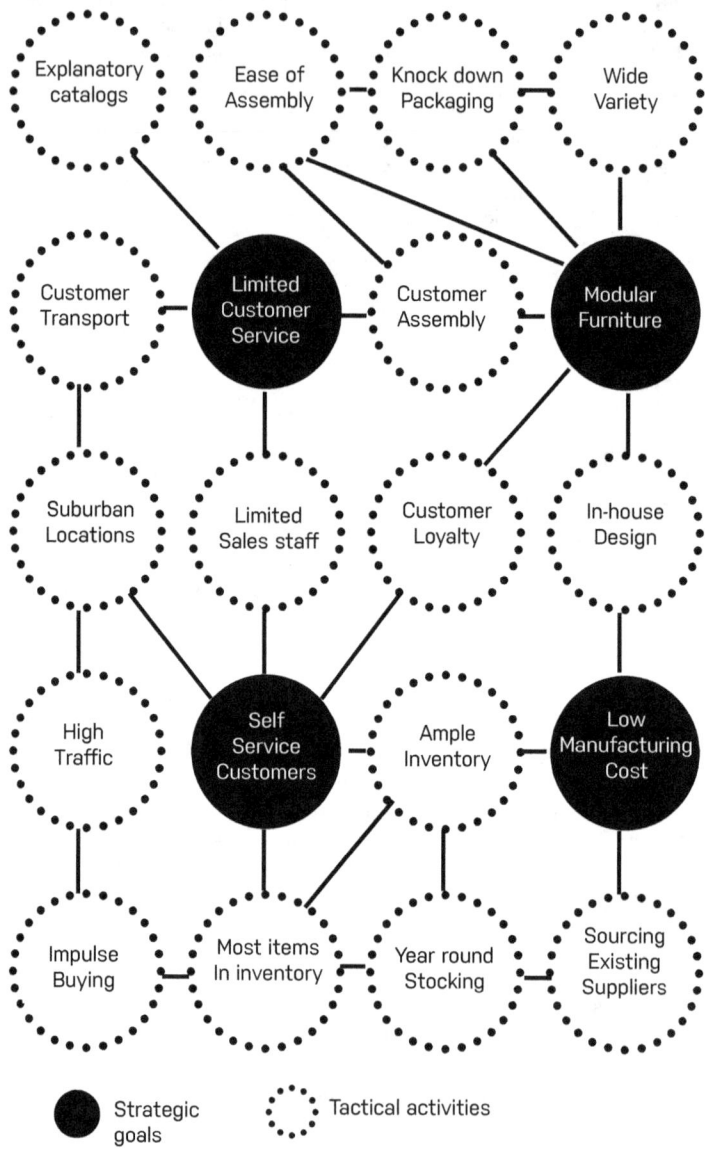

Source: Activity map for IKEA (after Porter)

6. You will have identified the root cause when asking "why" yields no further useful information.
7. Discuss the last answers and settle on the most likely systemic cause.
8. Fix the root problem

FLY-ON-THE-WALL

WHAT
Observation method where the observer remains as unobtrusive as possible and observes and collects data relevant to a research study in context with no interaction with the participants being observed. The name derived from the documentary film technique of the same name.

WHO
Alex Bavelas 1944
Lucy Vernile, Robert A. Monteiro 1991

WHY
1. Low cost
2. No setup necessary
3. Can observe a large number of participants.
4. Objective observations
5. Compared to focus groups, setup, data collection, and processing are much faster.

CHALLENGES
1. No interaction by the observer.
2. Observer cannot delve deeper during a session.
3. No interruption allowed
4. Observer cannot obtain details on customer comments during a session

HOW
1. Define activity to study
2. Select participants thoughtfully
3. Choose a context for the observation
4. Carefully observe the interaction or experience. This is best done by members of your design team.
5. It is important to influence the participants as little as possible by your presence.
6. Observe but do not interact with participants while observing them in context.
7. Capture Data
8. Identify issues
9. Identify needs
10. Create design solutions based on observed and experienced human needs.

FOCUS GROUPS

WHAT
Focus groups are discussions usually with 6 to 12 participants led by a moderator. Focus groups are used during the the design of products, services and experiences to get feedback from people. They are often conducted in the evening and take on average two hours. 8 to 12 questions are commonly explored in a discussion.

> "The purpose of focus groups is not to infer, but to understand, not to generalize but to determine a range, not to make statements about the population but to provide insights about how people perceive a situation."
>
> Richard A. Krueger

WHO
Robert K. Merton 1940 Bureau of Applied Social Research.

WHY
1. Low cost per participant compared to other research methods.
2. Easier than some other methods to manage

CHALLENGES
1. Removes participants from their context.
2. Requires a skilled moderator.
3. Focus group study results may not be generalizable.
4. Focus group participants can influence each other.

HOW
1. Select a good moderator.
2. Prepare a screening questionnaire.
3. Decide incentives for participants.
4. Select facility.
5. Recruit participants. Invite participants to your session well in advance and get firm commitments to attend. Remind participants the date of the event.
6. Participants should sit around a large table. Follow discussion guide.
7. Describe rules. Provide refreshments.
8. First question should encourage talking and participation.
9. The moderator manages responses and asks important questions
10. Moderator collects forms and debriefs focus group.
11. Analyze results while still fresh.
12. Summarize key points.
13. Run additional focus groups to deepen analysis.

IDEATION DECISION MATRIX

WHAT
A process to lead the group to consensus on a specific solution Ideas are listed and each member ranks the ideas: 1=best, 2=2nd best, ...n=least favorite. Rankings are collated, added and the top 3-5 LOWEST totals are used in the next step.

WHEN?
1. You have time between ideation and synthesis phases.
2. You have used a computer or email so circulation of the brainstorm list is fast and easy

CHALLENGES
1. Should obtain informed consent.
2. May not be ideal for research among vulnerable people.
3. May be a relatively expensive research method.
4. May be time-consuming.
5. Best used with other methods.
6. Technology may be unreliable.
7. Method may be unpredictable.

BENCHMARKING MATRIX FOR PRODUCT DESIGN

Criteria	A	B	C	D	E	F	G	H	I
Usability	1	2	3	1	4	1	1	2	3
Speed to market	2	1	1	2	2	4	2	1	4
Brand compatibility	2	4	0	2	2	4	0	4	4
Roi	2	3	1	1	4	1	1	3	3
Fits strategy	1	1	1	4	0	3	1	2	2
Aesthetic appeal	2	4	0	2	2	4	0	4	4
Differentiation	2	2	2	0	1	1	3	3	0
Tooling cost	2	2	1	1	1	2	0	4	3
Fits distribution	2	2	3	1	2	1	4	0	3
Uses our factory	3	3	5	3	0	3	2	1	3
Fits trends	1	3	2	2	1	3	4	3	2
Total	21	26	23	18	20	23	21	24	29

DISCOVERY PHASE

BENEFITS MAP

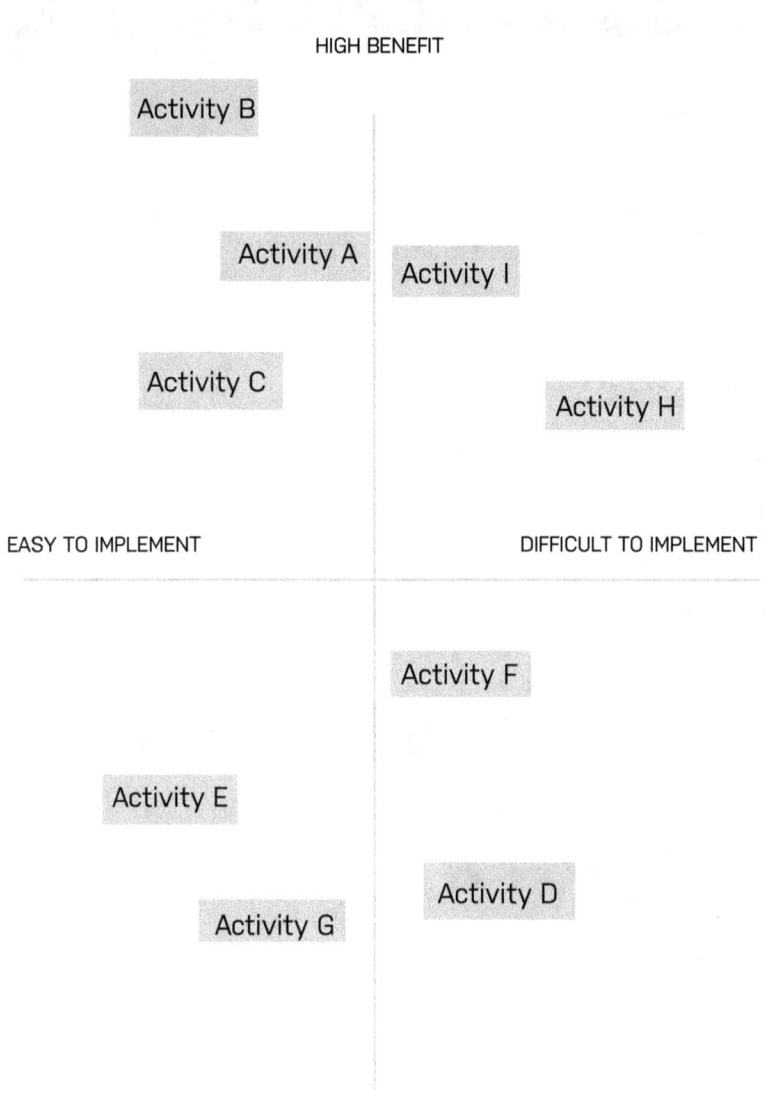

8. Has to be carefully analyzed.

HOW
1. Define subject of study
2. Define participants
3. Gather data images and insight statements.
4. Analyze data.
5. Identify insights
6. Rank insights
7. Produce criteria for concept generation from insights.
8. Generate concepts to meet needs of users.

WHY
1. Effective (members use measures to reach agreement)
2. Time-sensitive (agreement is quick)
3. Easy (one form, 4 steps)
4. Everyone's evaluation is valid
5. Math is used to consolidate
6. Highest Result = Consensus

HOW
1. Each person puts a value from 5(high) to 1(low) on each ideas for their effectiveness and then for feasibility.
2. Total values by criteria.
3. Multiply total effectiveness by total feasibility.
4. Highest product is your chosen solution.

INTERVIEWS

PLANNING INTERVIEWS

WHY
1. More in-depth information than other methods.
2. Uncover tacit or day to day knowledge not available from secondary sources.
3. Low costs .
4. Understand the end user point of view.

CHALLENGES
1. Doesn't yield quantitative information.
2. Transcribing interviews takes time.
3. Some subjects may not want to be recorded.
4. Interviews are best conducted in situ or in the context of use of a design.
5. Both the interviewer and interviewee have some biases.

PLANNING
1. What information do you need to uncover?
2. Is interviewing the best way to uncover the information that you need?
3. Who should you interview?
4. How will you identify the interviewees?
5. What is their experience and diversity of experience?
6. Where should the interviews be conducted?
7. When should you conduct the interviews?
8. How should you conduct the interviews?
9. List your goals.
10. How will the information be used?
11. How will you communicate the findings?
12. What is your primary question?
13. How many people should you interview?
14. How long will the interviews take and how long will it take to transcribe the interviews?
15. It takes 4 to 6 hours to transcribe one recorded hour of an interview.
16. Who is your audience and what method will you use to communicate with them?
17. What is the timeline? Create a timeline that addresses

the following: preliminary research, locating interviewees, conducting interviews, transcribing the interviews, analyzing the transcripts, and formulating the finalized product of your project. Formulate rough deadlines to keep yourself on track.
18. Who will conduct the interviews?
19. Do the interviewers need to be trained?
20. Be aware of and minimize interviewer bias interviewees may respond differently to different interviewers based upon differences in interview style, age, race, class, gender, or culture.
21. What language will interviews be conducted in?
22. Is interpretation needed during the interview?
23. What tools or equipment will you need?
24. You will need tape, video, or digital recorders to record the interviews. A computer is needed transcribe the interview.
25. Who will transcribe the interviews?
26. What resources, people and money, will be needed?
27. How will you address confidentiality? Will you need a non disclosure agreement?
28. How will the data be analyzed?
29. Who will write the report or communicate the findings? materials?

CONDUCTING THE INTERVIEW
1. Create a list of people to interview.
2. Contact them and set up a time to meet.
3. Allow 2 hours face to face for each interview.
4. The best quality data is gathered face to face.

CREATE THE INTERVIEW GUIDE
1. An interview guide is a set of questions that you plan to ask during the interview.
2. Your interview guide is designed to guide you through the process.
3. An interview guide directs the conversation to make sure that desired content is covered.
4. It creates uniformity when you interview multiple interviewees or have multiple interviewers.

Adapted from Ash Maurya, Running Lean, 2012

PROBLEM DEFINITION INTERVIEW

WHAT
Identify your target audience. Test your assumptions about the audience and their needs. Interview at least ten people. Ask the participants to rank their top three needs. Ask the participant how each problem should be solved. How do the participants solve the problems today?

A SCRIPT FOR THE PROBLEM INTERVIEWS

WELCOME
Explain the interview process and the purpose of the interview.

COLLECT BACKGROUND INFORMATION
Ask introductory questions and collect necessary background information: "Before we go to the

problems, I would like to know....how often / with whom / do you...?"

TELL A STORY
Illustrate the top problems you want to explore. "Let me tell you about the problems we are tackling...do any of these resonate with you?"

PROBLEM RANKING
State the top 3 problems and ask the interviewee to rank them. Ask if the interviewee has any other problems related to the issue

EXPLORE CUSTOMER'S WORLDVIEW
Go through each problem and ask the interviewees how they address them today.

WRAP-UP
Ask for permission to follow-up.

DOCUMENT RESULTS.
Document thoughts that you did not have time to write down while interviewing.

Adapted from Ash Maurya, Running Lean, 2012

INTERVIEWING

WHAT
Interviewing is a method of ethnographic research that has been described as a conversation with a purpose.

WHY
1. Contextual interviews uncover tacit knowledge about people's context.
2. The information gathered can be detailed.
3. The information produced by contextual inquiry is relatively reliable

CHALLENGES
1. End users may not have the answers
2. Contextual inquiry may be difficult to challenge even if it is misleading.
3. Keep control
4. Be prepared
5. Be aware of bias
6. Be neutral
7. Select location carefully

WHEN
1. Know Context
2. Know User
3. Frame insights

HOW
1. Contextual inquiry may be structured as 2 hour one on one interviews.
2. The researcher does not usually impose tasks on the user.
3. Go to the user's context. Talk, watch listen and observe.
4. Understand likes and dislikes.
5. Collect stories and insights.
6. See the world from the user's point of view.
7. Take permission to conduct interviews.
8. Do one-on-one interviews.
9. The researcher listens to the user.
10. 2 to 3 researchers conduct an interview.
11. Understand relationship between people, product and context.
12. Document with video, audio and notes.

WRITING AN INTERVIEW GUIDE

HOW
1. Plan in advance what you want to achieve
2. Research the topic
3. Select a person to interview.
4. Meet them in their location if possible.
5. Set a place, date, and time.
6. Be sure he or she understands how long the interview should take and that you plan to record the session.
7. Start with an open-ended question. It is a good way to put the candidate at ease,
8. Tape record the interview if possible.
9. Decide what information you need
10. Write down the information you'd like to collect through the interview. Now frame your interview questions around this information.
11. Prepare follow-up questions to ask.
12. Research the person that you are interviewing
13. Check your equipment and run through your questions.
14. Use neutral wording
15. Do not ask leading questions or questions that show bias.
16. Leave time for a General Question in the End
17. The last question should allow the interviewee to share any thoughts or opinions that they might want to share, such as "Thank you for all that valuable information, is there anything else you'd like to add before we end?"
18. Bring your questions to the interview
19. Explore the answers but return to your list of questions to follow your guide.
20. Record details such as the subject's name contact and details
21. Take detailed notes
22. Use empathy tools to encourage your participant to share information.
23. Final question: "Is there anything you think I should have asked that I didn't?"
24. Transcribe the interview
25. Write out both sides of the conversation, both question and answer.
26. Never change what the interviewee said or how they said it.
27. Outline the important points.
28. Edit the transcript for clarity, flow, and length.
29. Tell a story
30. Add details from your notes appearance and personality of your subject, ambient sounds, smells, visuals.
31. Check the facts.

Source: adapted from The Art of Interview" by Anne Williams

INTERVIEWING METHODS
CONTEXTUAL INQUIRY

WHAT
Contextual inquiry involves one-on-one observations and interviews of activities in the context. Contextual inquiry has four guiding principles:
1. Context
2. Partnership with users.
3. Interpretation
4. Focus on particular goals.

WHO
Whiteside, Bennet, and Holtzblatt 1988

WHY
1. Contextual interviews uncover tacit knowledge about people's context.
2. The information gathered can be detailed.
3. The information produced by contextual inquiry is relatively reliable

CHALLENGES
1. End users may not have the answers
2. Contextual inquiry may be difficult to challenge even if it is misleading.

HOW
1. Contextual inquiry may be structured as 2 hour one on one interviews.
2. The researcher does not usually impose tasks on the user.
3. Go to the user's context. Talk, watch listen and observe.
4. Understand likes and dislikes.
5. Collect stories and insights.
6. See the world from the user's point of view.
7. Take permission to conduct interviews.
8. Do one-on-one interviews.
9. The researcher listens to the user.
10. 2 to 3 researchers conduct an interview.
11. Understand relationship between people, product and context.
12. Document with video, audio and notes.

CONTEXTUAL LADDERING

WHAT
Contextual laddering is a one-on-one interviewing technique done in context. Answers are further explored by the researcher to uncover root causes or core values.

WHO
Gutman 1982, Olsen and Reynolds 2001.

WHY
1. Laddering can uncover underlying reasons for particular behaviors.
2. Laddering may uncover information not revealed by other methods.
3. Complement other methods
4. Link features and product attributes with user/customer values

CHALLENGES
1. Analysis of data is sometimes difficult.
2. Requires a skilled interviewer who can keep the participants engaged.
3. Laddering may be repetitive
4. Sometimes information may not be represented hierarchically.

HOW
1. Interviews typically take 60 to 90-minutes.
2. The introduction. The researcher gives information about the length of the interview, content, confidentiality and method of recording.

3. The body of the interview. The researcher investigates the user in context and documents the information gathered.
4. Ask participants to describe what kinds of features would be useful in or distinguish different products.
5. Ask why.
6. If this answer doesn't describe the root motivation ask why again.
7. Repeat step 3. until you have reached the root motivation.
8. Wrap up. Verification and clarification

E-MAIL INTERVIEW

WHAT
With this method an interview is conducted via an e-mail exchange.

WHY
1. Extended access to people.
2. Background noises are not recorded.
3. Interviewee can answer the questions at his or her own convenience
4. It is not necessary to take notes
5. It is possible to use online translators.
6. Interviewees do not have to identify a convenient time to talk.

CHALLENGES
1. Interviewer may have to wait for answers.
2. Interviewer is disconnected from context.
3. Lack of communication of body language.

HOW
1. Choose a topic
2. Identify a subject.
3. Contact subject and obtain approval.
4. Prepare interview questions.
5. Conduct interview
6. Analyze data.

EXTREME USER INTERVIEW

WHAT
Interview experienced or inexperienced users of a product or service in order to discover useful insights that can be applied to the general users.

WHY
Extreme user's solutions to problems can inspire solutions for general users. Their behavior can be more exaggerated than general users so it is sometimes easier to develop useful insights from these groups.

CHALLENGES
1. Keep control
2. Be prepared
3. Be aware of bias
4. Be neutral
5. Select location carefully

HOW
1. Do a timeline of your activity and break it into main activities
2. Identify very experienced or very inexperienced users of a product or service in an activity area.
3. Explore their experiences through interview.
4. Discover insights that can inspire design.
5. Refine design based on insights.

GROUP INTERVIEW

WHAT
This method involves interviewing a group of people.

WHY
People will often give different answers to questions if interviewed on=on=-one and in groups. If resources are available it is useful to interview people in both situations.

CHALLENGES
Group interview process is longer than an individual interview

HOW
1. Welcome everyone and introduce yourself
2. Describe the process.
3. Ask everyone to introduce themselves.
4. Conduct a group activity or warming-up exercise.
5. Break the larger group into smaller groups of 4 or 5 people and give them a question to answer. Ask each participant to present their response to the larger group.
6. Allow about 25 minutes.
7. Ask each interviewee to write a summary.
8. Collect the summaries.
9. Ask if have any further comments.
10. Thank everyone and explain the next steps.
11. Give them your contact details.

GUIDED STORYTELLING

WHAT
Guided storytelling is interview technique, where the designer asks a participant to walk you through a scenario of use for a concept. Directed storytelling guides participants to describe their experiences and thoughts on a particular topic.

WHO
Whiteside, Bennet, and Holtzblatt 1988

WHY
Guided storytelling uncovers tacit knowledge.

CHALLENGES
1. Keep control
2. Be prepared
3. Be aware of bias
4. Be neutral
5. Select location carefully

HOW
1. Contextual inquiry may be structured as 2 hour one on one interviews.
2. The researcher does not usually impose tasks on the user.
3. Go to the user's context. Talk, watch listen and observe.
4. Understand likes and dislikes.
5. Collect stories and insights.
6. See the world from the user's point of view.

DAY IN THE LIFE

After scanning the daily British newspapers, The Queen reviews her correspondence.

If there is an Investiture - a ceremony for the presentation of honors and decorations - it begins at 11.00am and lasts just over an hour.

The Queen will often lunch privately. Every few months, she and The Duke of Edinburgh will invite a dozen guests from a wide variety of backgrounds to an informal lunch.

| 7 am | 8 am | 9 am | 10 am | 11 am | 12 pm | 1 pm | 2 pm |

Every day, 200-300 letters from the public arrive. The Queen chooses a selection to read herself and tells members of her staff how she would like them to be answered

A series of official meetings or 'audiences' will often follow. The Queen will see a number of important people.

In the afternoons, The Queen goes out on public engagements. The Queen prepares for each visit by briefing herself on whom she will be meeting and what she will be seeing and doing

140 DISCOVERY PHASE

DOT VOTING

CONCEPT 1

● ● ● ●   ● ●

CONCEPT 2

● ●

CONCEPT 3

● ● ● ●

CONCEPT 4

● ● ●

CONCEPT 5
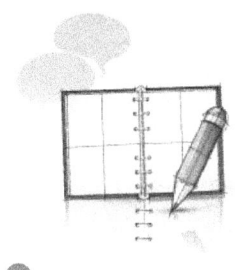
●

CONCEPT 6

● ● ● ●   ●

7. Take permission to conduct interviews.
8. Do one-on-one interviews.
9. The researcher listens to the user.
10. 2 to 3 researchers conduct an interview.
11. Understand relationship between people, product and context.

MAN IN THE STREET INTERVIEW

WHAT
Man in the street interviews are impromptu interviews recorded on video. They are usually conducted by two people, a researcher and a cameraman.

WHY
1. Contextual interviews uncover tacit knowledge.
2. The information gathered can be detailed.

CHALLENGES
1. Keep control
2. Be prepared
3. Be aware of bias
4. Be neutral
5. Ask appropriate questions
6. Select location carefully
7. Create a friendly atmosphere, interviewee to feel relaxed.
8. Clearly convey the purpose of the interview.
9. This method results in accidental sampling which may not be representative of larger groups.

HOW
1. Decide on goal for research.
2. Formulate about 10 questions related to topic
3. Use release form if required.
4. Conduct a preliminary interview.
5. Select location. It should not be too noisy or have other distracting influences
6. Approach people, be polite. Say, "Excuse me, I work for [your organization] and I was wondering if you could share your opinion about [your topic]."
7. If someone does not wish to respond, select another subject to interview.
8. Limit your time. Each interview should be no be longer than about 10-minutes.
9. Conduct 6 to 10 interviews

NATURALISTIC GROUP INTERVIEW

WHAT
Naturalistic group interview is an interview method where the participants know each other prior to the interview and so have conversations that are more natural than participants who do not know each other.

WHY
1. This method has been applied in research in Asia where beliefs are informed by group interaction.
2. Can help gain useful data in cultures where people are less willing to share their feelings.

CHALLENGES
Familiarity of participants can lead to Group-think.

HOW
1. The interview context should support natural conversation.
2. Select participants who have existing social relationships.
3. Group the participants in natural ways so that the conversation is as close as possible to the type of discussion they would have in their everyday life.
4. Groups should be no larger than four people for best results.

ONE-ON-ONE INTERVIEWS

WHAT
The one-on-one interview is an interview that is between a researcher and one participant in a face-to-face situation.

WHY
1. The best method for personal information
2. Works well with other methods in obtaining information to inform design.
3. Can be used to exchange ideas or to gather information to inform design

CHALLENGES
1. Keep control
2. Be prepared
3. Be aware of bias
4. Be neutral
5. Select location carefully
6. Record everything
7. Combine one on one interviews with group interviews.

HOW
1. May be structured as 2 hour one on one interviews.
2. Select the questions and the subjects carefully.
3. Create interview guide,
4. Conduct a pre-interview to refine the guide.
5. The researcher does not usually impose tasks on the user.
6. Go to the user's context. Talk, watch listen and observe.
7. Understand likes and dislikes.
8. Collect stories and insights.
9. See the world from the user's point of view.
10. Take permission to conduct interviews.
11. Understand relationship between person, product and context.
12. Document with video, audio and notes.

STRUCTURED INTERVIEW

WHAT
In a structured interview, the researcher prepares a list of questions, script or an interview guide that they follow during the interview. Most interviews use a structured method.

INTERVIEW GUIDE
1. 4-5 distinct topics or questions
2. Distinct probes for each topic
3. Specific order
4. Order from general to specific
5. Begin with most important questions
6. Builds in transitions among topics

WHY
1. A structured interview is often used for phone interviews.

2. It is easy to analyze the results.
3. Structured interviews are often used by quantitative researchers.

TESTING THE INTERVIEW GUIDE
1. Are the questions phrased in a way that will elicit the information that you're seeking?
2. Are the questions clear?
3. Are the questions biased?
4. Are any of them closed ended?
5. Do any need expansion?
6. Did you use any double negatives?

CHALLENGES
1. Respondents may be less likely to discuss sensitive experiences.

HOW
1. The researcher should follow the script exactly.
2. The interviewer is required to show consistency in behavior across all interviews

ANALYSIS
1. Familiarization
2. Transcribing
3. Organizing
4. Coding
5. Reducing data
6. Displaying data
   - Helps organize data
   - See areas where analysis is complete
   - See patterns & themes
   - See how data "fits" theory
7. Drawing & Verifying Conclusions
8. Inductive: categories and themes emerge (grounded theory)
9. Deductive: processes of "fitting" the data into categories and themes (framework analysis)

PHOTO ELICITATION INTERVIEW

WHAT
Photos are used by a researcher as a focus to discuss the experiences, thoughts and feelings of participants.

WHY
1. A method sometimes used to interview children.
2. Photos can make starting a conversation with a participant easier.
3. Photos can uncover meaning which is not uncovered in a face to face interview.

CHALLENGES
1. Photos can create ethical questions for the researcher.
2. A researcher may show bias in selecting subject of photos.

HOW
1. Define the context.
2. Select the participants
3. Either researcher or participant may take the photos.
4. Researcher analyses photos and plans the interview process
5. Researcher shows the photos to the participant and discusses their thoughts in relation to the photographs.
6. The interview is analyzed by the researcher.
7. Create a list of insights.

UNSTRUCTURED INTERVIEW

WHAT
Unstructured interviews are interviews where questions can be modified as needed by the researcher during the interview.

INTERVIEW GUIDE
1-2 broad topics

WHY
1. A useful technique for understanding how a subject may perform under pressure.
2. Unstructured interviews are used in ethnographic case studies
3. Respondents may be more likely to discuss sensitive experiences.

CHALLENGES
1. Interviewer bias is unavoidable.

HOW
Researchers need a list of topics to be covered during the interview.

The interviewer and respondents engage in a formal interview in that they have a scheduled time to sit and speak with each other and both parties recognize this to be an interview.
1. The interviewer has a clear plan of the focus and goal of the interview.
2. There is no interview guide.
3. The interviewer builds rapport with subject.
4. Questions are open-ended.
5. Unstructured interviews are used for developing an understanding of an as-of-yet not fully understood topic.

TELEPHONE INTERVIEW

WHAT
This style of interview is conducted via telephone.

WHY
Wide geographical access
1. Allows researcher to reach hard to reach people.
2. Allows researcher to access closed locations.
3. Access to dangerous or politically sensitive sites

CHALLENGES
1. Lack of communication of body language.
2. Interviewer is disconnected from context.

HOW
1. Choose a topic
2. Identify a subject.
3. Contact subject and obtain approval.
4. Prepare interview questions.
5. Conduct interview
6. Analyze data.

MIXED METHOD RESEARCH

WHAT
Mixed methods research is a design for collecting, analyzing, and mixing both quantitative and qualitative data in a single study or series of studies to understand a research problem.

> *Mixed methods research is a systematic integration of quantitative and qualitative methods in a single study for purposes of obtaining a fuller picture and deeper understanding of a phenomenon."*

Huey Chen

> *Mixed methods research is a set of procedures that should be used when integrating qualitative and quantitative procedures reflects the research question(s) better than each can independently. The combining of quantitative and qualitative methods should better inform the researcher and the effectiveness of mixed methods should be evaluated based upon how the approach enables the investigator to answer the research question(s) embedded in the purpose(s) (why the study is being conducted or is needed; the justification) of the study."*

Newman, Ridenour, Newman & DeMarco, 2003

Qualitative and quantitative research provide a better understanding of users than either method can provide alone. Mixed methods research is becoming increasingly popular.

> *Combining qualitative and quantitative methods has gained broad appeal in public health research. The key question has become not whether it is acceptable or legitimate to combine methods, but rather how they will be combined to be mutually supportive and how findings achieved through different methods will be integrated."*

NIH, Office of Behavioral and Social Science Research

QUALITATIVE:
1. Working with unfamiliar subjects.
2. When data is complex ambiguous or unclear
3. When you wish to understand meaning.
4. When you require flexibility.
5. For studying issues in detail

QUANTITATIVE
1. When the data is clearly defined
2. When metrics are known
3. When detailed numerical data is required
4. When repeatability is important
5. When generalizable across populations is needed

WHY USE MIXED METHODS?
Greene, Caracelli, and Graham (1989) identified the five purposes or rationales of mixed methodological studies:
1. Triangulation (i.e., seeking convergence and corroboration of results from different methods studying the same phenomenon),

2. Complementarity (i.e., seeking elaboration, enhancement, illustration, clarification of the results from one method with results from the other method),
3. Development (i.e., using the results from one method to other method),
4. Initiation (i.e., discovering paradoxes and contradictions that lead to a reframing of the research question), and
5. Expansion (i.e., seeking to expand the breadth and range of inquiry by using different methods for different inquiry components).

WHEN TO USE IT
1. When you want to combine the advantages of quantitative (trends, large numbers, generalization) with qualitative (detail, small numbers, in-depth)
2. When you want to validate your findings
3. When you want to expand your quantitative findings
4. Both approaches have strengths and weaknesses

Some research methods such as interviews and observations can be either quantitative or qualitative. Quantitative data can be generalized to the
larger population. In qualitative research subjects are selected because they have experienced the central phenomenon.

WHY USE MIXED METHODS?
1. Together quantitative and qualitative data provide both precise measurement and generalizability of quantitative research and the in-depth, complex picture of qualitative research
2. To validate quantitative results with qualitative data
3. Our quantitative data provide a general explanation and we need to follow-up with participants and have them explain the quantitative results
4. When outcomes to be measured are not enough; and need to be complemented by understanding
5. Quantitative data may fail to provide specific reasons, explanations or examples
6. Qualitative research provides data about meaning and context
7. Findings are often not generalizable because of the small numbers & narrow range of participants
8. Qualitative research can provide specific examples of quantitative data.
9. Wit quantitative research it may be difficult to see the overall pattern
10. Selection of research methods should be made after the research questions are asked
11. Some methods work well in some contexts but not in other contexts
12. Mixed methods are used when one method only was is insufficient
13. If the results lead to divergent results, then more than one explanation is possible

SATURATION
Saturation occurs:
1. When no new information (redundancy) is obtained *Source Lincoln & Guba, 1985; Patton, 1990*
2. Through the constant comparison of data Recurrent patterns and themes are seen

Source Glaser & Strauss, 1967, Cutcliffe & McKenna, 2002

MOBILE DIARY STUDY

WHAT
A mobile diary studies is a method that uses portable devices to capture a person's experiences in context when and where they happen such as their workplace or home. Participants can create diary entries from their location on mobile phones or tablets.

WHY
1. Most people carry a mobile phone.
2. It is a convenient method of recording diary entries.
3. It is easier to collect the data than collecting written diaries.
4. Collection of data happens in real time.
5. Mobile devices have camera, voice and written capability.

CHALLENGES
1. Can miss non-verbal feedback.
2. Technology may be unreliable.

HOW
1. Define intent
2. Define audience
3. Define context
4. Select the online diary study tool based.
5. Set up the diary study tool, create user accounts, and design study activities
6. Prepare introductory email or letter to participants, with study details and dates
7. Prepare the diary kit
   - User account online login details
   - Types of feedback
   - Contact details
   - Information about what to do regarding additional questions, user account issues,
8. Conduct online Meet & Brief sessions with participants
9. Create activity and assignment prompts can be written or video.
10. Monitor diary entries and maintain engagement with participants to keep them on task
11. Update and set next tasks
12. Respond to participant inquiries, diary entries, or ensure technical support issues are being resolved
13. Pose additional questions or suggest alternative scenarios to gain deeper insights
14. Make notes and compile data to refer to for follow-up interviews and final data insights report
15. Conduct timely, final in-depth interviews to further probe and validate data revealed during the study
16. Thank participants and ensure compensation is given as applicable

BENEFITS
1. Participants record their experiences in their natural environment rather than an unrelated, unnatural environment such as a lab.
2. Participants more likely to capture influential external factors such as time, location, social or environmental triggers, etc.
3. Researchers can collect participant observations in longer durations + Diary studies offer participants more time for in-depth consideration and opportunities for creativity than traditional-type research sessions, allowing participants a few days per activity/question

SAMPLE INTERVIEW CONSENT FORM

Research should, be based on participants' freely volunteered informed consent. The researcher has a responsibility to explain what the research is about and who will see the data. Participants should be aware that they can refuse to participate; confidentiality, and how the research will be used.

The information contained within this book is strictly for educational purposes. If you wish to apply ideas contained in this book you are taking full responsibility for your actions. There are no representations or warranties, express or implied, about the completeness, accuracy, reliability, suitability or availability with respect to the information, products, services, or related graphics contained in this book for any purpose. Any use of this information is at your own risk.

Purpose of the research
The purpose of this project is [purpose]. *Provide a brief, usually one-paragraph, explanation of what the research is about and state why the subject is being asked to participate [e.g., inclusion/exclusion criteria]*

What we will ask you to do
If you agree to be in this study, you are asked to participate in a recorded interview. The interview will include questions about [topic] , The interview will take about [duration] minutes to complete. With your permission, we would also like to tape-record the interview.

Risks and benefits
There is the risk that you may find some of the questions about [topic] to be sensitive. *[Describe any possible benefit to the participants or others that may reasonably be expected from the research; then describe any reasonably foreseeable risks or discomforts to the participants, or state "there are no foreseeable risks," if none are identified.]*

Compensation:
There will be [amount of compensation] [type of compensation] compensation. *[Specify whether participants will be compensated and if so, the amount. If amount will be prorated for any reason, state this.]*

Taking part is voluntary
Taking part in this interview is completely voluntary. You may skip any questions that you do not want to answer. If you decide not to take part or to skip some of the questions, it will not affect your current or future relationship with Cornell University. If you decide to take part, you are free to withdraw at any time.

Your answers will be confidential
The records of this project will be kept private. In any sort of report we make public we will not include any information that will make it possible to identify you. Research records will be kept in a locked file; only [who] will have access to the records. [Regarding the storage of the tape, who will keep it, where will it be stored, after the transcription is done?] If we tape-record the interview, we will destroy the tape after it has been transcribed, which we anticipate will be within [duration] months of its taping.
If you have questions: [contact]

If you have questions
The researchers conducting this study are [researchers]. Please ask any questions you have now. If you have questions later, you may contact [name] at [email] or at [phone].

Statement of Consent
I have read the above information, and have received answers to any questions I asked. I consent to take part in the project. In addition to agreeing to participate, I also consent to having the interview tape-recorded. I understand the information presented above and that: My participation is voluntary, and I may withdraw my consent and discontinue participation in the project at any time. My refusal to participate will not result in any penalty.

You will be given a copy of this form to keep for your records.

Interviewee Signature ....Date ....
In addition to agreeing to participate, I also consent to having the interview tape-recorded.

Researcher's Signature ....Date ....
This consent form will be kept by the researcher for at least [duration] years beyond the end of the project and was approved by the [Organization] on [date].

This consent form will be kept by the researcher for at least [duration] years beyond the end of the project and was approved by the [Organization] on [date].

DRAWBACKS
1. Researchers do not observe participants in their natural environment or collect their own real-time data
2. Participants may have a belief bias, adjust behaviors, or have difficulty recalling events
3. Researchers must trust participants on what they record or observe about their experiences and emotional behaviors
4. Finding the right respondents who can be creative is a MUST, which means recruiting might take longer to avoid selecting candidates that might plateau or withdraw before the study is complete

MYSTERY SHOPPER

WHAT

Mystery Shopping is a method used to anonymously evaluate products and services, operations, employee integrity, merchandising, and product quality. Mystery shoppers perform tasks such as purchasing a product, asking questions, registering complaints and then provide feedback about their experiences. Mystery shopping evaluation generates around $1.5 billion per annum and is growing.

MYSTERY SHOPPING IS ALSO KNOWN AS:
1. Secret Shopping
2. Experience Evaluation
3. Anonymous Audits
4. Mystery Customers
5. Digital Customers
6. Virtual Customers

WHO

Originally used in the 1940s as a way of evaluating employee integrity.n the 1940's, Wilmark coined the term "mystery shopping". In the 1970's and 80's, Shop 'n Chek popularized mystery shopping. Since 2010, mystery shopping has become a common form of evaluation in the medical tourism industry and in the UK in customer services provided by local authorities and other non-profit organizations such as housing associations and churches. some fast-food restaurants are mystery-shopped three times a day and shoppers are rotated.

Source: Newhouse 2004: 2

WHO USES MYSTERY SHOPPING?
User include:
1. Banks
2. Gas stations
3. Retailers
4. Car dealers
5. Apartments
6. Manufacturers
7. Call Centers
8. E-Commerce services
9. Government agencies
10. Hospitals
11. Associations
12. Franchise operations
13. Promotions agencies Hotels
14. Restaurants
15. Movie Theaters
16. Recreation parks
17. Transportation systems
18. Fitness/health centers
19. Property management firms
20. Freight/courier services

WHO PROVIDES MYSTERY SHOPPING SERVICES?
21. Consultants
22. Marketing Firms
23. Private Investigators
24. Merchandising Companies
25. Advertising agencies

CHALLENGES
1. Time-consuming
2. Employees may resist
3. Ethical management

BENEFITS OF MYSTERY SHOPPING
1. Metrics for service performance.
2. Improves customer retention.
3. Ensures service quality..
4. Competitive analyses.
5. Compliments marketing research data.
6. Identifies training needs and sales opportunities.
7. Educational tool.
8. Monitors employee integrity.

USE OF THE INTERNET
1. Many websites use mystery shopping.
2. May be easier to implement online.

HOW
1. Define objectives.
2. Program & questionnaire design.
3. Create evaluation form for mystery shopper.
4. Recruit shoppers.
5. Train shoppers.
6. Conduct evaluation.
7. Analyze data.
8. Report conclusions and recommendations.
9. Review findings.
10. Implement actions.

OBJECTIVES & GOALS
Identify and define actionable goals.

QUESTIONNAIRE DESIGN
11. Design questionnaires to provide objective, observational feedback
12. Cover: greeting, customer service, facility cleanliness and orderliness, speed of service, product quality and employee product knowledge
13. Ask only "yes" and "no" questions. Ask for clarification of no questions.
14. Include a "general comments" section
15. Use a scoring system. Give a weighting to the most important questions.

RECRUITING SHOPPERS
1. Mystery shoppers should match "real customer" profiles.
2. Mystery shoppers are often employed as part-time contractors.
3. Recruit through classified advertising, Internet or referrals.
4. There may be special requirements such as wearing

glasses.
5. Shoppers may be asked to complete test shops during recruiting.

DATA COLLECTION
1. Provide shoppers with specific shopping tasks and clear written guidelines
2. Be consistent
3. Mystery shopper observations are limited to a choice of fixed alternatives

DATA PREPARATION
1. Check and validate each report.
2. Run quality control checks
3. Track data using relational database.

REPORTING
1. Process reports within 30 days.
2. The reports should be actionable.

REVIEW FINDINGS
1. Share the reports with training personnel.
2. An ongoing program is more effective than irregular audits.

HOW TO CHOOSE A MYSTERY SHOPPING PROVIDER
3. Experience
4. Reputation
5. Resources
6. Location

HOW TO MAKE THE MOST OF MYSTERY SHOPPING PROGRAMS
1. Inform employees of the program.
2. Promote the program.
3. Action the findings.
4. Take a positive approach.
5. Apply to employee training.
6. Share the findings
7. Evaluate only actionable issues.
8. Use yes/no questions
9. Limit use of open questions.
10. Benchmark and track trends.

Source: Adapted from Mark Michelson

OBSERVATION

WHAT
This method involves observing people in their natural activities and usual context such as work environment. With direct observation the researcher is present and indirect observation the activities may be recorded by means such as video or digital voice recording.

WHY
1. Allows the observer to view what users actually do in context.
2. Indirect observation uncovers activity that may have previously gone unnoticed

CHALLENGES
1. Observation does not explain the cause of behavior.
2. Obtrusive observation may cause participants to alter their behavior.
3. Analysis can be time-consuming.
4. Observer bias can cause the researcher to look only where they think they will see useful information.

HOW
1. Define objectives
2. Define participants and obtain their cooperation.
3. Define The context of the observation: time and place.

4. In some countries the law requires that you obtain written consent to video people.
5. Define the method of observation and the method of recording information. Common methods are taking written notes, video or audio recording.
6. Run a test session.
7. Hypothesize an explanation for the phenomenon
8. Predict a logical consequence of the hypothesis
9. Test your hypothesis by observation
10. Analyze the data gathered and create a list of insights derived from the observations.

RESOURCES
Notepad computer
Pens
Camera
Video camera
Digital voice recorder

COVERT OBSERVATION

WHAT
Covert observation is to observe people without them knowing. The identity of the researcher and the purpose of the research are hidden from the people being observed.

WHY
1. This method may be used to reduce the effect of the observer's presence on the behavior of the subjects.
2. To capture behavior as it happens.
3. Researcher is more likely to observe natural behavior

CHALLENGES
1. The method raises serious ethical questions.
2. Observation does not explain the cause of behavior.
3. Can be difficult to gain access and maintain cover
4. Analysis can be time-consuming.
5. Observer bias can cause the researcher to look only where they think they will see useful information.

HOW
1. Define objectives.
2. Define participants and obtain their cooperation.
3. Define The context of the observation: time and place.
4. In some countries the law requires that you obtain written consent to video people.
5. Define the method of observation and the method of recording information. Common methods are taking written notes, video or audio recording.
6. Run a test session.
7. Hypothesize an explanation for the phenomenon.
8. Predict a logical consequence of the hypothesis.
9. Test your hypothesis by observation
10. Analyze the data gathered and create a list of insights derived from the observations.

RESOURCES
Camera
Video Camera
Digital voice recorder

DIRECT OBSERVATION

WHAT
Direct Observation is a method in which a researcher observes and records behavior events, activities or tasks while something is happening recording observations as they are made.

WHO
Radcliff-Brown 1910
Bronisław Malinowski 1922
Margaret Mead 1928

WHY
To capture behavior as it happens.

CHALLENGES
1. Observation does not explain the cause of behavior.
2. Analysis can be time-consuming.
3. Observer bias can cause the researcher to look only where they think they will see useful information.
4. Obtain a proper sample for generalization.
5. Observe average workers during average conditions.
6. The participant may change their behavior because they are being watched.

HOW
1. Define objectives.
2. Make direct observation plan
3. Define participants and obtain their cooperation.
4. Define The context of the observation: time and place.
5. In some countries, the law requires that you obtain written consent to video people.
6. Define the method of observation and the method of recording information. Common methods are taking written notes, video or audio recording.
7. Run a test session.
8. Hypothesize an explanation for the phenomenon.
9. Predict a logical consequence of the hypothesis.
10. Test your hypothesis by observation
11. Analyze the data gathered and create a list of insights derived from the observations.

RESOURCES
Notepad computer
Pens
Camera
Video Camera
Digital voice recorder

INDIRECT OBSERVATION

WHAT
Indirect Observation is an observational technique whereby some record of past behavior is used than observing behavior in real time. Humans cannot directly sense some things, we must rely on indirect observations with tools such as thermometers, microscopes, telescopes or X-rays.

WHY
1. To capture behavior or an event as it happens in it's natural setting.

2. Indirect observation uncovers activity that may have previously gone unnoticed
3. May be inexpensive
4. Can collect a wide range of data

CHALLENGES
1. Observation does not explain the cause of behavior.
2. Analysis can be time-consuming.
3. Observer bias can cause the researcher to look only where they think they will see useful information.
4. Observe average workers during average conditions.
5. The participant may change their behavior because they are being watched.

HOW
1. Define objectives.
2. Make direct observation plan
3. Define participants and obtain their cooperation.
4. Define The context of the observation: time and place.
5. In some countries the law requires that you obtain written consent to video people.
6. Define the method of observation and the method of recording information.
7. Run a test session.
8. Hypothesize an explanation for the phenomenon.
9. Predict a logical consequence of the hypothesis.
10. Test your hypothesis by observation
11. Analyze the data gathered and create a list of insights derived from the observations.

NON-PARTICIPANT OBSERVATION

WHAT
The observer does not become part of the situation being observed or intervene in the behavior of the subjects. Used when a researcher wants the participants to behave normally. Usually this type of observation occurs in places where people normally work or live.

WHY
12. To capture behavior as it happens.

CHALLENGES
1. Observation does not explain the cause of behavior.
2. Analysis can be time-consuming.
3. Observer bias can cause the researcher to look only where they think they will see useful information.
4. Obtain a proper sample for generalization.
5. Observe average workers during average conditions.
6. The participant may change their behavior because they are being watched.

HOW
1. Determine research goals.
2. Select a research context
3. The site should allow clear observation and be accessible.
4. Select participants
5. Seek permission.
6. Gain access

7. Gather research data.
8. Analyze data
9. Find common themes
10. Create insights

PARTICIPANT OBSERVATION

WHAT

Participant observation is an observation method where the researcher participates. The researcher becomes part of the situation being studied. The researcher may live or work in the context of the participant and may become an accepted member of the participant's community. This method was used extensively by the pioneers of field research.

WHO
Radcliff-Brown 1910
Bronisław Malinowski 1922
Margaret Mead 1928

WHY
1. The goal of this method is to become close and familiar with the behavior of the participants.
2. To capture behavior as it happens.

CHALLENGES?
1. May be time-consuming.
2. May be costly.
3. The researcher may influence the behavior of the participants.
4. The participants may not show the same behavior if the observer was not present.
5. May be language barriers.
6. May be cultural barriers.

7. May be risks for the researcher.
8. May be sensitive to privacy, and confidentiality.

HOW
1. Determine research goals.
2. Select a research context
3. The site should allow clear observation and be accessible.
4. Select participants
5. Seek permission.
6. Gain access
7. Gather research data.
8. Analyze data
9. Find common themes
10. Create insights

OVERT OBSERVATION

WHAT

A method of observation where the subjects are aware that they are being observed.

WHO
Radcliff-Brown 1910
Bronisław Malinowski 1922
Margaret Mead 1928

WHY
To capture behavior as it happens.

CHALLENGES
1. Observation does not explain the cause of behavior.
2. Analysis can be time-consuming.
3. Observer bias can cause the researcher to look only where they think they will see useful information.

HOW
1. Define objectives.
2. Define participants and obtain their cooperation.
3. Define The context of the

observation: time and place.
4. In some countries the law requires that you obtain written consent to video people.
5. Define the method of observation and the method of recording information. Common methods are taking written notes, video or audio recording.
6. Run a test session.
7. Hypothesize an explanation for the phenomenon.
8. Predict a logical consequence of the hypothesis.
9. Test your hypothesis by observation
10. Analyze the data gathered and create a list of insights derived from the observations.

STRUCTURED OBSERVATION

WHAT
Particular types of behavior are observed and counted like a survey. The observer may create an event so that the behavior can be more easily studied. This approach is systematically planned and executed.

WHY
1. Allows stronger generalizations than unstructured observation.
2. May allow an observer to study behavior that may be difficult to study in unstructured observation.
3. To capture behavior as it happens.
4. A procedure is used which can be replicated.

CHALLENGES
1. Observation does not explain the cause of behavior.
2. Analysis can be time-consuming.
3. Observer bias can cause the researcher to look only where they think they will see useful information.

HOW
1. Define objectives.
2. Define participants and obtain their cooperation.
3. Define The context of the observation: time and place.
4. In some countries the law requires that you obtain written consent to video people.
5. Define the method of observation and the method of recording information. Common methods are taking written notes, video or audio recording.
6. Run a test session.
7. Hypothesize an explanation for the phenomenon.
8. Predict a logical consequence of the hypothesis.
9. Test your hypothesis by observation
10. Analyze the data gathered and create a list of insights derived from the observations.

UNSTRUCTURED OBSERVATION

WHAT
This method is used when a researcher wants to see what is naturally occurring without predetermined ideas. We use have an open-ended approach to observation and record all that we observe.

WHY
1. To capture behavior as it happens.

2. Observation is the most direct measure of behavior

CHALLENGES
1. Replication may be difficult.
2. Observation does not explain the cause of behavior.
3. Analysis can be time-consuming.
4. Observer bias can cause the researcher to look only where they think they will see useful information.
5. Data cannot be quantified
6. In this form of observation there is a higher probability of observer's bias.

HOW
1. Select a context to explore
2. Take a camera, note pad and pen
3. Record things and questions that you find interesting
4. Record ideas as you form them
5. Do not reach conclusions.
6. Ask people questions and try to understand the meaning in their replies.

PERSONAL INVENTORY

WHAT
This method involves studying the contents of a research subject's purse, or wallet. Study the things that they carry every day.

WHO
Rachel Strickland and Doreen Nelson 1998

WHY
1. To provide insights into the user's lifestyle, activities, perceptions, and values.
2. To understand the needs priorities and interests.

HOW
1. Formulate aims of research
2. Recruit participants carefully.
3. Document the contents with photographs and notes
4. ask your research subject to talk about the objects and their meaning.
5. Analyze the data.

> *The participant is asked to bring their 'most often carried bag' and lay the objects they carry on a flat surface, talking through the purpose and last-use of each item. Things to look out for where the bag is kept in the home and what is clustered around it, what is packed/repacked on arrival/departure, and the use of different bags for different activities."*
>
> Jan Chipchase

RESOURCES
Camera
Notepad computer

PROBLEM DEFINITION INTERVIEW

WHAT
The problem interview is all about testing your assumptions about a problem and to whom it is a problem.

HOW
State the top 1-3 problems and ask the interviewee to rank them.
Go through each problem and ask the interviewees how they address them today. General rule of thumb: you are done with the problem interviews when.
6. You have a must-have problem.
7. You can identify the demographics.
8. Of an early adopter
9. You can describe how customers.
10. Solve this problem today
11. You should interview at least ten people.

A SCRIPT FOR THE PROBLEM INTERVIEWS

WELCOME: SET THE STAGE.
Shortly, explain how the interview works. "Thank you for taking the time...We are currently...."

COLLECT BACKGROUND INFORMATION
Ask introductory questions and collect necessary background information: "Before we go to the problems, I would like to know.... how often / with whom / do you...?"

TELL A STORY TO SET THE CONTEXT
Illustrate the top problems you want to explore with your interviewee. "Let me tell you about the problems we are tackling...do any of these resonate with you?"

PROBLEM RANKING
State the top 1-3 problems and ask the interviewee to rank them. Ask if the interviewee has any other problems related to the discussed issue that she would like to add.

EXPLORE CUSTOMER'S WORLD-VIEW
Go through each problem and ask the interviewees how they address them today. Let them go to as much detail as they wish. Consider (and ask if necessary) how they rate the problems: "must-have", "nice to have", or "don't need".

WRAP-UP
If you have a solution already in mind, give a conceptual description of what you have in mind in order to maintain
interest. Then ask for permission to follow-up.

DOCUMENT RESULTS.
Take a few minutes to document your thoughts, that you did not have time to write down while interviewing.

Adapted from Ash Maurya, Running Lean, 2012

RECRUITMENT BRIEF

At the beginning of each phase, you must work as a team to:

1. Write your research questions
2. Decide what user research

activities will help you answer your questions
3. Identify the target audience.
4. Decide recruitment method
5. Review your research.
6. Select your space and gather your materials.

A recruitment brief is the instructions that you will send to a recruiting company.
They will create a screener.

Always provide the agency with a written brief.

In your brief, you should cover:
1. Research dates.
2. Research location
3. The number of participants
4. A description of the people you would like to recruit.
5. Incentives

REVIEWING THE SCREENER
The agency will provide you with a screener. Check the screener to ensure that it aligns with your needs.

SERVICE SAFARI

WHAT
A service safari is a research method for understanding services. By using a service you will be able to understand how that service works and what the experience is like. A service safari could be used to find out information about a specific service.

When carrying out a service safari you should think about:
6. Different stages which make up the service
7. People involved in delivering the service and what they do
8. What objects you use or interact with
9. What spaces the service takes place in
10. What information is available to people
11. How people involved in delivering the
12. Service contribute to the experience.

Taking photos or video will help you to find out more about the service you are using

HOW
1. What is the service?
2. What information is there?
3. What makes this service work well?
4. What are users doing?
5. What products are used?
6. What makes this service not work well?
7. Who is involved?
8. What is the space like?

SHADOWING

WHAT
Shadowing is observing people in context. The researcher accompanies the user and observes user experiences and activities. It allows the researcher and designer to develop design insights through observation and shared experiences with users.

WHO
Alex Bavelas 1944
Lucy Vernile, Robert A. Monteiro 1991

WHY
1. This method can help determine the difference between what subjects say they do and what they really do.
2. It helps in understanding the point of view of people. Successful design results from knowing the users.
3. Define intent
4. Can be used to evaluate concepts.

CHALLENGES
1. Selecting the wrong people to shadow.
2. Hawthorne Effect, The observer can influence the daily activities under being studied.

HOW
1. Prepare
2. Select carefully who to shadow.
3. Observe people in context by members of your design team.
4. Capture behaviors that relate to product function.
5. Identify issues and user needs.
6. Create design solutions based on observed and experienced user needs.
7. Typical periods can be one day to one week.

RESOURCES
Video camera
Digital still camera
Notepad computer
Laptop Computer

MAPPING METHODS

CURRENT STATE MAPS
With a current-state journey map, you can:
1. Identify pain points and their causes.
2. Identify gaps in what you are offering customers.
3. Improve the efficiency and effectiveness of a current service or customer experience.
4. Craft a better customer experience for a product service or brand.
5. Plan systematically what your organization is delivering to customers.
6. Implement a more efficient system of touchpoints.
7. Understand how customers behave across multiple channels.
8. Identify where your current customer experience or service is most likely to fail.
9. Unite your team with the common goal of a better customer experience.
10. Identify opportunities for feedback or measurement.
11. Develop metrics for progress towards goals.
12. Align your organization with a better customer experience.

FUTURE STATE MAPS
1. With a future-state journey map, you can:
2. Plan a future service or customer experience.
3. Define a new service with better customer experience than your existing service.
4. Implement a new service or customer experience.
5. Develop a product or service road-map.
6. Envision the ideal customer experience or service.
7. Identify the infrastructure needed to create a new service or customer experience.
8. Plan for hiring new staff
9. Drive positive change in your organization.
10. Develop empathy for customers.

WHAT'S THE DIFFERENCE, BETWEEN A BLUEPRINT AND A JOURNEY OR EXPERIENCE MAP?

A customer journey map captures how your customer is feeling emotionally across touchpoints over time.

A service blueprint captures the service or experience delivery process across touch points and the elements that make up the service including the things customers see and do not see.

The two types of maps complement each other. The order in which you create them depends on your goals.

SERVICE BLUEPRINT
1. Define employees roles about the customer experience.
2. Identify areas of service improvement.
3. Identify points where moments of truth will occur.
4. Capturing Dynamic Processes
5. Service blueprinting allows the capturing of dynamic processes in a visual manner.
6. A blueprint is one of few methods that allow you to visually convey events that change over time.
7. Relatively few methods allow for this type of dynamic, and at the same time visual, representation.
8. To identify where your customer experience is most likely to fail.
9. Opportunities for improvements
10. To plan and implement a new customer experience.
11. To implement metrics to measure your customer experience.
12. To audit and improve your service evidence or touchpoints.

EXPERIENCE MAP
1. To identify customer pain points and gaps in your touchpoints
2. To design a new service or experience with a focus on optimizing your customer's experience.
3. To audit the customer experience.
4. To develop new touch points to improve the customer experience.

USER STORIES

WHAT
User stories describe a user and the reason why they need to use the service you're building. You must use user stories when building your service - they're essential to building and running a service that meets user needs.

WHAT TO INCLUDE
They should include:
1. The person using the service (the actor)
2. What the user needs the service for (the narrative)
3. Why the user needs it (the goal)

FORMAT
They have the following format:

As a... [who is the user?]

I needxxxx
So thatxxxx

FOCUS ON THE GOAL
The most important part of a user story is the goal. This helps you:

Make sure you're solving the need
Decide when the story is done and a

user need is met
If you're struggling to write the goal then you should reconsider why you think you need that feature.

WHAT-HOW-WHY

WHAT

The What-How-Why method is a tool to help develop a deeper understanding of stakeholders.

You start with concrete observing what the behavior is then How the person is behaving then finally go to and then finally develop a model for Why. What are the underlying factors driving the behavior?

HOW

You should divide activities into What, How and Why.

4. Record concrete observations of what is happening. What is the person doing? What is happening in the background? What is the person holding? Try to be as objective as possible.

5. How is the person doing what they are doing? Record how the person is doing their activity. Try to describe the emotional impact of performing the task.

6. Develop a theory for why the person is doing what they are doing? What are the underlying emotional drivers behind what you have observed? Make educated guesses regarding motivation and emotions.

7. Test your assumptions with stakeholders.

Source: adapted from Rikke Dam and Teo Siang, Interactive Design Foundation

WWWWWH

WHAT

Who, What, Where, When, Why, and How? is a method for getting a thorough understanding of the problem, It is used to obtain basic information in police investigations. A well-known golden rule of journalism is that if you want to know the full story about something you have to answer all the five W's. Journalists argue your story isn't complete until you answer all six questions.

1. Who is involved?
2. What occurred?
3. When did it happen?
4. Where did it happen?
5. Why did it occur?

WHO

Hermagoras of Temnos, Greece 1st century BC.

WHY

This method helps create a story that communicates clearly the nature of an activity or event to stakeholders.

HOW
1. Ask the questions starting with the 5 w's and 1 h question words.
2. Identify the people involved
3. Identify the activities and make a list of them.
4. Identify all the places and make a list of them.
5. Identify all the time factors and make a list of them.
6. Identify causes for events of actions and make a list of them.
7. Identify the way events took place and make a list of them.
8. Study the relationships between the information.

I keep six honest serving men. They taught me all I knew. Their names are what and why and when and how and where and who."

Rudyard Kipling

SOME WWWWWH QUESTIONS

WHO
1. Who is affected?
2. Who believes that the problem affects them?
3. Needs the problem solved?
4. Does not want the problem to be solved?
5. Could stand in the way of a solution?

WHEN
1. Does it happen
2. Doesn't it happen?
3. Did it start?
4. Will it end?
5. Is the solution needed?
6. Might it happen in the future?
7. Will it be a bigger problem?
8. Will it improve?

WHERE
1. Does it happen?
2. Doesn't it happen
3. Else does it happen?
4. Is the best place to solve the problem

WHY
1. Is this situation a problem?
2. Do you want to solve it?
3. Do you not want to solve it?
4. Does it not go away?
5. Would someone else want to solve it?
6. Can it be solved?
7. Is it difficult to solve?

WHAT
1. May be different in the future
2. Are its weaknesses?
3. Do you like?
4. Makes you unhappy about it?
5. Is flexible?
6. Is not flexible?
7. Do you know?
8. Do you not understand?
9. How have you solved similar problems?
10. Are the underlying ideas?
11. Are the values involved?
12. Are the elements of the problem and how are they related?
13. What can you assume to be correct
14. Is most important
15. Is least important
16. Are your goals?
17. Do you need to discover?

05
EXPERIENCE MAPS

EXPERIENCE MAPS

WHAT

Experience maps are diagrams that allow a designer or manager to describe the elements of a customer experience in concise terms.

A journey map focuses on identifying touch points, An experience map focuses on the emotions your customer experiences. In practice, many people use these terms interchangeably. The particular lanes included can be mixed and matched to your goals.

Customer journeys depict what customers really want. These methods help us to understand interactions from users' point of view. They must be developed from your customers' perspective. They are a framework to craft a better customer experience. With these tools you can identify problem areas and opportunities for improvement.

Maps are usually created to help understand a particular segment or persona. The more complex your service or customer experience, the more value there is in mapping the customer journey and experience.

HISTORY

The origin of journey and experience mapping is less apparent than Service Blueprints, but they have been used at least since 1991 (Whittle & Foster, 1991).
Several sources mention these methods from 2006 (Parker & Heapy, 2006; Voss & Zomerdijk, 2007). The detailed application is still evolving (Følstad et al., 2013). Følstad defines a customer journey as the process a customer goes through to reach a particular goal. The value of these techniques is greatest when the complexity of the route is higher. Customer journey maps describe not only what a customer experiences but also the customer's response to those experiences.

Wechsler (2012) describes internal workshops for creating customer journey maps. The analysis of customer journeys may also concern quantitative measurement of the customer's experience. In the scientific literature, such analysis is typically conducted as part of the mapping process to quantify changes in experiential quality during the customer journey (Trischler & Zehrer, 2012). Kankainen et al. (2012) describe the use of customer journeys for co-design, where customers formulate "dream journeys". In 2007 the British Government published guidelines on customer journey mapping (HM Government, 2007).

WHY

Journey and experience mapping can be used for the following purposes:

1. Understand the collective experiences of customer segments
2. To create a more streamlined, consistent, and efficient customer experience.
3. Create a more seamless customer experience across business departments and channels.
4. Design a new service or product customer experience
5. Allocate people and resources more effectively.
6. Develop alignment across departments of an organization.
7. Craft a better customer experience.
8. Expose places where your service or customer experience may fail.
9. Craft a better customer experience
10. Strategic and tactical innovation
11. Building and sharing knowledge
12. Designing the moments of truth
13. Understand competitive positioning
14. Understanding the ideal experience
15. Reveal the truth from your customer's perspective
16. Identify opportunities
17. Empathize with your custom
18. Designing and improving Systems
19. Develop a better product road map
20. Take cost & complexity out of the system
21. Prioritize competing deliverables
22. Plan for hiring
23. Bring different parts of your business together to work to improve the customer experience
24. Build knowledge of customer behaviors and needs across channels
25. Identify specific areas of opportunity to drive ideation and innovation
26. Make intangible services tangible.
27. Develop customer insights
28. Understand where friction exists between the needs of different market segments
29. Introduce metrics for what matters most for your customers.
30. Align your offerings to brand promise.
31. Identify failure points.
32. Improve efficiency.
33. Imagine future product and

PARTS OF AN EXPERIENCE MAP

Phase	PREPARE	ENTER

- Physical Evidence
- Physical evidence Channel 1
- Physical evidence Channel 2

Map channels of interest such as instore or web

- Customer Actions
- Customer thinking
- Customer saying
- Customer feeling
- Customer Goals
- Customer Needs

a horizontal row of boxes is called a swimlane or a lane

- Pain points/ frustrations
- Challenges/ Barriers
- Moments of truth
- Actors/ stakeholders
- Environments

Map factors of interest such as instore or web

- Expectations
- Risks
- Opportunities

brainstorm with stakeholders how to improve the experience

- Emotional Journey

EXPERIENCE MAPS

| EXPERIENCE | EXIT |

understand what your customer is thinking by interviewing them

understand customer pain points through research

map positive or negative experience based on your research data for your persona

service experiences.
34. More Holistic thinking.
35. Making better decisions.
36. A living document that can evolve with your business.
37. Is a holistic view of key touch points and interactions personas have with the brand.
38. Communicate the experience visually.
39. Promotes better coordination of across channels.

A MAP HELPS YOU

1. Plan your product or service offering most efficiently for various customer segments.
2. Evaluate customer experience gaps or fail points before they occur.
3. Identify opportunities to improve you customer experience.
4. identify ways to improve your touchpoints and remove duplication.
5. You can create a map as a concept for a customer's ideal future experience.
6. Put all stakeholders on the same page so that you can reach a common understanding and agreement on how to move forward towards your organizational goals.
7. Helps make measures of success clear.
8. From analyzing your map recommendations and a plan to reach your objectives can be put into place.

HOW TO BUILD AND EXPERIENCE MAP

Here is a list of stages that you can complete creating a Service Blueprint. Consider the blueprint to be a living document that will develop and improve, so it doesn't have to be perfect first time. Concentrate on your customers and their point of view.

SELECT YOUR TEAM

Care should be taken in choosing your team. As many groups and diverse points of view involved in design delivery and use of the service as possible should be represented.

1. Keep groups to six people or less.
2. If your total group size is larger than six break the large group into smaller groups of six or less.
3. Have a diverse team with different genders, age, occupations and seniority represented.
4. Have at least two or three "T" shaped people. That is, people with two or more areas of expertise such as technology and management or management and design. This makes the team more flexible and helps group collaboration. This experience can be gained through education or work. Look for people with at least 10,000 hours of experience in each of two areas. That corresponds to three or four years of work

experience in each area.
5. Involve external and internal stakeholders such as customers, suppliers, internal business management, engineering, design, marketing, distribution, IT and sales. Have customer-facing people where possible because they better understand the customer's perspective.

CREATE YOUR GOAL STATEMENT
1. What is the problem, unmet needs or opportunities that you wish to analyze?
2. Create a clear outline of customer goals and needs that is compatible with your goals and with an outcome that satisfies them.
3. Who are the stakeholders?
4. Where is the service or experience delivered?
5. When is the service or experience provided?
6. What are the channels?
7. Why is there a need for a new design solution?
8. Do you want to enhance the customer experience?
9. Do you wish to engage your customers more effectively?
10. Do you wish to create a more efficient process?
11. Define your goals in a statement.

DEFINE YOUR TARGET AUDIENCE SEGMENT AND THEIR NEEDS
The most successful products services and experiences target precise customer segments.

GATHER YOUR EXISTING RESEARCH
Start by auditing internal customer experience data that has been previously gathered. Do you have existing research? Where are the gaps in your knowledge?

Interviews are one of the most usual methods used to gather data. Ask them to walk you through their experience and talk about their problems, needs desires and feelings at each stage. Start by talking to between five and twenty people as a minimum sample size. Ask them what touch points they are engaging at each phase. Ask them where they are experiencing problems or frustrations in achieving their goals. Document your interviews or observations by using video or a digital recorder.

To be useful, your map needs to be based on real and truthful information.

REVIEW YOUR EXISTING RESEARCH
Review existing research Identify gaps in data and create a list of recurring customer experience problems.

CREATE A RESEARCH PLAN TO FILL THE GAPS
1. What do you still need to

COFFEE SHOP EXPERIENCE MAP

time	0 mins	10	20	30	40
	EVALUATE		**ENTER**		
touch points	Home Interior	Internet Laptop	Car	Car park Coffee shop exterior	Coffee shop interior Menu board
doing	At home decides to go out to have a coffee	Checks location of coffee shop on Internet	Drives car to coffee shop	Parks and enters coffee shop	Selects drink and waits in line to order
thinking	Should I call a friend?	Which coffee shop should I go to?	Will be able to park close?	Will there be a long queue?	Should I have a latte or a drip coffee?
pain points	Friend not answering	Hard to park at best coffee shop	No parking place available shop	Queue takes 20 minutes	Too many choices on menu
feeling	HAPPY / NEUTRAL / UNHAPPY — ZONE OF CUSTOMER UNHAPPINESS				
opportunities	Improve web site	differentiate coffee shop from other coffee shops	Make more parking available.	Order coffee Online. Add second cash register.	Reduce number of options

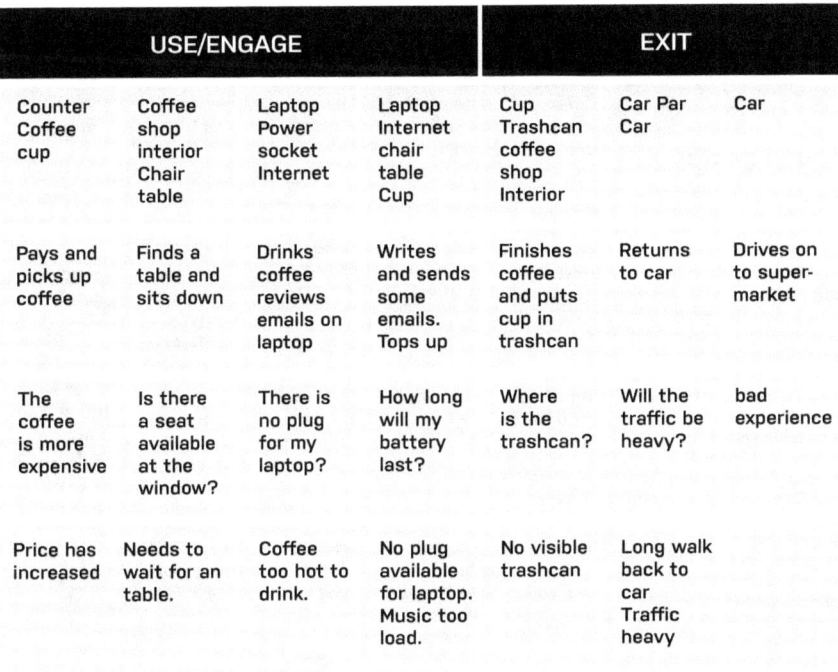

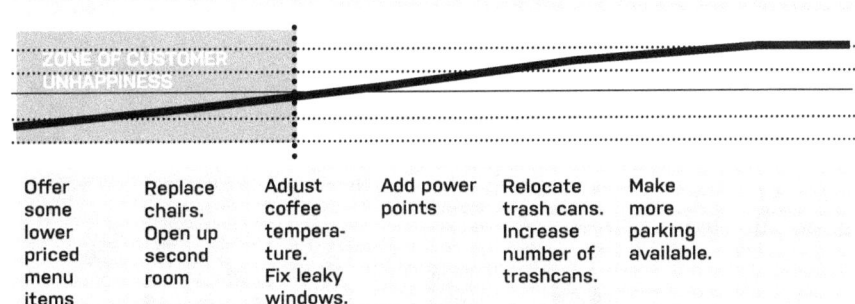

EXPERIENCE MAPS 175

AIR TRAVEL EXPERIENCE MAP

time	0 days	1	5		10
	RESEARCH		**BOOK FLIGHT**		
touch points	home laptop web	home laptop web	home laptop web	home laptop web	home laptop web
doing	research lights travel sites	select preferred options	book flight	receive confirmation save itinerary	receive check-in email
thinking	can i find a price that i can afford?	Do they have hidden costs?	The web site is hard to use	I don't need the loyalty program	what is the easiest way to go to the airport?
pain points	The web site is hard to use	cannot find baggage charges	return flight has two stops Too many choices on menu	cancellation policy not clear	
feeling	HAPPY / NEUTRAL / UNHAPPY (ZONE OF CUSTOMER UNHAPPINESS)				
opportunities	Improve brand awareness monitor web site customer experience	clarify baggage charges improve incentives for first time flyers	Heuristic evaluation of web site Reduce number of options	evaluate and optimize loyalty program communicate benefits more clearly	sell services related to day of travel

176 | EXPERIENCE MAPS

PRETRAVEL		TRAVEL					
home laptop web	home laptop web clothes bag	phone taxi traffic curb	security check point	coffee seating airline desk flight board	plane seating overhead bin entertainment	airport lounge baggage handling taxi rank	
receive loyalty program email	check-in at home pack bag	order cab travel to airport	security check bag	lounge buy coffee board flight	chat to traveler watch movie	deboard plane pick up bag	
If the experience is good I might join the loyalty program	Is there a seat available at the window?	will i miss my flight?	Will I drop something important?	Is there room for my bag in the overhead?	are movies free?	have they lost my bag:"	
Price has increased	no window seat available	high traffic cab charge high	no one at bag check long line	coffee too hot Poor internet reception Flight board not in lounge area	The movies are not the type of movies I prefer	wait 30 minutes at bag carousel	
Address barriers to signing up to loyalty program	improve interface for seat selection when booking	partner with taxi company to provide reduced cab fee for loyalty program customers	review bag check process add curb bag check	Evaluate Internet services provided during lounge waiting	Research customer segements to better understand entertainment preferences	review bag handling faster bag processing for loyalty customers	

EXPERIENCE MAPS

know?
2. What questions do you need to ask?
3. How many people will you study?
4. What type of people will you research?
5. What will be the context of the research?
6. What methods will you use?
7. When will you select and screen the subjects, conduct the research and report on findings?

SYNTHESIZE YOUR RESEARCH
Put each potentially useful piece of information on a separate post-it note. Put the post-it notes on a wall and ask your team to organize the customer's comments into related groups or themes. Which issues are most significant to more customers? Build a hierarchy of issues.

APPOINT YOUR MODERATOR

SELECT AND PREPARE YOUR WORKSPACE
A safe space is a large room with plenty of natural light with a large table and sufficient chairs for your team.
Some useful materials
1. A large wall
2. Butcher paper
3. Masking tape
4. Mobile dry erase boards
5. Dry erase markers
6. Sharpies
7. Adhesive notes in 5 colors
8. Digital camera
9. Tripod

IDENTIFY YOUR TARGET SEGMENT/S TO MAP
Identifying customer segments.

CREATE A PERSONA FOR EACH TARGET SEGMENT
Create 3 to 6 personas to cover all your customers.

IDENTIFY STAKEHOLDERS
A stakeholder is someone who may be in some way influenced by your design when it is complete and marketed.

HOLD STAKEHOLDER WORKSHOPS
Organize a workshop, and guide internal and external stakeholders through the process of creating the first draft. Go over the user experience in detail and discuss the experience from the perspective of customers and diverse stakeholders,

SELECT THE SERVICE TO BE MAPPED
Select your journey or experience to map. We suggest starting small with part of an experience that is important or problematic. For example rather than mapping an entire customer journey for air travel from New York to London, map a part of it that is important such as selecting the airline and booking the travel online. Then explore several challenging sub-journeys before tackling the whole journey.

DECIDE PRESENT OR FUTURE SERVICE TO MAP

It is most usual to first map your existing customer experience. A current state map can help identify ways to make your existing customer experience better or more efficient.

After mapping your existing service you may be interested in creating a map as a scenario for a future service or customer experience.

SELECT START AND END POINTS OF THE CUSTOMER EXPERIENCE

Define the scope in terms of time and customer activities.

SELECT CHANNELS TO MAP

Some examples of channels include
1. In-store experience
2. Face to face
3. Print
4. Web
5. Call center
6. Tablet app
7. TV
8. Mobile phone

The channel defines the opportunities and constraints of a touchpoint. You can map all channels on one map in parallel lanes. This type of map is called a multichannel map. You can map just one channel per map and create as m,any separate maps as you have channels.

START SMALL

Consider picking a specific scenario or sub-activity of your entire customer experience.

DRAFT THE MAP

Use a large wall or table. Create your first rough draft using post-it notes. When it is complete photograph and share it with as many internal and external stakeholders as possible and ask for their feedback. If insights don't fit on a single map, keep maps simple by creating one map for each persona.

CREATE THE STORY

What are the main elements of the customer experience from a customer perspective? What parts of their experience leave a lasting impression on them either positive or negative.

MAP USER ACTIONS & ACTIVITIES STEP-BY-STEP

Start at the beginning of the service or experience and list each thing a customer commonly does step by step. Put each sub- activity on a separate post-it note. For example, if the activity is visiting a coffee shop the activities may include.
1. At work decide to get a coffee on the way home
2. Check the location of coffee shops on the Internet.
3. Select coffee shop
4. Go to car
5. Drive to coffee shop
6. Park
7. Enter coffee shop

8. Stand in line
9. Order
10. Pick up coffee
11. Find table
12. Sit down
13. Drink coffee
14. Read news on tablet
15. Pack up
16. Return to car
17. Drive home
18. Reflect on the experience.

Describe each activity on a separate post-it note and place them in a line on your wall or table. Continue till your team is happy that all important activities have been included.

MAP TIME
How long does each customer activity usually take? Does a stage usually last ten seconds or ten minutes. Place the time taken on a post-it note above each stage of customer activity.
Time to consider:
1. Critical periods service actions, such as response to a proposal.
2. Duration of each service step, such as airline check-in
3. Time between service steps such as walking to a hotel room after check-in.
4. End to end service experience.

BUILD THE MAP
Now you are ready to create the map.

MAP USER ACTION PHASES
Break the list of customer activities into four or six phases of sub-activities. Some examples of phases of activities are:

1. Explore
2. Evaluate
3. Engage
4. Experience

1. Aware
2. Join
3. Use
4. Develop
5. Leave

1. Research
2. Evaluate and compare
3. Commit
4. Use and Monitor
5. Refine and review

MAP THE PHYSICAL EVIDENCE STEP-BY-STEP
Physical evidence is usually the lane shown at the top of a blueprint. Services consist of the interactions with people, the processes, and the physical proof of the experience. Designed objects in the service environment are sometimes referred to as "physical evidence" because they are physical proof of service that has taken place. Physical evidence is the tangible things that help to communicate and perform the service and influence a customer's perception of a service.

Physical evidence is the visible manifestation of service. It conveys to customers whether the service provider cares about their customers and whether they trust their customers. Physical facilities and staff appearance; and uniforms. Physical evidence should be considered important by the customer and the promise implied by these tangible objects should be delivered. A bank card is an example of physical evidence of a service. It helps a bank differentiate their service from another bank. It separates the service from the seller.

Other examples of physical evidence are
1. The building
2. The interior
3. The car park
4. Internal signs.
5. Packaging.
6. Promotional materials
7. Web pages.
8. Paperwork
9. Brochures.
10. Stationery
11. Billing statement
12. Furnishings.
13. Signs
14. Uniforms and employee dress.
15. Business cards.
16. Mailboxes.

MAP THE PAIN POINTS

A pain point is any part of the customer experience that they find people disturbing, frustrating, urgent or uncomfortable. Many customer needs are for things the end users don't clearly understand or can articulate. A pain point is a problem for your customer and a problem and an opportunity for you. Solving pain points create value for you and your customer. "customer pain" is a synonym

evidence cues are what customers use to evaluate service quality.

Physical evidence can convey intended and unintended messages to customers. Physical evidence is the interface between a service provider and a customer. Key to delivering a successful service is to clearly identify a simple, consistent message, and then manage the evidence to support that message.

" Well-prepared small details represent sincerity in serving guests which reflects the hotel's good service spirit. For example, welcome fruit, an electric kettle and fresh flowers in hotel rooms are service evidence that often evoked delight as they show the hotel's thoughtfulness"

"For example, a research participant talked about disappointment caused by "fake" hangers in a hotel room's closet. She complained: They're not real hangers, because they're attached to the railing. So
if you want to take out a hanger and then hang it on a chair or hang it on a door, you can't, because there's no hook... That's kind of a fake hanger. It shows that they think I'm going to steal the hangers. So it makes me feel not trusted."

Source: Kathy Pui Ying Lo Loughborough University

Physical evidence includes the service providers building/

for "customer needs". Customers spend money to combat pain or to pursue pleasure. Examples of service pain points are airport security lines, hospital directions, or the cost of travel. A pain point is the why customers choose you if you offer a solution to their need. If you engage your customers and listen, they'll tell you their pain points

To identify customer 'pain-points':
1. In-depth interviews with customer-facing internal employees
2. Requests from your most valuable customers.
3. Customer interviews.
4. Customer focus groups.
5. Review of customer support or warranty claims to identify persistent problems.
6. Review of competitor offerings.
7. You can list the root causes of pain for your customers at each stage.

CUSTOMER OR STAKEHOLDER COMMENTS
List significant or representative comments in a lane. What do customers think?

MAP BRAND IMPACT
List brand impact of touchpoints and customer comments in a lane.

KEY PEOPLE
Identify internal owners of experiences that support customer's needs.

CUSTOMER NEEDS
Do customers have unrecognized needs that could be addressed? What do customers want to accomplish at each stage of interaction?

MAP CONNECTIONS
Use arrows to illustrate the flow of responsibility who is driving the service at any moment and should be initiating service action:

1. Model expectations of "proactive" provider activity.
2. Model the customer responsibility for next steps.
3. Model partner expectations.
4. Define points of hand-off between roles, such as from backstage to onstage.

MAP MOMENTS OF TRUTH
Map those interactions that have the most impact on the customer. A moment of truth is an interaction between a customer and a service provider that allows the end user to form an impression of the organization. For example waiting in line in a coffee shop. A moment of truth is a point in time when a customer can make a judgment about the value of a service delivery and a business relationship. Identifying moments of truth and improving their outcomes is a focus of service blueprinting.

ROOT CAUSE OF PAIN
Ask why the experience is painful for the customer. If necessary, ask why several times to understand the cause of the pain.

MAP BARRIERS
What are the obstacles to the optimal experience for the customer at each stage of their interaction?

ADD PHOTOS OR PICTURES WHERE POSSIBLE
Maps sometimes have a lane of photographs that show pain points or other aspects of customer activities. Use pictures if they are the best way of communicating something. For example lack of cleanliness on a train platform.

IDENTIFY POINTS OF FAILURE
Where is the experience failing or likely to fail?

OPPORTUNITIES
Brainstorm ways to change to better meet customer needs.
1. Brainstorm ways to change to meet better customer needs.
2. Bullet these ideas in a separate lane stage by stage.
3. What is the ideal customer experience
4. Analyze every touch point
5. Identify physical evidence at each phase - moment of truth
6. Simplify and refine the process
7. Remove pain points and surprises.
8. Add touchpoints that are missing
9. Build scenarios.
10. Think about extreme users, new users, average users.

PHOTOGRAPH THE DRAFT
Photograph the whole blueprint and photograph the blueprint in sections with sufficient resolution to enable you to transfer the map into a graphics program such as Adobe Illustrator or InDesign.

CREATE A PRESENTATION COPY
Photograph the whole map and photograph the map in sections with sufficient resolution to enable you to transfer the map into a graphics program such as Adobe Illustrator or InDesign. Templates can be used for future maps.

DISTRIBUTE TO STAKEHOLDERS FOR FEEDBACK
Distribute draft to internal and external stakeholders for feedback. Circulate you map as widely as possible to get feedback from internal departments, executives, external customers and stakeholders.

REFINE THE MAP BASED ON THE FEEDBACK
Does it tell the story of your customer's experience that is complete, from beginning to end? Is it understandable to people outside the team? Are

LIST CUSTOMER ACTIVITIES STAGE-BY-STAGE

stages	EVALUATE	ENTER	USE/ENGAGE		EXIT
touch points					
doing					
thinking			customer activities		
feeling					
pain points					
opportunities					

LIST THE PHASES OF CUSTOMER ACTIONS

stages	EVALUATE	ENTER	USE/ENGAGE		EXIT
touch points					
doing		Review customer activities Identify 4 to 6 phases			
thinking					
feeling					
pain points					
opportunities					

the insights actionable? Does it inspire and support a change in strategy? Does it communicate the necessary information, without further explanation? Simplify the map. Identify gaps and do further research to fill the gaps. Gaps in touchpoints may suggest opportunities to add new touchpoints.

ITERATE
Distribute the refined map to other stakeholders and refine the map again.

BRAINSTORM THE IDEAL EXPERIENCE
Put together what you have learned to generate a better experience for your customers that you can implement. Develop step-by-step corrective actions for fail points.

RAPID PROTOTYPING
Experience prototyping is the most efficient way to implement an improved service. The goal is to observe customers interacting with the new experience and obtain their feedback about the experience. Use methods such as:
1. Video prototyping
2. Role-playing
3. Desktop walkthroughs
4. Bodystorming
5. Paper prototyping
6. Empathy tools
7. Wireframing
8. Service staging
9. Wizard of Oz
10. Start with low-fidelity methods and move to higher fidelity prototyping methods as you find clarity with the best design direction.

SERVICE STAGING
Test the refinements in a staged setting. Sets up space that imitates the real environment, but with simple props to represent physical objects.

CONDUCT USER STUDIES IN THE TARGET CONTEXT
Test with target users iteratively and refine the service until the pain points have become points of pleasure for customers.
1. Do people understand the service
2. Do people see the value of the service?
3. Do people understand how to use it?
4. Is the experience positive?
5. What ideas do the customers have that could improve the service?

IMPLEMENT THE SERVICE
The end purpose of a blueprint is to take action and improve the journey and drive the ROI to justify the investment.
After the new service design is tested, the design team documents the new experience and creates implementation guidelines to roll out of the new service across the organization. The service blueprint is now a tool to communicate the new design.

1. Use your map for employee

LIST THE TOUCHPOINTS STAGE-BY-STAGE

stages	EVALUATE		ENTER		USE/ENGAGE				EXIT		
touch points							touchpoints				
doing											
thinking											
feeling											
pain points											
opportunities											

LIST CUSTOMER THOUGHTS STAGE-BY-STAGE

stages	EVALUATE		ENTER		USE/ENGAGE				EXIT		
touch points											
doing											
thinking											
feeling					customer thoughts						
pain points											
opportunities											

training.
2. Map upcoming product launches or your desired future state

MEASURE YOUR PROGRESS TOWARDS YOUR GOALS

Define ways of tracking your progress towards measurable goals.
1. Net Promoter Score and customer loyalty measures
2. Customer satisfaction measures
3. Quantitative assessments of the customer emotions.
4. Metrics of customer effort
5. The measure of the performance of each touchpoint.
6. New sales.
7. Increased loyalty and retention of customers
8. The increase in revenue per customer.
9. More sales.
10. Reduced costs
11. Better delivery processes.
12. Better quality
13. Increased competitiveness

> *Design thinking is a particularly effective approach for problems in a world filled with accelerated uncertainty. Most problem-solving methodologies are based on predictability. We are typically taught how to take data from the past and project it into the future. That doesn't work very well when you're trying to create a new future that's not dependent on information from the past.*
>
> *Design thinking asks that we learn our way into the future through a process of experimentation and prototyping."*

Jeanne Liedtka
strategy professor at the University of Virginia's Darden Graduate School of Business

MULTI-CHANNEL MAP

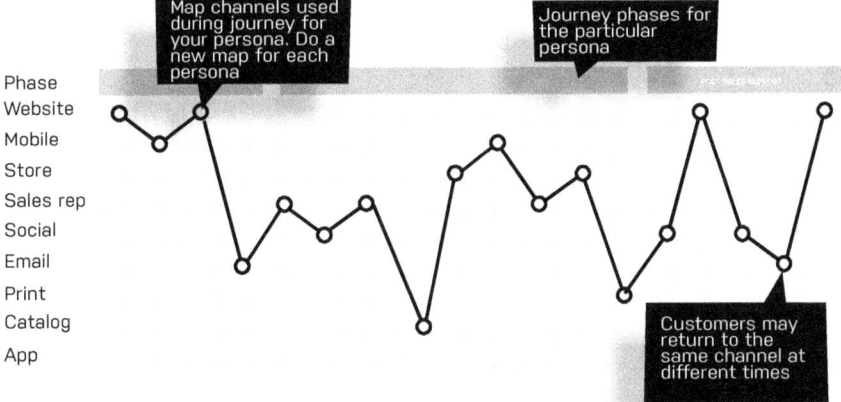

EXPERIENCE MAPS 187

LIST HOW THE CUSTOMER IS FEELING

stages	EVALUATE		ENTER		USE/ENGAGE				EXIT		
touch points											
doing											
thinking											
feeling											
pain points					feeling good, bad or neutral						
opportunities											

LIST PAIN POINTS STAGE-BY-STAGE

stages	EVALUATE		ENTER		USE/ENGAGE				EXIT		
touch points											
doing											
thinking											
feeling											
pain points											
opportunities					pain points						

EMOTIONAL JOURNEY MAP

WHAT
An emotional journey map is a map that visually illustrates people's emotional experience throughout an interaction with an organization or brand.

WHY
1. It provides a focus for discussion.
2. It focuses on what may make your customers unhappy
3. Provides a visually compelling story of customer experience.
4. Customer experience is more than interaction with a product.
5. By understanding the journey that your customers are making, you will be in a position to make informed improvements.

CHALLENGES
1. Customers often do not take the route in an interaction that the designer expects.
2. Failure to manage experiences can lead to lost customers.

HOW
1. Define the activity of your map. For example, it could be a ride on the underground train.
2. Collect internal insights.
3. Research customer perceptions.
4. Analyze research.
5. Map journey.
6. Across the top of the page do a timeline Break the journey into stages using your customer's point of view
7. Capture each persona's unique experience.
8. Use a scale from 0 to 10. The higher the number, the better the experience.
9. Plot the emotional journey.
10. Analyze the lease pleasant emotional periods and create ideas for improving the experience during those periods.
11. Create a map for each persona.

MULTI-CHANNEL MAP
Interactions can cross channels, touchpoints or physical evidence and take place in multiple contexts. More than 50% of companies according to one study have little understanding of the complex nature of their customer's typical purchase routes. Customers desire seamless interactions across channels and touchpoints. A multichannel map can help uncover opportunities for your business to improve the customer experience.

AS YOU FILL THE BOXES BRAINSTORM WITH YOUR TEAM OPPORTUNITIES TO IMPROVE THE SERVICE BY IMPROVING THE PAINPOINTS

stages	EVALUATE	ENTER	USE/ENGAGE	EXIT
touch points				
doing				
thinking				
feeling				
pain points				
opportunities				

EMOTIONAL JOURNEY MAP

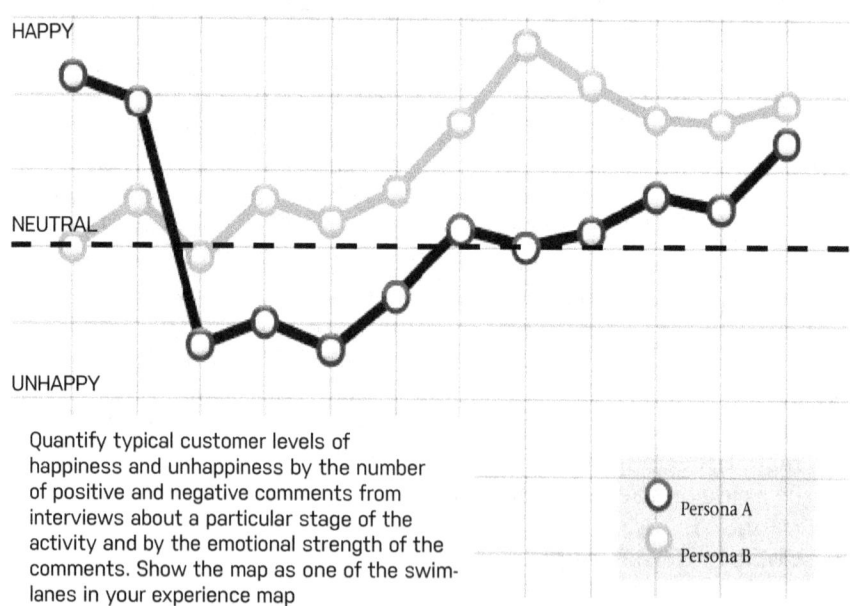

Quantify typical customer levels of happiness and unhappiness by the number of positive and negative comments from interviews about a particular stage of the activity and by the emotional strength of the comments. Show the map as one of the swim-lanes in your experience map

Persona A
Persona B

8 am 9 am 10 am 11 am 12 pm 1 pm 2 pm 3 pm 4 pm 5 pm 6 pm 7 pm

EXPERIENCE MAPS

EXERCISE ONE
EXPERIENCE MAP
Autonomous vehicle ride hailing service

BACKGROUND
Experience mapping is a strategic process of capturing and communicating complex interactions and experiences. The activity of mapping builds knowledge and consensus across your organization, and the map helps build seamless customer, user or employee experiences.

INSTRUCTIONS
1. Choose a service, customer, user, or employee experience you find interesting, that you will be able to find people to interview about, and that you believe can be improved by some intervention. It should involve at least 12 steps and take at least 30-minutes on average.
2. Interview at least 4 Users: Discover user's emotional state throughout the experience. Try to understand what they feel, what they care about, and what that implies.
3. Create an experience map to describe the customer or employee journey.
4. What is the customer or employee doing? Break the experience down into at least one dozen activities that take place over at least 30-minutes
5. List the touchpoints that the employee or customer engages through the activities at each stage of their activity. These can be websites, vehicles, buildings, devices, interior spaces, people or other tangible physical things.
6. List what the customer or employee is thinking about at each stage.
7. What does the person want or need at each stage?
8. List how the customer is feeling at each stage, are they happy, frustrated, bored, confused or experiencing some other emotions.
9. What are the pain points at each stage where the person has negative feelings?
10. What are the opportunities to improve the experience or pain points at each stage?
11. Plot the most important points within the experience. The most successful experience maps will communicate creatively, demonstrate emotional insights, and clearly identify where lapses can be prevented or repaired by providing people with a better solution.

DELIVERABLES
Four personas representing the most important user groups for the service experience.
One experience map of one to two pages as a PDF file.

06
GLOSSARY

GLOSSARY

In this short glossary I have brought together a collection of terms used in Design Thinking, service design and user-centered design.

These fields are emerging areas of design and I believe will become the most significant areas of design this century. There are many terms that are used and these terms are still evolving.

At the back of this work you will find a list of my other publications if you would like more in-depth information about any of these fields.

I hope that you will find this collection useful.

A-B TEST
Testing technique where a percentage of site visitors are shown an alternate version of a design. The effectiveness of the two designs is then compared.

ACTOR
A person involved in the creation, delivery, support, or use of a service.

AFFINITY DIAGRAM
A tool used to organize a large number of ideas, sorting them into groups based on their natural relationships, for review and analysis

AFFORDANCES
The qualities of a design or material that affects or suggests how it can be used. For example, the affordances of a hammer (weight, handle and and grip, scribed head, etc) suggest it should be used for striking objects. Looking at affordances is especially useful when analyzing how designs or materials prompt certain behaviors. (eg. "When all you have is a hammer, everything looks like a nail."
Source dSchool Stanford

ANALOGOUS SITUATIONS
An analogous situation is a situation from another area or industry that may relate to an area of focus for a design and may suggests ways to improve it.

ANALYTIC INDUCTION
A qualitative research method that begins with a rough hypothesis, which is modified through the examination of cases that don't fit the hypothesis.

ANALYTICS
A broad term that encompasses a variety of tools, techniques and processes used for extracting useful information or meaningful patterns from data.

ARTIFACTS
Physical service touchpoints. For example the New York Underground map

BACKSTAGE/ BACKOFFICE
Backstage activities are those taken by the service delivering company employees that are not visible to the customer. Backstage actions are actions that impact customers.

Backstage actions are separated from onstage service delivery by the line of visibility. Activities above the line of visibility are seen by the client while everything below it is invisible. On an aircraft, the taking of an order for a meal is an onstage or front-stage action, and the preparation of the food is a backstage action if it is not seen by the traveler.

BETA LAUNCH
The limited launch of a software product with the goal of finding bugs before final launch.

BIAS
A one-sided viewpoint, inclination or a partial perspective. An interviewer might inadvertently bias an interviewee's answers by asking a "loaded" question, in which a desired answer is presupposed in the question.

BODYSTORMING
Prototyping method,
Service situations are be acted out,for example for example at the hotel reception. The design team cast the roles, practice the situation. often with the input of end users The purpose is to prototype and test interactions to better understand and refine them.

BRAINSTORMING
Brainstorming is a group or individual creativity approach where design solutions are generated by members of the team in a collaborative session.

A method for generating ideas, intended to inspire the free-flowing sharing of thoughts of an individual or a group of people, typically while withholding criticism in order to promote uninhibited thinking.

CARD SORTING
A technique using either cards or software, whereby users generate an information hierarchy that can then form the basis of an information architecture or navigation menu.

A technique to investigate how users tend to group. The users are given a set of cards containing individual item names and are told to sort them into related piles and label the groups. Card sorting provides insight into the user's mental model and suggests the structure and placement of items on a Website.
Source: Human Factors International

CAUSATION
A relationship between an event (the cause) and a second event (the effect), where the second event is a consequence
of the first event.
Source: Human Factors International

CHANNEL
A medium for communication or delivery. Most services use more than one channel. For example phone, email, in-store or website.

CLOSED QUESTIONS Questions that elicit a yes/no response.

CO-DESIGN
Process in which the design team directly engages end users to assist in the design to access knowledge that is crucial to develop successful design solutions.

The designers should provide ways for people to engage with each other as well as instruments to communicate, be creative, share insights and envision their own ideas. The co-design activities can support different levels of participation, from situation in which the external figures are involved just in specific moments to situations in which they take part to the entire process, building up the service together with the designers.

COGNITIVE DISSONANCE A PET technique in changing impression. Cognitive dissonance refers to the discomfort caused by holding two or more conflicting (dissonant) beliefs at the same time. People seek to reduce the discomfort by changing one of the beliefs, thus returning to a state of 'consonance'. So, for example, someone holding the belief that "I am a smart consumer," may be faced with the dawning realization that "I paid too much for that car." The two beliefs are in conflict (dissonant) and therefore uncomfortable, so one of the beliefs must change. To avoid undermining positive self-belief, and because it is difficult to get a different car, the user's attitude about the car will change, so that it is seen as more valuable, and therefore worth the price paid.
Source: Human Factors International

COMPARISON TESTS Usability test that compares two or more designs. Examples might be comparing alternative wireframes, comparing before and after designs, or a comparing a design against competitor designs.
Source: Human Factors International

CONCEPTUAL MODEL
A model constructed by the users in their mind to understand the working or the structure of objects, based on their mental model and previous experience, to speed up their understanding. Also called mental model.
Source: Human Factors International

CONFIRMATION BIAS
The tendency to search for, notice, and interpret information in a way that confirms one's beliefs or opinions.
Source: Human Factors International

CONTEXTUAL INQUIRY
A semi-structured field interviewing method based on a set of principles that allow it to be molded to different situations. This technique is generally used at the beginning of the design process and is good for getting rich information, but can be complex and time-consuming.

CODE
a word chosen to represent an idea, topic, or event that is an important theme of the interviews. After these words are decided on, they are connected to colors or symbols used to mark passages of the transcripts.

CODING
The process of marking passages of the interview's transcript that are about the same thing. By same thing we mean-the passages have the same phrases repeated in them or they talk about the topic in the same way. These passages are marked with a name,the code, which is usually connected to a longer explanation of what the

passages have in common. Codes stress what themes run through the interview or the collection of interviews.

COLLABORATIVE DESIGN
Inviting input from users, stakeholders and other project members.

COLLECTIVE INTELLIGENCE
Collective intelligence is shared knowledge that comes from the collaboration of a group of people and is expressed in consensus decisio-making. Collective intelligence requires openness, sharing ideas, experiences and perspectives.

CONTEXT
Context
The world the service belongs to. The context is the specific frame in which the service takes place. Exploring and defining the context means setting the project boundaries in terms of limits but also opportunities. Context is external elements that surround and influence design. These items can be physical and non-physical and cultural. The environmental context relates to the time, the day, the location, the type of place and any other physical aspect that could influence your design. The surrounding context influences the success of design.

CONTEXTUAL INQUIRY
Interviewing users in the location that they use the product or service, to understand their tasks and challenges.

CONVERGENT
Process of Narrowing down ideas through synthesis.

CROSS-DISCIPLINARY COLLABORATION
Combines the wisdom and skills of different professional disciplines working in close and flexible collaboration. Each team member requires disciplinary empathy allowing them to work collaboratively with other discipline members. Design teams can include anthropologists, engineers, educators, doctors, lawyers, scientists, etc. in the innovative problem-solving process.

CULTURAL PROBE
Cultural probes are sets of simple artifacts (such as maps, postcards, cameras, or diaries) that are given to users for them to record specific events, feelings or interactions in their usual environment, in order to get to know them and their culture better. Cultural probes are used to uncover aspects of culture and human interaction like emotions, values, connections, and trust.

CUSTOMER JOURNEY
The customer journey is a graphical representation of how the customer perceives and experiences the service interface over time It often also shows the phases before and after the interaction with the service. A customer journey map is a tool to explore, visualize, understand and refine an end user experience.

DECOY STRATEGY
A PET technique in changing impression linked to the Contrast Principle. People want to compare things before making decisions and like to make easy comparisons. So you can persuade them to select one of a small number of easily compared choices by introducing another choice that can't easily be compared. For example,

you are more likely to get people to purchase a front loader washing machine, if you give them two front loader choices (easily compared) by contrast to a third choice of a top-loader (less easy to compare). In another example, you can increase sales of an item, by offering a similar, but inferior item at about the same price. It's easy to compare them, recognize the contrast in quality, and conclude that the better quality item represents
exceptional value.
Source: Human Factors International

DEDUCTIVE ANALYSIS
A type of analysis that begins with theoretically derived hypotheses then tests them with data that were collected in accordance with the theoretical context.

DIARY STUDY
Asking users to record their experiences and thoughts about a product or task in a journal over a set period of time.

DIVERGENT
Expansive idea generation and exploration of ideas.

EMPATHIZE
This term is sometimes used to encompass the Understand and Observe steps or as a replacement for them. The use of this emotional term helps remind designers that they must always consider the human experience of real people. It's more than just seeing it from their perspectives, it's about understanding how they feel about it all and what it means to them.
Source: dSchool Stanford

EMPATHY
Principle in the Design Thinking process and human- centered design, in which the user's perspective is always represented.
Source: Libraries Toolkit

ENTRY POINTS
Position of access to a service, where people are able to engage the service as customers, providers, or stakeholders.

ETHNOGRAPHY
The process of gathering information about users and tasks directly from users in their normal work, home or leisure environment.

EVIDENCE
Service evidences are touch-points that represent parts of a service experience.

EVIDENCE-BASED DESIGN
Evidence-based design is the approach of basing design decisions on credible research to achieve the best possible outcomes. Evidence-based design emphasizes the importance of basing decisions on the best possible data for the best possible outcomes. The design is not based just on the designer's opinion.

EXPERIENCE DESIGN
The application of design processes with the goal of creating an appropriate experience for the person interacting with the
product. This process begins with understanding the needs and wants of the user. Analysis focuses on cognitive, emotional and motor aspects of the interaction and is
completed when the quality of the experience is measured with the developed product.

Source: Human Factors International

EXPERIENCE PROTOTYPING
Service experiences have components that are intangible, and change over time and have multiple touch-points. Services are prototyped different ways then physical products.
Experience Prototype is a representation, that
is designed to help us understand, explore or communicate what it feels like to engage with a product, space service or system.

EXIT POINTS
Point of disengagement of a service, by stakeholders.

EXTREME USER
A person who lies at the periphery of a group of users. Extremes can can include age, ability, occupation, experience, etc. Rather than designing for a composite or "average" user, a design team will oftentimes look to extreme users for surprising and actionable insights. Focusing on extreme users can lead to more innovative solutions, more profound insights about a group of users, and new, untapped markets for a product or service.
Source: dSchool Stanford

FIELD STUDY
A field study is a general method for collecting data about users, user needs, and product requirements that involves observation and interviewing. Data are collected about task flows, inefficiencies, and the organizational and physical environments of users.

FIVE WHYS
An analysis method used to uncover the root cause of a problem.

Example of the method:
A patient had the wrong leg amputated
1. Why: Patient gave consent for amputation the night before the proposed surgery to Registrar (who was not going to undertake procedure).
2. Why: Amputation site marked with a biro (wrong leg).
3. Why: Registrar unaware of hospital policy on amputation sites being marked with a skin pencil and with bodily part being fully visible to Doctor.
4. Why: The department had no induction procedures for new medical staff working in the department.
5. Why: Because "we've never been asked to".

Root Cause Analysis Tool Kit. NHS

FOCUS GROUPS
A direct data gathering method in which a small group (8–10) of participants are led in a semi-structured, brainstorming session to elicit rapid feedback

FORMATIVE EVALUATION
Formative evaluation is a type of usability evaluation that helps to 'form' the design for a product or service. Formative evaluations involve evaluating a product or service during development, often iteratively, with the goal of detecting and eliminating usability problems.

FREE LISTING
Free listing is a technique for gathering data about a specific domain or topic by asking people to list all the items they can think of that relate to the topic. It can be used to gather data in large group settings or in one-on-one interviews.

FRONTSTAGE/FRONTOFFICE
These are face-to-face between customers and employees. These are separated from the customer by the line of interaction.

GAMBLER'S FALLACY
The mistaken belief that if an event has occurred more frequently than normal, it will happen less frequently in the future, and vice-versa.
Source: Human Factors International

GAP ANALYSIS
A technique used to determine the difference between a desired state and an actual state, often used in branding and marketing. Gap analysis may address performance issues or perception issues.
Source: Human Factors International

GESTALT PRINCIPLES
Set of principles developed by the Gestalt Psychology Movement that established rules governing how humans perceive order in a complex field of objects. Gestalt principles of visual organization state that objects near each other, with same background, connected to each other, or having similar appearance are perceived as belonging to a group.
Source: Human Factors International

GROUNDED THEORY
A qualitative research method in which theory is developed after data has been gathered and analyzed.

GROUPTHINK
Groupthink is consensus of opinion without critical reasoning or evaluation of consequences or alternatives. Employees may self-censor themselves for fear of upsetting the status quo.

HCI
Human Computer Interaction involves the study, planning, and design of the interaction between people (users) and computers.

HEURISTICS
Best practices, principles, or rules of thumb. Established principles of design and best practices in interface design, used as a method of solving usability problems by using rules of thumb acquired from human factors experience.
Source: Human Factors International

HEURISTIC EVALUATION A usability evaluation method in which one or more reviewers, preferably experts, compare a software, documentation, or hardware product to a list of design principles, referred to as heuristics and identify where the product does not follow those principles. Evaluating a website or product and documenting usability flaws and other areas for improvement.

HICK-HYMAN LAW Demonstrates the relationship between the time it takes someone to make a decision and the number of possible choices he or she has. More choices will increase decision time.
Source: Human Factors International

HIGH-FIDELITY PROTOTYPE
A prototype which is quite close to the final product, with lots of detail and a good indication of the final proposed aesthetics and functionality.

HORIZONTAL PROTOTYPE
Prototypes that display a wide range of features without fully implementing all of them. Horizontal prototypes provide insights into users' understanding of relationships across a range of features.
Source: Human Factors International

HOW MIGHT WE?
A positive, actionable question that frames the challenge but does not point to any one solution.
Source: Libraries Toolkit

HUMAN-CENTERED
An approach to design that adapts the solution to the end user through understanding the end user. The understanding is developed through engaging the end user and testing a variety of possible solutions through an iterative design process.

INDUCTIVE ANALYSIS
A type of analysis that begins with collecting and analyzing data, after which hypotheses are made.

Putting the user and user's perspective at the center of a solution. Human-centered or people-centric design requires having empathy with the user to solve for their specific needs. This philosophy involves starting with people and desirability first, before moving on to feasibility and viability.
Source: Libraries Toolkit

INTERACTION DESIGN (IXD)
Sometimes referred to as IxD, interaction design strives to create meaningful relationships between people and the products and services that they use.

INSIGHTS
Ideas or notions expressed as succinct statements that interpret patterns in your research and can provide new understanding or perspective on the issue.
Source: Libraries Toolkit

INTERCEPT
Spontaneous, casual and brief conversations with users in a natural context. Unplanned interviews that garner live feedback for your mini-pilot.
Source: Libraries toolkit

INTERVIEW GUIDE
A list of questions to direct conversation and make sure key issues get discussed. The guide should be flexible to move with conversation but at the same time its main purpose is to keep the interview on topic.

INTERVIEWER BIAS
the influence of the interviewer on the interviewee, which affects responses

I-SHAPED PERSON
Someone who has deep skills and knowledge in one area but not a broad competency across other areas.

ITERATIVE CONSULTATIVE PROCESS
An iterative consultative process is a design process of inviting diverse stakeholders to review a design and give feedback in order to improve the design from their point of view.

ITERATE
The act of repeating a process with the aim of approaching a desired goal, target or result. Each repetition of the process is also called an iteration. In Design Thinking it refers to the cycles of prototyping, testing and revision.

ITERATIVE DESIGN PROCESS
Iterative design is the process of prototyping testing and refining a design in a series of repeated steps.

JOURNEY MAP
A visual representation of a particular person or persona's experience with a service. The experience is documented over time and often shows multiple channels.

LEADING QUESTION
a question that is phrased in a way that suggests to the interviewee an answer that the researcher prefers.

LEARNINGS
The most basic level of information you record from your research, including direct quotes, anecdotes, first impressions, notes on the environment, notes on what was most memorable or surprising, and more.
Source: Libraries Toolkit

LIKERT SCALE
A type of survey question where respondents are asked to rate the level on which they agree or disagree with a given statement on a numeric scale, e.g., 1-7, where 1 = strongly agree and 7 = strongly disagree. (Also see Rating Scale.)
Source: Human Factors International

LINE OF VISIBILITY
In a service blueprint this is a line that separates face to face customer employee interactions from customer employee interactions that are remote or not face to face.

LOADED WORD
a word that has positive or negative connotations and can influence the interviewee's response to a question.

LOW-FIDELITY PROTOTYPE
A quick and easy translation of high-level design concepts into tangible and testable artifacts, giving an indication of the direction that the product is heading. Prototypes that are simple, focused on one or two features. Low resolution prototyping allows a team to make their ideas tangible and gather feedback.

MASLOW'S HIERARCHY OF NEEDS
A theory of motivation, in which individuals' needs are described as a hierarchy, often illustrated as layers in a pyramid. Needs at each level must be met prior to an individual aspiring to the next level. Maslow's theory describes five levels: Physiological, Safety, Social, Esteem and Self-actualization. In PET we can design to meet needs at one or more of these levels. For example, a mobile phone may meet people's safety ('I need to contact you in an emergency'), social ('I like to keep in touch wherever I am') and self-esteem needs ('Look at my cool phone'), with somewhat different design considerations applying to each of these levels.
Source: Human Factors International

MINIMUM VIABLE PRODUCT

A minimum viable product is a simple version of a new product which allows a team to learn the maximum amount about customers with the least effort.
The goal of an MVP is to test fundamental business hypotheses as efficiently in the real-world as possible.

MODERATOR

A person that works with a group to regulate, but not lead, a discussion. Whereas a facilitator might take charge of a discussion to shepherd it in a specific direction, a moderator remains passive, without explicitly leading the process or driving a desired outcome. A moderator takes the lead from the participants, listening and intervening only when necessary to encourage further discussion or ask for clarity for other participants or audiences.

NEEDS

A necessary function or condition. There are a wide variety of human needs such as food, shelter, security, affection and self fulfillment.

OUTSIDE-IN PERSPECTIVE

This is the perception that people outside of an organization have of the organization and it's products and services such as customers and other stakeholders.

PAPER PROTOTYPE

Paper prototyping is the process of creating rough, often hand-sketched, drawings of a user interface, and using them in a usability test to gather feedback. A rough, often hand-sketched, drawing of a user interface, used in a usability test to gather feedback. Participants point to locations on the page that they would click, and screens are manually presented to the user based on the interactions they indicate.

PARADOX OF CHOICE

Limiting choice is a PET technique in changing impression. Paradoxically, people think they want many choices, but can, in fact, be overwhelmed by the complexities too many choices introduce to decision-making. So, people are more likely to be persuaded to make a purchase (or other decision) if you limit their choice to a small number, often no more than three or four.
Source: Human Factors International

PARTICIPATORY DESIGN

An approach that involves stakeholders such as clients, end users, community members in the design process to ensure that the design meets the needs of those it is serving as well as generating buy-in. A type of social research in which the people being studied have significant control over and participation in the research.

PERSONA

A persona is a fictitious identity that reflects one of the user groups for who you are designing. A representation of a user segment with shared needs and characteristics. In user-centered design and marketing, personas are archetypal characters that represent different user segments that might use a product or service in a similar way.

PLACEBO EFFECT

A PET technique in changing impression. In medicine, for example, you can achieve health improvements just by giving the impression you are treating

patients with a drug, even if you are giving them a 'placebo', a neutral substance with no known medical properties. There is evidence that the more expensive patients think the drug to be, the greater the placebo effect.
Source: Human Factors International

POINT OF VIEW OR POV
In Design Thinking, a POV means the point of view of a very particular person. Creating a point of view involves synthesizing the data gained in the Understand and Observe phases in order to create a common reference/inspiration for later ideation and prototyping. The idea is to focus on a real person, with many of the concrete details found during the Understand/Observe phases. One approach is to develop one or two concise sentences that express User+Need+Insight.
Good: "Mark is a shy, recent college graduate who needs a way to stay connected with the college community because he feels that his life could be more exciting. Alumni newsletters and college reunions need not apply."
Bad:"Mark needs a website to share pictures and news with the people he met in college because he feels lonely."
Source: dSchool Stanford

POWER OF EXPECTATION
A PET technique in changing impression. Presenting goods or services in a way that raises the expectation that they will be good, results in users perceiving them as better. A wellformatted report, for example will be seen as better written than a scruffy one, even if the text is exactly the same. Similarly, a well presented meal will not only be more tempting than the same food just thrown on the plate, but will also taste better (as every good chef knows!). So, in PET, if we design to give the expectation that goods and services will be good, they are more likely to be experienced as good.
Source: Human Factors International

PROBES
Areas you want to go more in-depth in an interview.

A technique used during in-depth interviews to explore the interviewee's emotions about the topic we're researching. The 'probing' questions asked gently nudge the interviewees to disclose their feelings and beliefs. For example: "How do you feel about shopping online?"
Source: Human Factors International

PROTOTYPE
A prototype is a model built to test a concept with end users in order to learn from. Prototyping helps understand real, working conditions rather than a theoretical conditions.

QUESTIONNAIRES
A research instrument consisting of a series of questions and other prompts for the purpose of gathering information from respondents.

REFRAMING
Reframe to create different perspectives and new ideas.

How to reframe:
1. Define the problem that you would like to address.
2. There is more than one way of looking at a problem. You could

also define this problem in another way as."
3. What if a male or female used it?
4. What if it was used in China or Argentina?
5. "The underlying reason for the problem is."
6. "I think that the best solution is."
7. "You could compare this problem to the problem of."
8. "Another, different way of thinking about it

RETURN ON INVESTMENT (ROI)
A monetary evaluation of benefits relative to the effort or expenditure invested; a measure of how much return, usually measured as profit or cost savings, results from a given use of money. In the context of usability, ROI is the monetary (or other) benefit gained as a result of an investment in good usability design.
Source: Human Factors International

REVERSE CARD SORT
A usability testing technique, opposite to that of a card sort, where participants are given a list of items to see if they can figure out where to find them. Their success validates the self evidence of the navigational structure of a design. Categories have already been made and labeled appropriately
Source: Human Factors International

ROLE-PLAY
Assign roles and act out scenarios with props and end users feedback to refine your design.

SATISFACTION SYSTEM
The satisfaction system is the system of how the products or services satisfy the customer's needs. It includes the product or service and its related products or service. It involves understanding how related products add value to the main product. Customers are interested in the entire system beyond the individual product.

RULE OF RECIPROCATION
The technique is built on a social rule where people given a gift feel compelled to give something back. For example: You give your customer a small gift. Later, they're likely to consider signing up for your new service.
Source: Human Factors International

SCALE
Service design considers micro and macro scales ,detailed interactions, and holistic overviews of an experience.

SCENARIOS
A scenario is a hypothetical narrative illustrating an event or series of events. It is a method of imagining a user experience in the real-world.

Use scenarios are a method of prototyping ideas in order to explore and refine them. Scenarios are short stories about people and activities that describe typical usage and focus on goals, actions and objects. Scenarios evoke reflection in design and provide a common reference point. Scenarios help express the requirements of the different stakeholders in a format that can be understood by the other stakeholders. They can be written, illustrated, acted or filmed. Scenario generating aims to predict how people could act in particular situations.

A concrete, often narrative, description of a user performing tasks in a specific context sufficiently detailed that design implications can be inferred.
Source: Human Factors International

SENSORIAL DESIGN
Sensorial Design is a term used to include the presentation of an experience in all senses. For example, Visual Design only covers visual expression and presentation to the visual sense. Audio Design includes the creation of music, sound effects, and vocals to communicate and entertain in the aural sense (hearing). Likewise, all of the other human senses (touch, smell, taste, etc.) are elements of an experience that can be designed.

SERVICE DESIGN
Design for experiences that reach people through many
different touch-points, and that happen over time.
British Standard for Service Design: BS 7000 -3, BS 7000 -10,BS EN ISO 9000

Service designs can be both tangible and intangible. Service design can involve artifacts, communication, context and behaviors. It
should be consistent, easy to use and have the strategic alliance.

Gillian Hollins, Bill Hollins, Total Design: Managing The Design Process in the Service Sector

SERVICE ECOLOGY
A service ecology is a system of people, objects and the relationships between them that form a service.

System in which the service is integrated: i.e. a holistic visualization of the service system. All the factors are gathered, analyzed and visualized: politics, the economy, employees, law, societal trends, and technological development. The service ecology is thereby rendered, along with its attendant agents, processes, and relations. *Mager 2009*

Ultimately, sustainable service ecologies depend on
a balance where the actors involved exchange value
in ways that is mutually beneficial over time.
Live/work 2008

SENSUALIZATION
Sensualization is the approach of considering the experience to be the total of the individual experiences of the five senses.

SERVICE
An exchange of value, involving tangible and intangible elements A system of products spaces human interactions and experiences.

SERVICE MOMENTS
Discrete points of interaction between a user and a service, often mapped out in a user journey. An example of a service moment is a patron placing a hold on a book, which can be done at home via the website, in the library via the website, or at the reference desk.
Source: Libraries Toolkit

SERVICE SYSTEM
The ecology of relationships, interactions, and contexts of a service. channels, resources, and

touchpoints, internal and external, that facilitate the delivering of a service.

STAKEHOLDER
A person, group, or organization directly or indirectly involved or affected by a product, service or experience.

Stakeholders include any individuals who are influence by the design. Specifically, the project team, end users, strategic partners, customers, alliances, vendors and senior management are project stakeholders

Possible stakeholders
1. Employees
2. Shareholders
3. Government
4. Customers
5. Suppliers
6. Prospective employees
7. Local communities
8. Global Community
9. Schools
10. Future generations
11. Ex-employees
12. Creditors
13. Professional associations
14. Competitors
15. Investors
16. Prospective customers
17. Communities

Why involve stakeholders?
1. Stakeholder analysis helps to identify:
2. Stakeholder interests
3. Ways to influence other stakeholders
4. Risks
5. Key people to be informed during the project
6. Negative stakeholders as well as their adverse effects on the project

SWIMLANES
An approach used in service design involving arranging descriptive boxes into rows (the "swim lanes") to provide additional context about how the steps are related. Work flow is represented over time and is usually read from left to right.

SYNTHESIS
The sense-making process in which research is translated and interpreted into insights that prompt design. Useful frameworks for synthesis include journeys, Venn diagrams, two by twos and maps.
Source: Libraries Toolkit

STAKEHOLDER MAP
A visual representation of the stakeholders in a service and the relationships between them.

SERVICE DESIGN
Service design is a form of conceptual design which involves the activity of planning and organizing people, infrastructure, communication and material components of a service in order to improve its quality and the interaction between service provider and customers.
Service design - Wikipedia, the free encyclopedia, https://en.wikipedia.org/wiki/Service_design (accessed March 20, 2016).

SOCIAL DESIGN
Design done for the social good or top positively impact society.

STRATEGIC DESIGN
Design that focuses on big picture systematic problems in order to increase an organization's future innovative and competitive advantage.

STORYBOARD

A storyboard is a graphic sequence of illustrations, words or images for the purpose of communicating a user scenario or experience. Storyboarding, was developed at Walt Disney during the early 1930s. A storyboard is a tool inspired by the film-making industry, where a visual sequence of events is used to capture a user's interactions. Depending on the audience, it may be an extremely rough sketch, purely for crystallizing your own ideas.

SUMMATIVE TESTING
Testing done to measure the success of the design in terms of human performance and preference.
Source: Human Factors International

THINK-ALOUD PROTOCOL

A direct observation method of user testing that involves asking users to think out loud as they are performing a task. Users are asked to say whatever they are looking at, thinking, doing, and feeling at each moment. This method is especially helpful for determining users' expectations and identifying what aspects of a system are confusing.

TOUCHPOINTS

A touchpoint is any point of contact between a customer and the provider of a service, product or experience. A touchpoint is where a potential customer or customer comes in contact with your brand before, during and after a transaction.

Identifying your touchpoints is an important step toward creating a journey map or a service blueprint. Each touchpoint is an opportunity to create a better customer experience. A touchpoint can be a physical, virtual or human point of interaction. Chris Risdon from Adaptive Path defines touchpoints in this way. 'A touchpoint is a point of interaction involving a specific human need in a specific time and place.' Laura Patterson of VisionEdge defines a touchpoint as " any customer interaction or encounter that can influence the customer's perception of your product, service, or brand."

TRANSCRIPTION

The process of turning audio or video recordings into a typed format.

T-SHAPED PERSON

A person who has deep competency in a particular subject area and broad knowledge and skills across a range of disciplines.

TWO BY TWO MATRIX

A type of framework with opposing axes showing a spectrum along a particular dimension on each axis. This framework is used to organized ideas within the four quadrants, or to demonstrate mappings of ideas across several dimensions.
Source Libraries Handbook

UNIQUE SELLING PROPOSITION

An exclusive message that concisely describes a product
against its competition, and which the business or brand can
use consistently in its advertising and promotion to achieve a cutting edge in the market.
Source: Human Factors International

UNMET NEEDS

Six principles that will ensure a design is compatible with user needs:
1. The design is based upon an

explicit understanding of users, tasks and environments.
2. Users are involved throughout design and development.
3. The design is driven and refined by user-centered evaluation.
4. The process is iterative.
5. The design addresses the whole user experience.
6. The design team includes multidisciplinary skills and perspectives.

Some Questions to ask:
1. Who are the users?
2. What are the users' tasks and goals?
3. What are the users' experience levels?
4. What functions do the users need from the design?
5. What information will be needed by end-users?,
6. In what form do they need it?
7. How do users think the design should work?

USABILITY
Is the ease of use and learning of an object, such as a book, software application, website, machine, tool or any object that a human interacts with.

USABILITY ROUND-TABLE
A meeting in which a group of end users is invited to bring
specific work samples and discuss the validity of an early
prototype.
Source: Human Factors International

USE CASES
A use case is a list of steps that define the interactions between a user and a system. Use cases, especially when used as requirements for software development, are often constructed in UML, with defined actors and roles.

USER-CENTERED DESIGN
A design process during which the needs of the user is considered at all times. Designers consider how a user is likely to use the product, and they then test the validity of their assumptions in real-world tests with actual users. Design that responds to user needs that is developed through engaging and understanding the point of view of users.

USER JOURNEY
The step by step journey that a user takes to reach their goal.

USER PROFILING
Based on research of user groups develop different character profiles to represent your users. These are also called personas.

USER VALIDATION
Process of testing to determine if the user's needs or requirements have been met

VALUE EXCHANGE
A service provider makes a promise to the service
recipient in exchange for some form of value. The movement of value from the service provider to the recipient is the value exchange.

VANITY METRICS
Data that make you feel good, but is not very useful or actionable such as new users gained per day or number of downloads. Vanity metrics do not reflect the key drivers of a business.

VERTICAL PROTOTYPE
Prototypes that display just a few complex features of a product and almost completely implement only these features. Vertical prototype tests provide insights into users' understanding of the complexity, issues, and problems of a specific feature.
Source: Human Factors International

VISUAL HIERARCHY
Refers to the overall page layout and its ability to lead the users' attention through the page elements. Effective visual hierarchies create an appropriate balance in composition that draws users to top levels of the hierarchy while optimizing visual access to important page level elements
Source: Human Factors International

WICKED PROBLEM
A wicked problem is a problem with contradictory, and changing requirements. The term 'wicked' is used, not in the sense of evil but rather its resistance to resolution.

Wicked problems are characterized by:
1. The solution depends on how the problem is framed.
2. Stakeholders have different world views and frames for understanding the problem.
3. The constraints of the problem and the resources needed to solve it change over time.
4. The problem is never solved definitively.

Source: Wicked problem:definition of wicked problem and synonyms http://brevard.ifas.ufl.edu/communities/pdf/SF_Wicked_Issues_Background_Defined_ (accessed March 20, 2016)

WIREFRAME
A rough guide for the layout of a website or app, either done with pen and paper or with wireframing software. The wireframe depicts the page layout and shows how the elements work functionally. It focuses on what a web interface does, not what it looks like. Wireframes can be sketches or computer images.

WIZARD OF OZ
A user-based evaluation of unimplemented technology where, generally unknown to the user, a human or team is simulating some or all the responses of the system.

WORKAROUND
A user's personal solution to a problem with a service or product, that circumvents the standard procedure. It is often temporary or makeshift. Observing these behaviors often leads to fruitful advances in insights and inspiration.
Source: Libraries Toolkit

07
INDEX

INDEX

Symbols

5 Whys 98
10x10 99
101 brainstorming 99
635 Method 99
.x 82, 109, 142, 154, 155, 156, 157, 158

A

Abductive logic: 40
Abductive thinking 40
abilities 108
Abilities 32
A-B test 193
action bias 121
activities 20, 114, 119, 136, 138, 159, 165, 179, 180, 184, 194
activity 114, 118, 129, 138, 139, 153, 156, 164, 179, 180, 189
Activity Map 128
actor 170, 193
acts 72
adaptability 32
adhesive notes 178
Adobe 183
affinity 118
affinity diagram 98, 106, 118, 193
affordance 193
age 55, 65, 67, 77, 108, 124
Age 55, 65, 67
agreement 172
Alam, I. 236
Allanwood, Gavin 236
Allport, Gordon 120
ambiguity bias 121
analgous situations 193
analysis 130
analytic induction 193
analytics 193

analyze 38, 53, 64, 114, 119, 133, 138, 145, 159, 189
anchoring bias 121
Angelis. J. 247
anthropopump 109
anthropump 5, 112
Antonelli, Paola 236
Anu, Valtonen 236
Apple 12, 109, 251
artifact 122
artifacts 193
Artifacts 193
Ash Maurya 134, 135, 160
attitudes 56, 68
audio 135
Australia 251
Autodesk 227

B

backoffice 193
backstage 193
backstory 31
Baines, T. 236
Balcioglu, Tevfik 236
Banerjee, Maithili 236
barriers 183
Bate, Paul 236
Bateson, Gregory 38
Battarbee, K. 236, 241
Bavelas, Alex 119, 129, 161
Becker, Ernest 112
behave 38, 49
behavior 38, 43, 49, 51, 60, 72, 74, 112, 120, 121, 138, 144, 153, 154, 155, 156, 157, 158, 159, 164
behavioral map 5, 112, 113
behavior segmentation 108
benchmarking 5, 47, 97, 98, 104, 107, 113, 131

Benedettini, O. 236
benefits 113
Benefit segmentation 108
benefits map 5, 113, 132
Benefits map 5, 113, 132
Bennet 136, 139
Berger, Warren 236
beta launch 194
Bettencourt, Lance 236
Beyer, Hugh 237
bias 5, 35, 45, 49, 73, 74, 107, 121, 122, 133, 134, 135, 136, 138, 139, 142, 143, 144, 145, 151, 153, 154, 155, 156, 157, 158, 159, 194, 195, 200
Biemans, W. G 237
Bitner, M. J. 237
blank 120
Bleuel, William H. 237
Blomkvist, J. 237
Blue Ocean 98
blueprint 163–251, 183–251, 207–251
Boas, Franz 38
body language 37, 58, 72, 138, 145
body storming 99, 185
bodystorming 194
Boucher, A. 239
boundary 114
boundary shifting 5, 114
Bowers, Micah 30
brainstorming 53, 64, 97, 99, 104, 109, 119, 170, 183, 194, 198, 234
brand 39, 59, 168, 172, 189, 207
Brax, S. 237
breaking down silos 80
British Design Council 100
Bruere, Robert W. 44, 45
Buchenau, M. 237
Bustinza, O 248
butcher paper 178
Buur, J. 248
Buxton, William (Bill) 237

C

camera 49, 114, 115, 120, 148, 178
camera journal 5, 98, 114
cameraman 142
Camp, Robert 113
Caracelli 146
cards 115, 116, 117, 124, 125
card sorting 99, 115, 194
car park 181
Carroll, J. M. 237
cash flow 23
causation 194
challenge 38, 44, 45, 49, 58, 59, 119, 135
channels 47, 52, 162, 168, 170, 172, 173, 179, 187, 189, 194, 201, 206
Charter, Martin 237
China 21, 25, 204, 251
Cipolla, Carla 237, 245
Cisco 227
citizenship status 108
Clatworthy, S. 237
closed card sort 5, 115
closed card sorting 115, 116
closed questions 194
clustering insights 97
Coate, Roger A. 60
Coates, Joseph F. 237
co-creation 51, 78, 79
code 195
co-design 99, 194
coding 144, 195
coffee 174, 175, 177, 179, 180
cognitive dissonance 121, 195
collaboration 37, 74, 78, 172
collaborative 194
collaborative design 196
collaborative spaces 37
collective intelligence 196
combine 143
common ground 98
communities 33, 51, 206, 209
comparison tests 195

competitive advantage 61, 82, 113, 207
competitive positioning 47, 168
competitive products 97
competitive strategy 113
competitors 206
complex 30, 47, 125, 146, 147, 167, 189, 191, 195, 199, 209
complexity 46, 109, 167, 168, 209
concept 114, 116, 119, 133
conceptual model 195
Condon, Patrick M. 238
confirmation bias 195
conflict 31
conflicting needs 47
conflicts of interest 122
connections 37
consensus matrix 6
consistency 61
constraints 97, 109
consumption 24
context 31, 38, 45, 49, 58, 97, 106, 108, 117, 119, 129, 130, 133, 135, 136, 137, 138, 139, 142, 143, 144, 145, 147, 148, 153, 154, 155, 156, 157, 158, 159, 160, 161, 162, 178, 185, 196, 197, 200, 204, 205, 206
contextual 135, 136, 137, 139, 142
contextual inquiry 6, 123, 135, 136, 137, 139, 195, 196
contextual interviews 135, 137, 142
contextual laddering 137
convergent 98, 196
convergent thinking 42
conversation 135, 136, 143, 144
conversation cards 116
Cooper, Alan 53, 54, 64, 238
Cornell University 149
Corsten, Hans, 238
Cottam, H. 238
covert 154
covert observation 6, 154
critical thinking 41

cross-disciplinary collaboration 196
cross-disciplinary teams 77
cultural 117, 124
cultural inventory 117
cultural probe 117, 196
cultural probes 117, 196
culture 82, 97
Curedale, Rob 228, 233
curiosity 32
curious 107
curiousity 35
current state maps 162
customer 10, 39, 47, 48, 52, 54, 64, 129, 137, 163, 167, 168, 171, 172, 173, 178, 179, 180, 181, 182, 183, 184, 185, 186, 188, 189, 207
customer experience 46, 47, 48, 51, 71, 162, 163, 167, 168, 172, 173, 179, 181, 183, 189, 207
customer journey 196
customers 39, 47, 52, 53, 54, 64, 66
customer segments 107, 168, 172, 173, 178
customer's perspective 168, 173
customization 24

D

Dam, Rikke 164
Danish Design Center 12, 28
Darden School of the University of Virginia 61
data 38, 44, 45, 53, 54, 64, 114, 119, 120, 129, 133, 137, 138, 142, 145, 148, 159, 171, 173
data analysis 72, 86
day experience method 118
day in the life 5, 98, 119, 140
day in the life study 5, 119, 140
DCC 226, 227
de Bono, E. 238

De Brentani, U. 238
debriefing 124
deck of cards 115, 116
decoy strategy 196
deductive analysis 197
deductive logic 40
DeFillippi, R. 241
De Jong, J. P. 238
deliverables 97
Dell 251
demographic segmentation 52, 108
Denmark 29
Descriptive question matrix 126, 127
desert island 98
Design Community College 2, 3, 228, 229, 230, 231, 232, 233, 234
design problem 109
design process 42, 119
design teams 251
design thinking 97
design thinking process 77, 79, 86, 97, 98, 104, 197
desktop walkthroughs 185
Despain, Wendy 238
development process 28, 29, 82, 85
diaries 44
diary methods 59, 120
diary study 120, 197
Díaz-Kommonen, L 238
differentiation 23, 32, 97
digital camera 120, 178
Dimitriadis, S. 247
direct observation 6, 154
disabilities 108
discovery 5, 104, 106, 107
Discovery Phase 61, 106
Discovery Process 107
Disney method 99
distribution segmentation 52
divergent 42, 197
divergent thinking 42

document 97, 135
Donald Norman 59
Doorley, Scott 238
dot voting 6, 99, 119, 141
double diamond design process model 100
draft 178, 179
dry erase markers 178
Duarte, Nancy 238

E

Easingwood, C. 245
Edison, Thomas 76, 78
education 18, 50, 56, 65, 68, 77, 108
Edvardsson, B. 238
Eisenhower, Dwight D. 82
E-mail 138
E-mail interview 138
emotional 124, 125, 189
emotional journey map 189
emotion cards 6, 120, 124, 125
emotions 33, 38, 53, 64, 71, 108, 124, 126, 164, 167, 187, 191, 196, 203
empathize 168
empathy 49, 53, 58, 63, 64, 86, 98, 108, 114, 185, 197
employees 10–251, 55, 66
employee training 99
empowered teams 77, 80
end user 60, 107, 133, 182, 196, 200
engineering 173
entrepreneurship 50
entry points 197
entry Points 197
environments 170
ethnicity 56, 68
ethnographic frameworks 109
ethnographic methods 48, 49, 112
ethnography 49, 54, 64, 197
Europe 52, 251

evaluation matrix 99
Evenson, S. 238, 240
evidence 170, 197
evidence-based design 197
exit points 198
expectations 23, 46, 47, 48, 74, 108, 182, 207
experience 30, 37, 39, 47, 59, 97, 108, 129, 163, 167, 168, 170, 171, 172, 173, 178, 179, 180, 185, 189, 207, 251
experience design 71, 197
experience maps 98, 108, 167, 168, 191
experience problems 46, 173
experience prototyping 185, 198
experiences 38, 48, 59, 65, 119, 138, 144, 145, 167, 168, 172, 173, 189
extreme user 138, 198
extreme user interview 138

F

facilitating 72, 77, 86
failure 47, 48, 60, 81, 86, 106, 168, 183
false causality 121
family size 56, 67
Fazlagic, Amir Jan 238
feedback 104, 148, 179, 185
feeling 188
feelings 170
Festinger, Leon 121
field study 198
findings 45, 178
Fisher, A.G.B. 18
Fitzsimmons, James A. 238
Fitzsimmons, Mona J. 238
five whys 6, 125, 198
flexibility 82
fly-on-the-wall 6, 129
focus 10, 55, 56, 59, 66, 68, 119, 120, 129, 136, 144, 189
Focus 233, 234

focus groups 6, 98, 106, 123, 129, 130, 182, 198, 233, 234
follow-up sessions 112
Følstad 167
Ford 12, 17, 227
formative evaluation 198
Foster 167
frame 135
framework 19, 144, 167, 207
framing bias 121
free association 98
free listing 198
Frei, Frances 238
frontstage 199
frustrations 54, 66
Fulton Suri, J. 239
funding bias 122
future 41, 48, 162, 165, 168, 172, 179, 187

G

gain 53, 64, 142
gambler's fallacy 199
gap analysis 199
Garcia, Fausto 239
Garrett, Jesse James. 239
Gaver, Bill 117, 239
Gebauer, H., Krempl, R. 239
Gemmel, Paul 239
gender 56, 65, 67, 77, 97, 108
generalizability 147
generating ideas 194
geographic segmentation 52, 108
Germany 42
Gestalt principles 199
glossary 193
goal 47, 113, 116, 125, 142, 173
Goal grid 98
goals 28, 45, 47, 48, 49, 52, 53, 54, 64, 66, 70, 71, 74, 97, 98, 108, 116, 122, 126, 127, 128, 133, 136, 152, 156, 157, 162, 163, 165, 167, 170, 172, 173, 187, 205, 208

Goals 123, 152
goal statement 173
Goodwin, Kim 239
Google 35, 116
government 107, 152, 168, 206, 227
Graham 146
Gratton, Lynda 239
Gray, Dave 239
Greene 146
Griffin, A. 237
groan zone 102, 103
Grönroos, Christian 239
grounded theory 199
group 37, 39, 52, 53, 54, 55, 64, 66, 67, 97, 119, 139, 142, 143, 172, 251
group interview 6, 138, 139
Group interview 6, 139
groups 49, 52, 54, 56, 66, 68, 129, 138, 139, 142, 172
groupthink 119, 121, 142, 199
Guba 147
guided storytelling 6, 139
Guided storytelling 6, 139
Gutman 137

H

Halvorson, Kristina 239
Hamilton 251
HCI 199
health 20, 51, 61, 108
Heapy 167
Heapy, Joe 239
hear 58
Heath, Chip 239
Hermagoras of Temnos 164
Heskett, James L. 239
heuristic evaluation 199
heuristics 99, 199
Hick-Hyman Law 199
hierarchy 20, 97, 107, 116, 178, 194, 201, 209
high fidelity prototype 200

Hohman, L. 239
holistic thinking 48, 172
Hollins, Bill 239
Hollins, Gillian 239
Holmlid, S. 237, 240
Holtzblatt 136, 139
Holtzblatt, Karen 240
Hong Kong University of Science and Technology 25
horizontal prototype 200
Horovitz, Jacques 240
hospital 55, 66
Hostetter, Chelsea 31
hotel 180, 181
housing 56, 67
how might we? 200
HP 17, 227, 251
human-centered design 200
human factors 86, 199
human needs 30, 60, 129, 202
humor 30, 32

I

IBM 12, 17
idea 40, 97, 104, 119, 120, 143, 165, 185, 189
ideation 6, 47, 57, 104, 130, 168, 203
ideation decision matrix 6, 130
IDEO 51, 61
implementation 99, 104, 152, 162
impromptu interviews 142
improvement 167
income 56, 65, 67, 108
indirect observation 6, 153, 155
inductive analysis 200, 200–251
inductive logic 40
information 37, 41, 44, 55, 67, 120, 135, 136, 137, 138, 142, 143, 165
inhibition 119
innovate 82
innovation 12, 18, 23, 28, 35, 40,

46, 47, 49, 50, 51, 60, 71, 82, 83, 85, 86, 121, 168, 251
Innovation 82, 98, 121
Innovation bias 121
innovation diagnostic 82
insight 114, 116, 120, 133
insights 31, 37, 38, 39, 43, 53, 57, 64, 97, 98, 113, 114, 115, 116, 119, 120, 130, 133, 135, 137, 138, 139, 143, 144, 148, 154, 155, 156, 157, 158, 159, 161, 168, 179, 185, 189, 191, 194, 195, 198, 200, 206, 209
in-store 179
intangible 47, 168, 198, 205
Intel 227
interact 129
interaction design 200
interactions 37, 167, 172, 189
Interactions 189
Interactive Design Foundation 164
intercept 200
Internet device 57, 68
interview consent form 149
interviewer bias 200
interview guide 5, 110, 134, 136, 143, 144, 145, 200
interviewing 6, 75, 97, 98, 99, 106, 116, 117, 118, 120, 133, 134, 135, 136, 137, 138, 139, 142, 143, 144, 145, 147, 148, 160, 173, 182, 196
Interviewing methods 6, 136
interviews 38, 44, 54, 59, 64, 195, 196, 199, 200, 203, 233, 233–251, 233–251, 234, 234–251, 234–251, 234–251
Intille 118
Intuit 12, 71
intuition 32, 40, 49
investment 85
Iqbal, Majid 240
I-shaped person 200
iteration 104, 201
iterative consultative process 201
iterative design 201

J

Japan 21
Jastrow 115, 116
Jegou, François 242
Jehl, Francis 78
Johansson, M 240
Johne, A. 240
Johnson, Steven 240
Jonathan Ive 109
Jossey-Bass 102
journey 10–251, 162, 163, 167, 178, 187, 189, 207
journey map 162, 163, 167, 189, 201, 207
judgment 20, 35, 58, 79, 107, 119, 182

K

Kalbach, Jim 240
Kallenberg, R. 243
Kaner, Sam 102, 103, 240
Kaner,Sam 102, 103
Kankainen 168
Kankainen, A. 240
Kay, J. M. 236
Kelley, Tom 240
key differentiation 97
Kimbell, Lucie 240
King, Stanley 241
Kipling, Rudyard 165
Kolko, Jon 241
Koskinen, I. 236, 241
Krueger, Richard A. 130

L

laddering 59, 137
language 77, 108, 228, 229, 230, 231, 232, 233, 234
launch 104
Leadbeater, C. 238

leading question 201
Lee, Fred 241
Lehrer, M. 241
Liedtka, Jeanne 61, 241
life stage 56, 67
Lightfoot, H. W. 236
Likert scale 201
Lincoln 147
line of visibility 194, 201
listening 35, 49, 58, 70, 74, 107
listening skills 72, 73, 75
Lloyd, Vernon 241
loaded word 201
Lockton, Dan, 241
Lockwood, Thomas 241
lotus blossom method 99
low fidelity prototyping 201
Lucero, A. 241
Luckner and Nadler 102
Lusch Robert F. 238, 241, 248, 249

M

Maffei, S. 241
Mager, Birgit 241
Malinowski, Bonislaw 155, 157
Malinowski, Bronisław 49
Malterud, K. 242
management 172, 173
manager of logistics 72, 86
man in the street interview 142
Manning, Harley 242
manufacturing 104
Manzini, Ezio 242, 245
mapping 112, 113, 114, 119, 128, 162, 163, 167, 168, 172, 178, 179, 180, 183, 187, 189
mapping methods 38, 162, 171, 207, 230, 231
marketing 57, 68, 99, 152, 251
Marquez, Joe 242
Martin, Roger L. 242
masking tape 178
Maslow's hierarchy of needs 201

materials 104
Mathieu, V. 242
Mattelmäki, Tuuli 236, 241, 242, 248
McCarthy, J. 248
McQuilken, Lisa 243
Mead, Margaret 38, 155, 157
meaning 30, 63, 71, 144, 159
media 56, 68
Menor L.J. 243
Meroni, Anna 243
Merton, Robert K 130
methods 119, 228–251
metrics 47, 50, 146, 152, 162, 163, 168, 187, 209
Miettinen, Satu 236, 243
milestones 98
Miller, Luke 243
mind maps 52
mind Maps 98
minimum viable product 202
Miozzo, M. 241
mixed method research 145
mobile 36, 118, 148, 178, 179, 187
mobile diary study 148
mobility 108
moderator 120, 178
modify 113
Moenaert, R. K. 237
Moggridge, Bill 243
Möller, K. 243
moments of truth 168
Monteiro, Robert A 129, 161
Morelli, N. 243
Moritz, Stefan 243
Moser, Christian 243
multi-channel map 189
multidisciplinary 107, 109, 208
mystery shopper 151, 152, 153
Mystery shopper 151, 153

N

narrative 30, 163, 204, 205
nationality 56, 68, 108

naturalistic group interview 142
needs 30, 37, 38, 39, 47, 48, 49, 54, 55, 58, 60, 64, 66, 73, 97, 108, 109, 115, 119, 120, 129, 133, 136, 145, 159, 162, 165, 168, 170, 173, 183, 201, 202, 207
negative stakeholders 206
Nelson, Doreen 159
Nestle 227
New York Times 17, 21
Ngram 116
Nielsen, Jakob 115, 116
Nietzsche, Friedrich 78
Nike 12, 227
non-participant observation 156
non verbal 148
Norman, Donald A. 243
North America 251
notes 119, 135, 179, 180
Nudurupati, S. S. 243

O

objectives 104, 154, 155, 156, 157, 158, 172
observation 6, 38, 44, 54, 64, 98, 106, 108, 118, 119, 129, 153, 154, 155, 156, 157, 158, 159, 161, 233, 234
observation skills 72, 75
observe 35, 49, 58, 97, 98, 109, 119, 129, 135, 137, 139, 143, 154, 155, 156, 158, 162, 197, 203
observer 129, 153, 154, 155, 156, 157, 158, 159
occupation 56, 65, 67, 108
Oliva, R. 243
Olsen 57, 68, 137
Olsson, J. 238
one-on-one interview 135, 136, 137, 142, 143
open card sort 5, 115
opportunities 46, 51, 98, 122, 163, 167, 168, 172, 179, 181, 183, 189, 207
Ordanini, A. 241, 243
O'Regan, N. 248
organization 82, 85
Osterwalder, Alexander 244
outside-in perspective 202
overt observation 157

P

Pacenti, E. 244
packaging 181
pain 174, 176
pain points 162, 163, 171, 181, 182, 183, 184, 185, 186, 188, 190, 191
Pang, S. 244
Panicucci 103
Papastathopoulou, P. 244
paper prototyping 99, 185, 202
paradox of choice 202
Park, Albert 25
Parker, Sophia 244
Park, Robert 38
Parry, G 248
participant observation 157
participants 37, 72, 73, 74, 75, 112, 114, 115, 116, 117, 118, 119, 120, 123, 124, 125, 129, 130, 133, 134, 137, 138, 139, 142, 143, 144, 147, 148, 149, 151, 153, 154, 155, 156, 157, 158, 159, 161, 198, 202, 204, 227
participation 75, 81, 130, 150, 195, 202
participatory design 202
Patel, Raj 244
Patnaik, Dev 244
Patrício, L. 244, 246
Patton 43, 147
Pennington, S. 239
PepsiCo 17
perceptual maps 98
performance 97

permission 156, 157
Perry, C. 236
person 37, 40, 52, 59, 65, 136, 143
persona 31, 53, 54, 55, 57, 64, 65, 66, 67, 68, 98, 102, 167, 171, 179, 187, 189, 190, 202, 208
personal inventory 159
personalization 36
personas 98, 107, 112, 118, 172, 178
perspective 45, 58, 167, 168, 173, 178, 179
phase 42
photo elicitation interview 144
photograph 144, 183
physical evidence 180
PICTIVE 99
Pine, Joseph B. 244
Pinheiro, Tenny 244
Pink, Daniel H. 244
placebo effect 203
planning 6, 104, 133
pleasure 185
point of view 97, 98, 99, 104, 106, 107, 119, 133, 135, 137, 139, 143, 162, 167, 172, 189
point of view (POV) 30, 46, 49, 54, 58, 66, 201, 203, 208
points of failure 183
Polaine, Andrew 245
Polanyi, Michael 37
Pollak, L. 245
positive 171, 179, 185
Post-it-Notes 49–251, 179
POV 98
power of expectation 203
presentation 123, 183
Prestes Joly, M. 245
price 52
Priestner, Andy 245
primary research 44
print 179, 187
probes 203
problem 45, 97, 165, 167
problem definition interview 134, 159
Problem definition interview 134, 160
problems 39, 40, 41, 138, 165, 173
problem-solving 79, 196
problem statement 57, 109, 125
process 12, 28, 39, 40, 41, 42, 77, 82, 85, 107, 114, 119, 120, 139, 144, 153, 163, 178, 194, 196, 205, 208, 228, 229
product 30, 39, 48, 52, 53, 54, 55, 56, 59, 64, 66, 68, 85, 104, 113, 135, 137, 138, 142, 143, 162, 168, 172, 187, 189, 207, 251
product design 251
project goals 98
prototype 31, 37, 40, 51, 194, 198, 200, 201, 202, 203, 208, 209
prototyping 71, 99, 104, 107, 112
Pruitt, John 245
psychographic segmentation 52, 56, 68, 108

Q

qualitative research 82, 97, 147, 193, 199
quality 18, 19, 99
quality assurance 99
quantitative research 82, 97, 146, 147
Quesenbery, Whitney 245
question guides 104
questionnaires 44, 99, 203
questions 45, 58, 120, 136, 138, 139, 142, 143, 144, 145, 165, 173

R

Rada, J. 248
Radcliff-Brown, Alfred 38, 155, 157
Raddats, C. 245
rearrange 120

Reason, Ben 245
Recruitment brief 160
refine 104, 120, 138, 180
reframing 204
reframing matrix 98
Reinartz, W. J. 248
relationships 135
religion 108
report writer 72, 86
reputation 153
research 6, 37, 38, 43, 44, 45, 49, 54, 55, 59, 64, 66, 71, 82, 84, 97, 98, 106, 107, 108, 109, 112, 114, 116, 117, 120, 122, 123, 129, 130, 134, 135, 136, 142, 145, 146, 147, 148, 149, 152, 154, 156, 157, 159, 160, 161, 171, 173, 178, 180, 181, 185, 189, 193, 197, 199, 200, 201, 202, 203, 206, 208, 233, 251
researcher 114, 115, 116, 118, 120, 125, 135, 137, 138, 139, 142, 143, 144, 145, 146, 149, 150, 153, 154, 155, 156, 157, 158, 159, 161
research goals 156, 157
research plan 5, 97, 98, 106, 109, 122, 173
research questions 123
resources 38, 44, 45, 47, 49, 54, 59, 64, 72, 83, 85, 107, 115, 117, 119, 120, 134, 139, 159, 168, 206, 209
return on investment (ROI) 204
revenue 10–251
reverse 204
reverse card sort 204
Reynolds 137
Riddle, Matthew 118
Ries, Eric 245
risks 97, 149, 157, 170, 206
Rizzo, F. 245
roadmap 46
Roam, Dan 245

Robinson, Ken 245
Roger Martin 40
ROI 185
role-play 204
role playing 99, 185, 204
room 175, 180, 181
Rosati, Jerel A. 60
Royal College of Art 117
Royal Statistical Society 38
rule of reciprocation 204

S

Säde, S. 245
safety 61, 201
Sakichi Toyoda 125
Salvador, T. 246
Sampson S.E. 243
Sandén, Bodil. 245
Sanders, E.B.-N. 246
Sangiorgi, D 244
Sangiorgi, D. 246, 249
Sangiorgi, Daniela 243
Sano 115, 116
Sarmento, T. 246
satisfaction 10–251
satisfaction system 204
Sato, S. 246
scale 201, 204
SCAMPER 99
scenarios 97, 99, 122, 139, 148, 179, 183, 204, 205, 207
schedule 74, 97, 227
scheduler 72, 86
schools 206
Schrage, M. 246
Schwarz, Sven 246
scope 97, 179
script 124, 134, 160
script for the Problem Interviews 134, 160
secondary research 44, 45, 97
secondary users 55, 66
Seddon, John 246
Segelström, F. 237, 246

segmentation 47, 52, 54, 64, 107, 108, 168, 172, 173, 178
segments 47, 53, 55, 66, 203
Seland, G. 246, 247
sense of self 63
sensorial design 205
sensualization 205
separate 179, 180
service 71, 83, 85, 98, 104, 106, 107, 108, 113, 128, 129, 138, 149, 151, 152, 161, 162, 163, 167, 168, 172, 173, 179, 180, 181, 182, 185, 191
service blueprint 98, 163, 167
service blueprints 52
service design 26-251, 27-251, 50, 107, 204, 205, 206
service ecology 205
services 2, 7, 17, 18, 19, 20, 21, 22, 23, 24, 25, 28, 29, 30, 31, 37, 39, 46, 47, 48, 50, 51, 52, 53, 55, 56, 59, 64, 66, 68, 180, 193, 194, 196, 197, 198, 200, 201, 202, 203, 204, 205, 206, 207, 208, 209, 232, 233, 234
service safari 161
Service safari 161
service staging 185
service system 206
servitization 22, 23
shadowing 112, 161
shareholders 206
sharpies 178
Shop-alongs 110
shoshin 35
Shostack, L. 247
Siemens 227
six thinking hats 99
sketching 31, 99, 119, 209
Sleeswijk Visser, F. 247
smart goals 98
social 65
social design 206
Some WWWWWH questions 165

space 37
Spies, Marco 247
Srinivasan, R. 247
stage 56, 67, 180, 182, 184, 186, 188
stakeholder 55, 66, 82, 98, 99, 106, 107, 125, 178, 182, 206
stakeholders 46, 53, 55, 64, 66, 70, 79, 82, 86, 97, 99, 104, 106, 107, 108, 109, 117, 122, 123, 164, 170, 172, 173, 178, 179, 183, 185, 196, 197, 198, 201, 202, 205, 206, 209
Stanford University 227
status-quo bias 121
Steelcase 12, 227, 251
STEP 42, 138, 179, 180, 207
Stevens, E. 247
Steward, Julian Haynes 117
Stickdorn, Marc 247
Storey, C. 240
story 6, 30, 31, 135, 136, 160, 163, 164, 183, 189
storyboard 119
storyboarding 207
storyboards 207
storytelling 30, 139
strategic 39, 46, 82, 117, 121, 128, 168
strategic design 207
strategic misrepresentation 121
strategy 51, 75, 82, 97
Strickland, Rachel 159
structure 135, 137, 139, 143
structured interview 6, 143
structured observation 6
Structured observation 6, 158
style guides 99
subject 49, 114, 133, 136, 138, 142, 144, 145, 159
subjects 38, 114, 119, 120, 136, 143, 178
sub-journeys 178
success 54-251, 58-251, 66-251, 172-251

summative testing 207
suppliers 128, 173, 206
survey 99, 117, 118
surveys 43
Svanæs, D. 247
swimlane 167, 179, 182
swimlane, lanes 170, 206
SWOT analysis 107
synthesis 104, 130, 196, 206
systems 46

T

table 119, 175, 179, 180
tablet 57, 68, 179
tacit knowledge 37, 38, 135, 137, 139, 142
Taffe, S. 247
talk 138, 159
target audience 107, 108, 134, 161, 173
tasks 113, 114, 117, 125, 135, 137, 139, 143
Tatikonda, M.J. 243
team 70, 71, 72, 74, 76, 77, 78, 79, 82, 86, 97, 98, 99, 106, 107, 108, 113, 117, 119, 121, 122, 125, 129, 160, 162, 172, 178, 180, 185
teams 22, 28, 29, 36, 53, 54, 58, 66, 76, 77, 79, 83, 107, 109, 194, 196, 198, 201, 202, 206, 208, 209, 251
technique 129, 137, 145
techniques 49, 54, 64, 66
technologies 82
technology 172
telephone 145
Telephone interview 6, 145
Teo Siang 164
Teo Siang, 164
test 42, 193
testing 99, 104, 108, 122, 123, 134, 154, 155, 156, 158, 164, 185

testing plan 99
Tether, B. 247
Thackara, John 247
Thaler, Richard 247
The Design Ladder 27, 28
themes 72, 73, 144, 147, 157, 178, 196
think 37
think aloud protocol 99, 207
thinking 40, 41, 42, 48, 119, 170, 171, 172
Tim Brown 51, 61
time 37, 44, 52, 114, 119, 120, 130, 136, 138, 142, 148, 165, 179, 180, 189, 207, 251
time segmentation 52
Tischner, Ursula 237
Titchener, E.B. 58
Tongur, S. 247
tools 37, 136, 167
touch 120
touchpoints 39, 47, 59, 162, 163, 172, 179, 182, 183, 185, 186, 188, 189, 191, 193, 206, 207
Toyoda, Sakichi 125
Toyota 125
transcription 207
transformation 31
triangulation 43, 146
tripod 178
Trischler 168
trust 30, 50, 58, 78, 151, 180, 196
T-shaped people 200
T-shaped person 76, 77
Tufte, Edward Rolf 248
TV 57, 68, 179
two-by-two matrix 207
types of personas 55, 66

U

Ulaga, W. 248
underlying needs 106, 107
understanding 49, 52, 53, 58, 59, 119, 145, 159, 165, 167, 171,

172, 173, 185, 189
understand people 38
unique selling proposition 207
unmet needs 7, 31, 60, 83, 86, 98, 106, 107, 173, 208
unstructured interviews 6, 145
unstructured observation 158
usability 131, 195, 208
usability study 123
use cases 208
user 39, 53, 54, 55, 59, 64, 66, 67
user-centered design 193, 202, 208
user experience 108
user interviews 99
user journey 208
user profiling 208
users 37, 39, 53, 54, 55, 64, 66, 115, 133, 135, 136, 137, 138, 139, 142, 143, 159, 167, 178, 185
user stories 6, 163
user validation 208

V

Vaajakallio, K. 240, 248
value exchange 208
values 23, 30, 32, 52, 71, 106, 121, 133, 137, 159, 165, 196
Vandermerwe, S. 248
vanity metrics 208, 209
Vargo, S. L. 241, 248, 249
Vecchierini 236
Vendrell-Herrero, F. 248
Verganti, Roberto 248
Vermeulen, P. A. 238
Vernile, Lucy 129, 161
vertical prototype 209
video 135, 137, 142, 143
video prototyping 185
Viladàs, Xènia 248
vision 30, 46, 97, 104, 251
Visser, Froukje Sleeswijk 248
visual hierarchy 209

Voss 167
voting 119, 120, 141
VW 251

W

Walker, B. 239
wall 119, 129, 178, 179, 180
Walmart 17
want 39, 65, 136, 165, 167, 181
warming up exercise 98
Watanabe, Ken 248
Watkinson, Matt 248
web 45, 56, 57, 68, 179, 181
Wessels, G. 241
Westerlund, B. 248
Wetter-Edman, K. 248
What-How-Why 164
Whirlpool 12
white board 49
Whiteside, Bennet 136, 139
Whittle 167
wicked problems 209
Williams, Anne 136
Wilmark 151
wireframing 99, 185, 195, 209
withhold judgment 35, 58, 107
Wizard of Oz 99, 185, 209
workarounds 109, 209
wrap-up 6, 135, 160
Wright, P. 248
WWWWWH 98, 164, 165
WWWWWH questions 165

X

Xerox 113

Y

Ylirisku, S. 248
Young, Indi. 249
Young, Laurie 249
Yu, E. 249

Z

Zehrer 168
Zeithaml, Valarie A., 249
Zombie cats 98
Zomerdijk 167

COURSES & OTHER TITLES

DCC ONLINE COURSES
MORE INFORMATION HTTPS://DCC-EDU.ORG

OUR MISSION

Through our online programs, workshops and publications we provide skills to fulfill evolving work roles and to to create better solutions in a new economy. We provide quality education which is better value, more accessible, more flexible and more relevant for working global professionals. Online live, interactive continuing education courses that you can access from home, from work or anywhere with an internet connection.

ABOUT US

Our programs are for working designers and anyone seeking design and management training. Our online programs are presented direct from Los Angeles by some of the most experienced design professionals in the world. We offer introductory courses, five-week certificate programs and eight-week advanced certificate programs that meet once per week. The courses are delivered at a number at different times to fit your schedule and time zone. Our books have been specified as texts at many design and business schools including the University of California, Art Center Pasadena, Parsons Graduate Program, and Purdue University. We can present a custom program in your location anywhere in the world. We can tailor an online program to your schedule and needs. Contact us at info@curedale.com.

WHO HAS ATTENDED OUR COURSES?

Past participants in our on-line programs have included thousands of executives, design managers, designers from all design disciplines, architects, researchers, social scientists, engineers and other decision-makers from the following organizations including the following organizations. Tesla Motors, NASA, Kaleidoscope, Speckdesign, Intel, Nike, MillerCoors, Radiuspd, Gensler, Herman Miller,Trek bikes, Catalystnyc, Sylvania, Whipsaw, Berkeley University, Stanford University, Pininfarina, Inscape, Newbalance, MIT, Rhode Island School of Design,Tufts, Nokia, Steelcase, Mayo Clinic, Ocad, California State University Santa Barbara,University of Michigan,In Form, RIT,Honeywell, Columbia University,Nissan, Volkswagen, Sony, Nestle, Kraft Foods, Otterbox, Henry Ford Museum, Samsung, Ammunition, Siemens AG, Group, frog Design, Ziba Design, Plantronics, Luxion, Philips, Method, Visteon, Texas Instruments, Cisco, Mindspring, Hasbro, Dow Corning, Bressler Group, Reebok, Logitech, HP,CCS, Praxxis Design, Levi Strauss, NCSU, Design & Industry, Kensington, Symantec, Canberra University, Australian Government Department of Defence, Maya, Karten Design, Autodesk, Barco, Shutterstock, Lucid, Colgate, Starbucks, Sunbeam, Seimens.

OTHER TITLES
MORE INFORMATION HTTPS://DCC-EDU.ORG

DESIGN THINKING

DESIGN THINKING PROCESS AND METHODS MANUAL 4TH EDITION
Author: Robert A Curedale
Published by:
Design Community College Inc.
August 21, 2016
Paperback: 600 pages
Language: English
ISBN-10: 194080535X
ISBN-13: 978-1940805351

DESIGN THINKING PROCESS AND METHODS MANUAL 1ST EDITION
Author: Robert A Curedale
Published by:
Design Community College Inc.
Edition 1 January 2013
Paperback: 400 pages
Language: English
ISBN-10: 0988236214
ISBN-13: 978-0-9882362-1-9

DESIGN THINKING PROCESS AND METHODS MANUAL 3RD EDITION
Author: Robert A Curedale
Published by:
Design Community College Inc.
August 21, 2016
Paperback: 690 pages
Language: English
ISBN-10: 194080549X
ISBN-13: 978-1940805498

DESIGN THINKING POCKET GUIDE 2ND EDITION
Author: Curedale, Robert A
Published by:
Design Community College, Inc
Jun 01 2013
Paperback: 228 pages
ISBN-10: 098924685X
ISBN-13: 9780989246859

DESIGN THINKING QUICK REFERENCE GUIDE
Plastic laminated
Loose leaf one page
Author: Curedale, Robert A
Published by:
Loose Leaf: 1 pages
Publisher: Design Community College Inc.; 1st edition (2015)
ISBN-10: 194080518X
ISBN-13: 978-1940805184

DESIGN THINKING PROCESS & METHODS GUIDE 2ND EDITION
Author: Curedale, Robert A
Published by:
Design Community College, Inc
January 2016
Paperback: 422 pages
Language: English
ISBN-10: 1-940805-20-1
ISBN-13: 978-1-940805-20-7

DESIGN THINKING POCKET GUIDE 2ND EDITION

Author: Curedale, Robert A
Published by:
Design Community College, Inc
Jun 01 2013
Paperback: 228 pages
ISBN-10: 098924685X
ISBN-13: 9780989246859

DESIGN THINKING QUICK REFERENCE GUIDE

Plastic laminated
Loose leaf one page
Author: Curedale, Robert A
Published by:
Loose Leaf: 1 pages
Publisher: Design Community College Inc.; 1st edition (2015)
ISBN-10: 194080518X
ISBN-13: 978-1940805184

DESIGN THINKING TEMPLATES & EXERCISES

Author: Curedale, Robert A
Published by:
Design Community College,Inc
2016
eBook 51 pages
ISBN-10: 1-940805-16-3
ISBN-13: 978-1-940805-16-0

BRIEFING CHECK LISTS

PRODUCT DESIGN BRIEFING CHECKLIST

Author: Curedale, Robert A
Published by:
Design Community College, Inc.
Edition 1 2016
Paperback: 54 pages
Language: English
ISBN-10: 1940805317
ISBN-13: 978-1940805313

WEB DESIGN BRIEFING CHECKLIST

Author: Curedale, Robert A
Published by:
Design Community College, Inc.
Edition 1 November 2016
Paperback: 90 pages
Language: English
ISBN-10: 1940805287
ISBN-13: 978-1940805283

DESIGN THINKING PROCESS & METHODS GUIDE 2ND EDITION

Author: Curedale, Robert A
Published by:
Design Community College, Inc
January 2016
Paperback: 422 pages
Language: English
ISBN-10: 1-940805-20-1
ISBN-13: 978-1-940805-20-7

MAPPING METHODS

MAPPING METHODS 2 SET-BY-STEP GUIDE EXPERIENCE MAPS JOURNEY MAPS SERVICE BLUEPRINTS AFFINITY DIAGRAMS EMPATHY MAPS

Author: Curedale, Robert
Published by:
Design Community College, Inc.
March 17 2018
Paperback: 312 pages
ISBN-10: 1940805376
ISBN-13: 978-1940805375

SERVICE BLUEPRINTS

2nd Edition
Author: Curedale, Robert
Published by:
Design Community College, Inc.
April 2019
Paperback

CUSTOMER & USER JOURNEY MAPS STEP-BY-STEP GUIDE

2nd Edition
Author: Curedale, Robert
Published by:
Design Community College, Inc
April 2019
Paperback

EMPATHY MAPS STEP-BY-STEP GUIDE

2nd Edition
Author: Curedale, Robert
Published by:
Design Community College, Inc
April 2019
Paperback

AFFINITY DIAGRAMS STEP-BY-STEP GUIDE

2nd Edition
Author: Curedale, Robert
Published by:
Design Community College, Inc
April 2019
Paperback

CUSTOMER & USER EXPERIENCE MAPS STEP-BY-STEP GUIDE

2nd Edition
Author: Curedale, Robert A
Published by:
Design Community College, Inc.
February 2019
Paperback: 254 pages
Language: English
ISBN-10: 1-940805-46-5
ISBN-13: 978-1-940805-46-7

SERVICE BLUEPRINTS
First Edition
Author: Curedale, Robert
Published by:
Design Community College, Inc.
March 2016
Paperback: 152 pages
ISBN-10: 1940805198
ISBN-13: 978-1940805191

JOURNEY MAPS
First Edition
Author: Curedale, Robert
Published by:
Design Community College, Inc
March 2016
Paperback: 152 pages
Language: English
ISBN-10: 1940805228
ISBN-13: 978-1940805221

EMPATHY MAPS
First Edition
Author: Curedale, Robert
Published by:
Design Community College, Inc.
March 2016
Paperback: 152 pages
Language: English
ISBN-10: 1940805252
ISBN-13: 978-1940805252

AFFINITY DIAGRAMS
First Edition
Author: Curedale, Robert A
Published by:
Design Community College, Inc.
March 2016
Paperback: 128 pages
Language: English
ISBN-13 978-1940805269
ISBN-10 1940805269

MAPPING METHODS: FOR DESIGN AND STRATEGY
First Edition
Author: Curedale, Robert A
Published by:
Design Community College, Inc.
April 2013
Paperback: 136 pages
Language: English
ISBN-13 978-1940805269
ISBN-10 1940805269

SERVICE DESIGN

SERVICE DESIGN PROCESS & METHODS 3RD EDITION
Author: Curedale, Robert
Published by:
Design Community College, Inc
2018
Paperback: 532 pages
ISBN-10: 1940805368
ISBN-13: 978-1940805368

SERVICE DESIGN PROCESS & METHODS 2ND EDITION
Author: Curedale, Robert A
Published by:
Design Community College, Inc.
Edition May 2016
Paperback: 589 pages
Language: English
ISBN-10: 1-940805-30-9
ISBN-13: 978-1-940805-30-6

SERVICE DESIGN 250 ESSENTIAL METHODS
Author: Curedale, Robert A
Published by:
Design Community College, Inc.
Edition 1 Aug 01 2013
Paperback: 372 pages
Language: English
ISBN-10: 0989246868
ISBN-13: 9780989246866

SERVICE DESIGN POCKET GUIDE
Author: Curedale, Robert A
Published by:
Design Community College, Inc.
Edition 1 Sept 01 2013
Paperback: 206 pages
Language: English
ISBN-10: 0989246884
ISBN-13: 9780989246880

COLOR

DESIGNING WITH COLOR STEP-BY-STEP GUIDE
Author: Curedale, Robert A
Published by:
Design Community College, Inc.
Edition 1 July 01 2018
Paperback: 224 pages
Language: English
ISBN-10: 1940805384
ISBN-13: 978-1940805382

DESIGN METHODS

DESIGN METHODS 1
200 WAYS TO APPLY
DESIGN THINKING
Author: Robert A Curedale
Published by:
Design Community College Inc.
Edition 1 November 2013
Paperback: 396 pages
Language: English
ISBN-10:0988236206
ISBN-13:978-0-9882362-0-2

DESIGN METHODS 2
200 MORE WAYS TO
APPLY DESIGN THINKING
Author: Robert A Curedale
Published by:
Design Community College Inc.
Edition 1 January 2013
Paperback: 398 pages
Language: English
ISBN-13: 978-0988236240
ISBN-10: 0988236249

50 SELECTED DESIGN
METHODS
Author: Curedale, Robert A
Published by:
Design Community College, Inc.
Edition 1 Jan 17 2013
Paperback: 114 pages
Language: English
ISBN-10:0988236265
ISBN-13: 9780988236264

DESIGN RESEARCH

DESIGN RESEARCH
METHODS
150 WAYS TO
INFORM DESIGN
Author: Curedale, Robert A
Published by:
Design Community College, Inc.
Edition 1 January 2013
Paperback: 290 pages
Language: English
ISBN-10: 0988236257
ISBN-13: 978-0-988-2362-5-7

INTERVIEWS
OBSERVATION AND
FOCUS GROUPS
Author: Curedale, Robert A
Published by:
Design Community College, Inc.
Edition 1 Apr 01 2013
Paperback: 188 pages
Language: English
ISBN-10:0989246833
ISBN-13: 9780989246835

INTERVIEWS
OBSERVATION AND
FOCUS GROUPS
Author: Curedale, Robert A
Published by:
Design Community College, Inc.
Edition 1 Apr 01 2013
Paperback: 188 pages
Language: English
ISBN-10:0989246833
ISBN-13: 9780989246835

DESIGN RESEARCH

30 GOOD WAYS TO INNOVATE
Author: Curedale, Robert A
Design Community College, Inc.
Edition 1 November 2015
Paperback: 108 pages
Language: English
ISBN-10: 1940805139
ISBN-13: 978-1940805139

INTERVIEWS OBSERVATION AND FOCUS GROUPS
Author: Curedale, Robert A
Published by:
Design Community College, Inc.
Edition 1 Apr 01 2013
Paperback: 188 pages
Language: English
ISBN-10: 0989246833
ISBN-13: 9780989246835

INTERVIEWS OBSERVATION AND FOCUS GROUPS
Author: Curedale, Robert A
Published by:
Design Community College, Inc.
Edition 1 Apr 01 2013
Paperback: 188 pages
Language: English
ISBN-10: 0989246833
ISBN-13: 9780989246835

BRAINSTORMING

50 BRAINSTORMING METHODS
Author: Curedale, Robert A
Design Community College, Inc.
Edition 1 November 2015
Paperback: 108 pages
Language: English
ISBN-10: 1940805139
ISBN-13: 978-1940805139

DESIGN FOR CHINA

CHINA DESIGN INDEX THE ESSENTIAL DIRECTORY OF CONTACTS FOR DESIGNERS 2014
Author: Curedale, Robert A
Design Community College, Inc.
Edition 1 2014
Paperback: 384 pages
Language: English
ISBN-13: 978-1940805092
ISBN-101940805090

09
BIBLIOGRAPHY

BIBLIOGRAPHY

SERVICE DESIGN BIBLIOGRAPHY

Alam, I., & Perry, C. (2002). A customer-oriented new service development process. Journal of Services Marketing, 16(6), 515-534.

Allanwood, Gavin. User experience design: creating designs users really love. S.l.: AVA ACADEMIA, 2018.

Antonelli, Paola, and Patricia Juncosa Vecchierini. Design and the elastic mind. New York: Museum of Modern Art, 2008.

Antonelli, Paola (2009). The People. In Dietrich, Lucas (ed.). 60 Innovators Shaping Our Creative Future.
London, Thames & Hudson. pp. 394—399.

Anu, Valtonen, and Miettinen Satu. Service design with theory: discussions on change, value and methods. Rovaniemi: LUP, Lapland University Press, 2013.

Association, Harvard Business School. Service management. Harvard Business School Press, Boston, Mass., 1991.

Balcioglu, Tevfik (ed.) (1998). The Role of Product Design in Post-Industrial Society. Ankara, Middle East Technical University, Faculty of Architecture Press.

Baines, T., & Lightfoot, H. (2013). Made to serve: how manufacturers can compete through servitization and product service systems. John Wiley & Sons.

Baines, T. S., Lightfoot, H. W., Benedettini, O., & Kay, J. M. (2009). The servitization of manufacturing: A review of literature and reflection on future challenges. Journal of Manufacturing Technology Management, 20(5), 547-567.

Banerjee, Maithili. Service design: a comparative study of design and service in UK and India with the idea of introducing service design in India. Saarbrucken: VDM Verlag Dr. Muller, 2010.

Bate, Paul, and Glenn Robert. Bringing User Experience to Healthcare Improvement: The Concepts, Methods and Practices of Experience-Based Design. S.l.: Radcliffe Publishing Ltd, 2007.

Battarbee, K. (2003). Stories as shortcuts to meaning. In Koskinen, I., Battarbee, K., & Mattelmäki, T. (Eds.), Empathic Design. Finland: IT Press, 107–118.

Battarbee, K. (2004). Co-experience: understanding user experiences in social interaction. Doctoral dissertation, University of Art and Design Helsinki.
Berger, Warren. Glimmer: how design can transform your business, your life, and maybe even the world. London: Random House, 2011.

Bettencourt, Lance. Service innovation how to go from customer needs to breakthrough services. New York: McGraw-Hill, 2010.

Beyer, Hugh, and Karen Holtzblatt. Contextual design: defining customer-centered systems. San Francisco, Calif.: Morgan Kaufmann, 2009.

Biemans, W. G., Griffin, A., & Moenaert, R. K. (Forthcoming). New Service Development: How the Field Developed, Its Current Status and Recommendations for Moving the Field Forward. Journal of Product Innovation Management, 1-16.

Bitner, M. J. (1992). Servicescapes: The Impact of Physical Surroundings on Customers and Employees. Journal of Marketing, 56(2), 56-71.

Bitner, M.J., "Evaluating Service Encounters: The Effects of Physical Surroundings and Employee Responses," Journal of Marketing, vol. 54, no. 2, 1990, pp 69-82

Bleuel, William H., and Joseph D. Patton. Service management: principles and practices. Research Triangle Park, NC, U.S.A.: ISA Press, 1994.

Blomkvist, J., Holmlid, S., & Segelström, F. (2010). Service Design Research: Yesterday, Today and Tomorrow. In M. Stickdorn, & J. Schneider (Eds.), This is Service Design Thinking. Amsterdam, Netherlands: BIS Publishers.

Blomkvist, J. (2014). Representing Future Situations of Service: Prototyping in Service Design. Linköping, Sweden: Linköping University Electronic Press.

Blomkvist, J., & Segelström, F. (2014). Benefits of External Representations in Service Design: A Distributed Cognition Perspective. The Design Journal, 17(3), 331-346.

Brax, S. (2005). A manufacturer becoming service provider-challenges and a paradox. Managing Service Quality, (15), 142-155.

Buchenau, M. & Fulton Suri, J. (2000). Experience Prototyping. Proceedings of Designing Interactive Systems conference (DIS 2000). New York: ACM Press, 424–433.

Carroll, J. M. (2000). Five reasons for scenario-based design. Interacting with Computers, 13, 43- 60.

Charter, Martin & Tischner, Ursula (2001). Sustainable Solutions: Developing Products and Services for the Future. Sheffield, Greenleaf Publishing.

Cipolla, Carla (2009). Relational services and conviviality. In Miettinen, Satu & Koivisto, Mikko (eds.). Designing Services with Innovative Methods. Helsinki, University of Art and Design and Kuopio Academy of Design. pp. 232—245.

Clatworthy, S. (2013). Design support at the front end of the New Service Development (NSD) process: The role of touch-points and service personality in supporting team work and innovation processes. Oslo, Norway: Arkitekthøgskolen i Oslo.

Coates, Joseph F. (2009). Normative Forecasting. In Glenn, Jerome C. & Gordon, Theodore J. (eds.). Futures Research Methodology — Version 3.0. CD-rom. World Federation of United Nations Associations.

Condon, Patrick M. Design Charrettes for Sustainable Communities. Washington: Island Press, 2012.

Cooper, A. (1999). Inmates are Running the Asylum: Why High-Tech Products Drive Us Crazy and How to Restore the Sanity. SAMS, A Division of Macmillan Computer Publishing.

Corsten, Hans, Ralf Gössinger, and Anton Meyer. Service Management. Konstanz: UVK, 2014.

Cottam, H. & Leadbeater, C. (2004). HEALTH: Co-creating Services. UK: Red paper 01. Design Council.

de Bono, E. (1985/1999). Six Thinking Hats. First published in USA by Little, Brown and Company 1985, revised and updated edition published by First Back Bay 199, published in UK by Penguin Books 2000.

De Brentani, U. (2001). Innovative versus incremental new business services: different keys for achieving success. Journal of Product Innovation Management, 18(3), 169-187.

De Jong, J. P., & Vermeulen, P. A. (2003). Organizing successful new service development: a literature review. Management decision, 41(9), 844-858.

Díaz-Kommonen, L. Reunanen, M. & Salmi, A. (2009). Role playing and collaborative scenario design development. Proceedings of International Conference on Engineering Design (ICED'09). Stanford University, Stanford, CA, USA: The Design Society, 79-86.

Doorley, Scott, and Scott Witthoft. Make space: how to set the stage for creative collaboration. Hoboken, NJ: John Wiley & Sons, 2012.

Duarte, Nancy. Resonate: present visual stories that transform audiences. Chichester: John Wiley & Sons, 2010.

Evenson, S. (2005). Designing for Services. Proceedings of the Designing Pleasurable Products and Interfaces Conference (DPPI 2005). Netherlands, Eindhoven, 149-161.

Edvardsson, B., & Olsson, J. (1996). Key Concepts for New Service Development. The Service Industries Journal, 16(2), 140-164.

Edvardsson, Bo, Anders Gustafsson, Michael D. Johnson, and Bodil Sandén. New service development and innovation in the New Economy. Lund, Sweden: Studentlitteratur, 2002.

Lusch Robert, and Stephen L. Vargo. Service - dominant logic: premises, perspectives, possibilities. Cambridge: Cambridge University Press, 2014.

Fazlagic, Amir Jan. Service design. Warszawa: Akademia Finansów i Biznesu Vistula, 2013.

Fitzsimmons, James A., and Mona J. Fitzsimmons. New service development: creating memorable experiences. Thousand Oaks: Sage, 2000.

Fitzsimmons, Mona J. Service Management. London: McGraw-Hill Education - Europe, 2014.

Frei, Frances, and Anne Morriss. Uncommon Service How to Win by Putting Customers at the Core of Your Business. Boston: Harvard Business Review Press, 2012.

Fulton Suri, J. (2003). Empathic design: informed and inspired by other people's experience. In Koskinen, I., Battarbee, K., Mattelmäki, T. (Eds.). Empathic Design. Finland: IT Press, 51–57.

Gebauer, H., Krempl, R., & Fleisch, E. (2008). Service development in traditional product manufacturing companies. European Journal of Innovation Management, 11(2), 219-240.

Garcia, Fausto. New service development: creating a framework for the management of innovation in experience based firms. Saarbrücken: LAP, Lambert Academic Pub., 2010.

Garrett, Jesse James. The elements of user experience. Indianapolis: New Riders, 2011.

Gaver, W., Boucher, A., Pennington, S. & Walker, B. (2004). Cultural Probes and the value of Uncertainty. Interactions. Vol. 11 (No. 5). New York: ACM Press, 53–56.

Gemmel, Paul, Roland Van. Dierdonck, and Bart Van. Looy. Service Management an integrated approach. Harlow: Pearson, 2013.

Goodwin, Kim. Designing for the digital age: how to create human-centered products and services. Indianapolis, IN: Wiley Pub., 2009.

Gratton, Lynda (2011). The Shift. The Future of Work Is Already Here. London, Collins

Gray, Dave, Sunni Brown, and James Macanufo. Gamestorming: a playbook for innovators, rulebreakers, and changemakers. Farnham: OReilly, 2010.

Gronroos, Christian. Service management and marketing: managing customer relationships for service and manufacturing firms. Chichester: Wiley, 2000.

Grönroos, Christian. Service management and marketing: a customer relationship management approach. Chichester, West Sussex: Wiley, 2005.

Grönroos, Christian, Bo Edvardsson, and Jagdish N. Sheth. Service management. Los Angeles: SAGE Publications, 2013.

Grönroos, Christian. Service management and marketing: customer management in service competition. Hoboken, NJ: John Wiley & Sons, 2015.

Halvorson, Kristina, and Melissa Rach. Content strategy for the Web. Berkeley, CA: New Riders, 2012.

Heapy, Joe. Service design: design for new challenges. Farnham: Gower, 2012.

Heath, Chip, and Dan Heath. Switch: How to Change Things When Change Is Hard. S.l.: Random House US, 2013.

Heskett, James L., W. Earl. Sasser, and Christopher W. L. Hart. Service breakthroughs: changing the rules of the game. New York: Free Press, 1990.

Hohman, L. (2007). Innovation Games – creating breakthrough products through collaborative play. Addison-Wesley.

Hollins, Gillian & Hollins, Bill (1991). Total design: Managing the

Design Process in the Service Sector. London, Pitman

Holmlid, S. (2007). Towards an understanding of the challenges for design management and service design. International DMI Education Conference Design Thinking: New Challenges for Designers, Managers and Organizations, ESSEC Business School, Cergy-Pointoise, France.

Holmlid, S. (2007). Interaction design and service design: Expanding a comparison of design disciplines. Nordic Design Research, NorDes 2007. Stockholm.

Holmlid, S. & Evenson, S. (2006). Bringing design to services. Invited to IBM Service Sciences, Management and Engineering Summit: Education for the 21st century, New York.

Holtzblatt, Karen, and Hugh Beyer. Contextual design: using customer work models to drive system design. New York, NY: ACM, 2000.

Holtzblatt, Karen, and Hugh Beyer. Contextual design: evolved. San Rafael, CA: Morgan & Claypool, 2015.

Horovitz, Jacques, and Gerry Johnson. Service strategy. México: Pearson Educación, 2011.

Iqbal, Majid, and Sharon Taylor. Service strategy ITIL v3 core publications. London: TSO (The Stationery Office), 2007.

ISO 13407 (1999). Human-centred design processes for interactive systems. International Standard EN/ISO 13407:1999.
Johansson, M. (2005). Participatory Inquiry – Collaborative Design. Doctoral Dissertation, School of Engineering, Blekinge Institute of Technology, Sweden.

Johne, A., & Storey, C. (1998). New service development: a review of the literature and annotated bibliography. European journal of Marketing, 32(3/4), 184-251.

Johnson, Steven. Where good ideas come from: the natural history of innovation. Riverhead Hardcover, 2010.

Kankainen, A., Vaajakallio, K., Kantola, V. & Mattelmäki, T. (2011). Storytelling Group – a co-design method for service design. Journal of Behaviour & Information Technology. UK, London: Taylor & Francis, 1–10.

Kalbach, Jim. Mapping experiences: a guide to creating value through journeys, blueprints & diagrams. Beijing: OReilly, 2016.

Kaner, Sam, and Lenny Lind. Facilitators Guide to Participatory Decision-Making: Sam Kaner. Gabriola Island: New Society Publishers, 1998.

Kelley, Tom, and Jonathan Littman. The ten faces of innovation: IDEOs strategies for beating the devils advocate & driving creativity throughout your organization. New York: Currency/Doubleday, 2005.

Key element guide: service strategy. London: The Stationary Office, 2008.

Kimbell, Lucy. The Service Innovation Handbook Action-Oriented Creative Thinking Toolkit for Service Organizations. Amsterdam: BIS publishers, 2015.

King, Stanley, and Merinda Conley. Co-Design: a process of design participation. New York: Van Nostrand Reinhold, 1989.

Kolko, Jon. Exposing the magic of design: a practitioners guide to the methods and theory of synthesis. Oxford: Oxford University Press, 2015.

Koskinen, I., Battarbee, K. & Mattelmäki, T. (Eds.) (2003). Empathic Design. Finland: IT Press. Leadbetter, C. We-think, 2nd ed. London, England: Profile, 2009.

Koskinen, I. & Battarbee, K. (2003). Introduction to user experience and empathic design. In Koskinen, I., Battarbee, K. & Mattelmäki, T. (Eds.) Empathic Design. Finland: IT Press, 37–50.
Lee, Fred. If Disney ran your hospital: 9 1/2 things you would do differently. Bozeman, MT: Second River Healthcare Press, 2004.

Lehrer, M., Ordanini, A., DeFillippi, R., & Miozzo, M. (2012). Challenging the orthodoxy of value cocreation theory: A contingent view of co-production in design-intensive business services. European Management Journal, 30(6), 499-509.

Liedtka, Jeanne, Randy Salzman, and Daisy Azer. Design thinking for the greater good. New York: Columbia University Press, 2017.

Lloyd, Vernon, and Colin Rudd. Service design. London: TSO, 2007.

Lloyd, Vernon, and Sharon Taylor. Service design ITIL v3 core publications. London: TSO (The Stationery Office), 2007.

Lockton, Dan, David Harrison, and Neville A. Stanton. Design with Intent: 101 patterns for influencing behaviour through design. Berkshire, UK: Equifine, 2010.

Lockwood, Thomas. Design thinking: integrating innovation, customer experience, and brand value. New York: Allworth, 2010.

Lockwood, Thomas. Building design strategy: using design to achieve key business objectives. New York, NY: Allworth Press, 2010.

Lockwood, Thomas. Design thinking integrating innovation, customer experience and brand value. New York, NY: Allworth Press, 2011.

Lucero, A. (2009). Co-designing interactive spaces for and with designers: Supporting mood-board making. Doctoral Dissertation. Eindhoven University of Technology, Netherlands.

Lusch, R., Vargo, S. & Wessels, G. (2008). Toward a conceptual foundation for service science: Contributions from service-dominant logic. IBM Systems Journal. 47(1).

Maffei, S., Mager, B. & Sangiorgi, D. (2005). Innovation through service design. From research and theory to a network of practice. User's driven perspective. Proceedings of Joining Forces. University of Art and Design Helsinki.

Mager, Birgit. Service design a review. Köln: Köln Internat. School of Design, 2004.

Mager, Birgit. 10 service design basic cards. Köln: Fachhochsch.,

Fachbereich Design, 2006.

Mager, B. (2009). Service design as an emerging field. In Miettinen, S. & Koivisto. M. (Eds.) Designing Services with innovative methods. Finland: Publication series of the University of Art and Design Helsinki, 28–43.

Mager, Birgit. Deep dive: collecting relevant insights. Köln: Service Design Network, 2013.

Mager, Birgit. Touchpoint the journal of service design: vol. 6, nr 3 (2014): Blurring boundaries. Köln: Service Design Network, 2014.

Mager, Birgit (2008). Service Design. In Erlhoff, Michael & Marshall, Timothy (eds.). Design Dictionary: Perspectives on Design Terminology. Basel, Birkhäuser.

Malterud, K. (2001). Qualitative research: standards, challenges, and guidelines. The Lancet. Vol. 358, 483–488.

Manning, Harley, and Kerry Bodine. Outside in: the power of putting customers at the center of your business. Las Vegas: Amazon Publishing, 2012.

Manzini, E. (1993, June). Il Design dei Servizi. La progettazione del prodotto-servizio. Design Management(7).

Manzini, Ezio (1998). Products in a period of transition. In Balcioglu, Tevfik (ed.). The Role of Product Design in Post-Industrial Society. Ankara, Middle East Technical University, Faculty of Architecture Press. pp. 43—58

Manzini, Ezio & Jegou, François (2003). Sustainable Everyday: Scenarios of urban Life. Milan, Edizione Ambiente

Marquez, Joe. Library service design. Place of publication not identified: Rowman & Littlefield, 2016.

Martin, Roger L. The design of business: Why design thinking is the next competitive advantage. Boston, MA: Harvard Business Press, 2009.

Martin, Roger L. The opposable mind how successful leaders win through integrative thinking. Boston, MA: Harvard Business School Press, 2009.

Mathieu, V. (2001). Service strategies within the manufacturing sector: benefits, costs and partnership. International Journal of Service Industry Management ,12(5), 451-475.

Mattelmäki, Tuuli & Sleeswijk Visser, Froukje (2011). Lost in Co-X. Interpretations of co-design and co-creation. In Roozenburg, N. R. M. & Chen, L. L. & Stappers, P. J. (eds.) (2011). Diversity and Unity, Proceedings of IASDR2011, the 4th World Conference on Design Research, 31 October — 4th November 2011. Delft, The Netherlands

Mattelmäki, T. (2006). Design Probes. Doctoral Dissertation, University of Art and Design Helsinki, Publication series A 69, Finland.

Mattelmäki, T., Hasu, M. & Ylirisku, S. (2009). Creating Mock-ups of Strategic Partnerships. Proceedings of IASRD conference. Seoul, Korea.

Mattelmäki, T., Vaajakallio, K. & Yliriksu, S. (2007). Active@work-Design dealing with social change. Online proceedings of the Include conference 2007. London: Helen Hamlyn Research Center, RCA. http://www.ektakta.com/include_proceedings/

McQuilken, Lisa, and Steve Mennen. Services marketing. Geelong, Vic.: Deakin University, 2010.

Menor L.J., Tatikonda M.J., and Sampson S.E. 2002. New Service Development: Areas of Exploitation and Exploration, Journal of Operations Management, 20: 135-157.

Meroni, Anna & Sangiorgi Daniela (2011). Design for Services. Design for Social Responsibility Series. Farnham, Gower Publishing.

Meroni, Anna, and Daniela Sangiorgi. Design for Services. Abingdon, Oxon: Taylor and Francis, 2016.

Miettinen, Satu (2009). Designing Services with Innovative Methods. In Miettinen, Satu & Koivisto, Mikko (eds.). Designing Services with Innovative Methods. Helsinki, University of Art and Design and Kuopio Academy of Design. pp. 10—28

Miettinen, Satu, and Mikko Koivisto. Designing services with innovative methods. Helsinki: University of Art and Design, 2009.

Miller, Luke. The practitioners guide to user experience design. London: Piatkus, 2015.

Moggridge, Bill. Designing interactions. Cambridge, MA: MIT Press, 2007.

Möller, K., Rajala, R. & Westerlund, M. (2008). Service Innovation Myopia? A New Recipe for Client-Provider Value Creation. In California Management review. Vol. 50 (No. 3), CMB.berkeley.edu, 31-48.

Moritz, Stefan. Service design: practical access to an evolving field. S.I.: Lulu.com, 2009.

Morelli, N. (2006). Developing new product service systems (PSS): methodologies and operational tools. Journal of Cleaner Production, 14(17), 1495-1501.

Moser, Christian. User Experience Design. Springer Berlin Heidelberg, 2012.

Nielsen, L. (2002). From user to character: An investigation into user descriptions in scenarios. Proceedings of Designing Interactive Systems (DIS 2002). ACM Press, 99-104.

Norman, Donald A. The design of everyday things. NY, NY: Basic Books, 2013.

Norman, Donald A. Living with complexity. Place of publication not identified: Mit Press, 2016.

Nudurupati, S. S., Lascelles, D., Yip, N., & Chan, F. T. (2013) Eight challenges of the servitization. Frameworks and Analysis. Spring Servitization Conference Proceedings 2013, p8

Oliva, R., & Kallenberg, R. (2003). Managing the transition from products to services. International journal of service industry management, 14(2), 160-172.

Ordanini, A., & Parasuraman, A. (2010). Service innovation viewed through a service-dominant logic lens: a conceptual framework and empirical analysis. Journal of Service Research, 14(1), 3-23.

Osterwalder, Alexander, and Yves Pigneur. Business model generation a handbook for visionaries, game changers, and challengers. New York: Wiley&Sons, 2013.

Osterwalder, Alexander, Yves Pigneur, Greg Bernarda, Alan Smith, and Trish Papadakos. Value proposition design. Hoboken, NJ: Wiley, 2014.

Osterwalder, Alexander, Yves Pigneur, Gregory Bernarda, Alan Smith, and Trish Papadakos. Value Proposition Design: How to Create Products and Services Customers Want. Somerset: Wiley, 2015.

Osterwalder, Alexander, Yves Pigneur, Gregory Bernarda, Alan Smith, and Trish Papadakos. Value Proposition Design: How to Create Products and Services Customers Want. Somerset: Wiley, 2015.

Osterwalder, Alexander, Yves Pigneur, and Greg Bernarda. The big pad of 50 blank, extra-large business model canvases and 50 blank extra-large value proposition canvases: a supplement to business model generation and value proposition design. Hoboken: Wiley, 2017.

Pacenti, E., & Sangiorgi, D. (2010). Service Design Research Pioneers: An overview of Service Design research developed in Italy since the '90s. Design Research Journal(1.2010), 26-33.

Papastathopoulou, P., & Hultink, E. J. (2012). New Service Development: An Analysis of 27 Years of Research*. Journal of Product Innovation Management, 29(5), 705-714.

Pang, S. (2009). Successful Service Design for Telecommunications: A comprehensive guide to design and implementation. Chichester, UK: John Wiley & Sons, Ltd.

Parker, Sophia, and Joe Heapy. The journey to the interface: how public service design can connect users to reform. London: Demos, 2006.

Patel, Raj. The value of nothing: how to reshape market society and redefine democracy. London: Portobello, 2009.

Patnaik, Dev, and Peter Mortensen. Wired to care: how companies prosper when they create widespread empathy. Place of publication not identified: Distributed by Amazon Digital Services, 2011.

Patricio, L., Fisk, R., Falcão e Cunha, J., & Constantine, L. (2011). Multilevel service design: From customer value creation to consumer service experience blueprinting. Journal of Service Research. 14(2). 180-200.

Pine, Joseph B., and James H. Gilmore. The experience economy. Boston: Harvard Business Press, 2011.

Pinheiro, Tenny. The service startup: design gets lean; a practical guide to integrate design and lean startup. S.l.: Amazon.com, 2014.

Pink, Daniel H. Free agent nation: how Americas new independent workers are transforming the way we live. New York: Warner Books, 2001.

Pink, Daniel H. A whole new mind:

moving from the information age to the conceptual age. New York: Riverhead Books, 2006.

Pink, Daniel H. A whole new mind: why right-brainers will rule the future. London: MC, Marshall Cavendish, 2012.

Polaine, Andrew, Lavrans Løvlie, Ben Reason, and John Thackara. Service design: from insight to implementation. Brooklyn, NY: Rosenfeld Media, 2013.

Polaine, Andy, Lavrans Lvlie, and Ben Reason. Service Design: from Insight to Implementation. New York: Rosenfeld Media, 2013.

Pollak, L. (2008). Myths of Service Innovation. International DMI Education Conference Design Thinking: New Challenges for designers, Managers and Organizations. ESSEC Business School, Cergy–Pointoise, France.

Prestes Joly, M.; Cipolla, C.; Mazini, E. (2014) Informal, Formal, Collaborative – identifying new models of services within favelas of Rio de Janeiro. Proceedings from ServDes2014. Lancaster, United Kingdom.

Priestner, Andy, and Matt Borg. User experience in libraries: applying ethnography and human-centred design. Abingdon: Routledge, 2016.

Pruitt, John, and Jonathan Grudin. (2003). Personas: practice and theory. Proceedings of the 2003 conference on Designing for user experiences ACM, San Francisco, CA, USA.
 Quesenbery, Whitney, and Kevin Brooks. Storytelling for User Experience. Sebastopol: Rosenfeld Media, 2011.

Raddats, C., & Easingwood, C. (2010). Services growth options for B2B product-centric businesses. Industrial Marketing Management, 39(8), 1334-1345.

Reason, Ben, and Melvin Brand Flu. Service Design for Business. Wiley, 2015. Reichwald, Ralf, and Jessica Scheler. Service Innovation. Leipzig: CLIC, 2009.

Ries, Eric. Lean startup. Place of publication not identified: Portfolio Penguin, 2017.

Rizzo, F. (2010). Co-design versus User Centred Design: Framing the differences. In Guerrini, L. (Eds.) Notes on Design Doctoral Research. Franco Angeli Editore.

Roam, Dan. Unfolding the napkin: the hands-on method for solving complex problems with simple pictures. New York: Portfolio, 2009.

Robinson, Ken, and Lou Aronica. The element: how finding your passion changes everything. London: Penguin Books, 2010.

Säde, S. (2001). Cardboard mock-ups and conversations: Studies on user-centered product design. Doctoral Dissertation, University of Art and Design Helsinki, Publication series A 34, Finland.

Sandén, Bodil. The customers role in new service development. Karlstad: Faculty of Economic Sciences, Communication and IT, Business Administration, Karlstad University, 2007.
Sanders, E. B.-N. & Simons, G. (2009). A Social Vision for Value Co-creation in Design. In Open

Source Business Resource, December 2009: Value Co-Creation. http://www.osbr.ca/ojs/index.php/osbr/article/view/1012/973

Sanders, E.B.-N. (2006). Scaffolds for building everyday creativity. In Frascara, J. (Eds.) Design for Effective Communications: Creating Contexts for Clarity and Meaning. USA, New York: Allworth Press.

Sanders, E.B.-N. (2002). From User-Centered to Participatory Design Approaches. In Frascara, J. (Eds.) Design and the Social Sciences. Taylor & Francis Books Limited.

Sanders, E.B.-N. (2001). A New Design Space. Proceedings of ICSID 2001 Seoul: Exploring Emerging Design Paradigm, Oullim. Seoul, Korea, 317-324.

Sanders, E. B.-N. & Dandavate, U. (1999). Design for experiencing: New tools. Proceedings of the First International Conference on Design and Emotion. Delft University of Technology, Delft, Netherlands, 87-92.

Sanders, L., & Stappers, P. J. (2012). Convivial Design Toolbox: Generative Research for the Front End of Design. BIS.

Sangiorgi, D. (2011). Transformative services and transformation design. International Journal of Design, 5(2), 29-40.

Sangiorgi, D. (2009). Building Up a Framework for Service Design Research. 8th European Academy Of Design Conference, (pp. 415-420). Aberdeen, Scotland.

Sarmento, T., & Patrício, L. (2014). Incorporating the customer experience along different iterative cycles of service design. Proceedings from ServDes2014. Lancaster, United Kingdom.

Sato, S. & Salvador, T. (1999). Playacting and Focus Troupe: Theater techniques for creating quick, intense, immersive, and engaging focus group sessions. Interactions. Vol. 6 (No. 5). USA, New York: ACM, 35-41.

Schrage, M. (2000). Serious play: how the world's best companies simulate to innovate. USA: President and Fellows of Harvard College.

Schwarz, Sven, Freimut Bodendorf, and Carolin Durst. Service innovation: research perspective and future roadmap. Nürnberg: Lehrstuhl für Wirtschaftsinformatik im Dienstleistungsbereich, 2012.

Seddon, John. Systems thinking in the public sector: the failure of the reform regime ... and the manifesto for a better way. Axminster: Triarchy, 2008.

Segelström, F. (2013). Stakeholder Engagement for Service Design: How Service Designers Identify and Communicate Insights. Linköping, Sweden: Linköping Electronic Press.

Seland, G. (2009). Empowering End Users in Design of Mobile Technology Using Role Play as a Method: Reflections on the Role-Play Conduction. In M. Kurosu (Eds.) Human Centered Design HCII 2009. Springer-Verlag Berlin Heidelberg, 912-921.

Service design: a toolkit for the design of public services. Brussels: Namahan, 2011.

Service design: Continual service improvement; Service operation; Service strategy; Service transition. London: TSO, 2007.

Servicedesign: vejen til enkle løsninger. Kbh.: Erhvervs- og Byggestyrelsen, 2010.

Shostack, L. (1982). How to Design a Service. European Journal of Marketing(161), 49-63.

Shostack, G. Lynn. "Designing Services that Deliver", Harvard Business Review, vol. 62, no. 1 January - February 1984, pp 133–139

Sleeswijk Visser, F. (2009). Bringing the everyday life of people into design. Doctoral Dissertation, Technical University of Delft, Netherlands.

Sleeswijk Visser, F., Stappers, P.J., Van Der Lugt R. & Sanders, E.B.-N. (2005). Contextmapping: Experiences from practice. CoDesign Journal. Vol. 1 (No. 2). UK, London: Taylor and Francis, 119–149.

Spies, Marco. Branded interactions: creating the digital experience. London: Thames and Hudson, 2015.

Srinivasan, R. Services marketing. Place of publication not identified: Prentice-Hall Of India, 2014.

Stevens, E., & Dimitriadis, S. (2005). Managing the new service development process: towards a systemic model. European Journal of Marketing, 39(1/2), 175-198.

Stickdorn, Marc, Jakob Schneider, and Kate Andrews. This is service design thinking basics, tools, cases. Amsterdam: BIS Publishers, 2011.

Svanæs, D. & Seland, G. (2004). Putting the Users Center Stage: Role Playing and Low-fi Prototyping Enable End Users to Design Mobile Systems. Proceedings of the SIGCHI conference on Human factors in computing systems (CHI 2004). USA, New York: ACM Press, 479–486.

Taffe, S. (2015). The hybrid designer/ end-user: Revealing paradoxes in co-design. Design Studies. 40. 39-59.

Tether, B. (2008). Service design: time to bring in the professionals? In L. Kimbell, & V. P. Siedel (Eds.), Designing for Services - Multidisciplinary Perspectives: Proceedings from the Exploratory Project on Designing for Services in Science and Technology-based Enterprises (pp. 7- 9). Oxford, UK: Saïd Business School.

Thackara, John. In the bubble: designing in a complex world. Cambridge, MA: MIT Press, 2006.

Thaler, Richard, and Cass Sunstein. Nudge: improving decisions about health, wealth, and happiness: Rev. and exp. ed. New York: Penguin, 2009.

Tongur, S. and Angelis. J. (2013) Disruptive innovation and servitization - Competitive advantage through product service value propositions. Spring Servitization Conference Proceedings 2013, p.147.

Touchpoint the journal of service design. Köln: Service Design Network,

2009-.
Tufte, Edward Rolf. Envisioning information. Cheshire, CT: Graphics Press, 2017.

Ulaga, W., & Reinartz, W. J. (2011). Hybrid offerings: how manufacturing firms combine goods and services successfully. Journal of Marketing, 75(6), 5-23.

Vaajakallio, K., Mattelmäki, T. & Lee, J-J. (2010a). "It became Elvis" – Co-design lessons with Children". Interactions Magazine. July / August. ACM, 26–29.

Vandermerwe, S., & Rada, J. (1989). Servitization of business: Adding value by adding services. European Management Journal 6 (4): 314 – 324.

Vargo, S. L., & Lusch, R. F. (2008). Service-dominant logic: continuing the evolution. Journal of the Academy of marketing Science, 36(1), 1-10.

Vendrell-Herrero, F., Parry, G., Bustinza, O. F., & O'Regan, N. (2014). Servitization as a Driver for Organizational Change. Strategic Change, 23(5-6), 279-285

Verganti, Roberto. Design-driven innovation: changing the rules of competition by radically innovating what things mean. Boston, MA: Harvard Business Press, 2014.
 Viladàs, Xènia. Design at your service: how to improve your business with the help of a designer. Barcelona: Index Books, 2011.

Visser, Froukje Sleeswijk. Service design by industrial designers. Delft: TU Delft, ID Studio Lab, 2013.

Watanabe, Ken. Problem Solving 101: A Simple Book for Smart People. 2013.

Watkinson, Matt. The ten principles behind great customer experiences electronic resou. Harlow: Financial Times, 2013.

Westerlund, B. (2009). Design Space Exploration: co-operative creation of proposals for desired interactions with future artifacts. Doctoral Dissertation, Kungliga Tekniska högskolan, Stockholm, Sweden.

Wener, R.E., "The Environmental Psychology of Service Encounters," in Czepiel, J.A., Solomon, M.R. and Suprenant, C.F. (eds), The Service Encounter: Managing Customer Interactions in Service Businesses, Lexington Books, 1985

Wetter-Edman, K. (2014). Design for Service – A framework for articulating designers' contribution as interpreter of users' experience. PhD Thesis. Gothenburg, Sweden: Litorapid Media AB.

Wright, P. & McCarthy, J. (2008). Empathy and Experience in HCI. Proceedings of the twenty-sixth annual SIGCHI conference on Human factors in computing systems (CHI 2008) Dignity in Design. USA, New York: ACM, 637–646.

Ylirisku, S. & Buur, J. (2007). Designing with video. Focusing the user-centred design process. UK, London: Springer-Verlag.

Ylirisku, S. & Vaajakallio, K. (2007). Situated Make Tools for envisioning ICTs with ageing workers. Online Proceedings of the Include conference 2007. London: Helen Hamlyn Research

Center, RCA. http://www.ektakta.com/include_proceedings

Yliriskö, S., Vaajakallio, K., Buur, J. (2007). Framing innovation in co-design sessions with everyday people. Online Proceedings of Nordic Design Research (Nordes07). Stockholm, Sweden: http://www.nordes.org/upload/papers/104.pdf

Vaajakallio, K. (2008). Design Dialogues: Studying co-design activities in an artificial environment. Copenhagen working papers on design. No. 2, Danmarks Designskole.

Vaajakallio, K. & Mattelmäki, T. (2007). Collaborative Design Exploration: Envisioning Future Practices with Make Tools. Proceedings of Designing Pleasurable Products and Interfaces (DPPI07). University of Art and Design Helsinki, 223–238.

Van Looy, B., Gemmel, P. and Van Dierdonck, R., Services Management: An Integrated Approach, 2nd ed., Esse, UK, Prentice Hall, p.231

Vargo, S. & Lusch, R. (2008). From goods to service(s): divergences and convergences of logics. Industrial Marketing Management. Vol. 37, 254–259.

Young, Indi. Mental models: aligning design strategy with human behavior. Brooklyn, NY: Rosenfeld Media, 2008.

Young, Laurie. From products to services: insight and experience from companies which have embraced the service economy. Chichester, England: John Wiley & Sons, 2008.
Yu, E., & Sangiorgi, D. (2014). Service Design as an approach to New Service Development:

reflections and future studies. Proceedings of the Fourth Service Design and Innovation conference, ServDes (pp. 194-204). Linköping, Sweden: Linköping University Electronic Press.

Zeithaml, Valarie A., Mary Jo Bitner, and Dwayne D. Gremler. Services marketing: integrating customer focus across the firm. New York, NY: McGraw-Hill Education, 2018.

•

ABOUT THE AUTHOR

Rob Curedale was born in Australia and worked as a designer, director and educator in leading design offices in London, Sydney, Switzerland, Portugal, Los Angeles, Silicon Valley, Detroit, and Hong Kong. He designed or managed the design of over 1,000 products as a consultant and in-house design leader for the world's most respected brands. Rob has three decades experience in every aspect of product development and design research, leading design teams to achieve transformational improvements in operating and financial results. Rob's design scan be found in millions of homes and workplaces around the world and have generated billions of dollars in corporate revenues.

DESIGN PRACTICE
HP, Philips, GEC, Nokia, Sun, Apple, Canon, Motorola, Nissan, Audi VW, Disney, RTKL, Governments of the UAE,UK, Australia, Steelcase, Hon, Castelli, Hamilton Medical, Zyliss, Belkin, Gensler, Haworth, Honeywell, NEC, Hoover, Packard Bell, Dell, Black & Decker, Coleman and Harmon Kardon. Categories including furniture, healthcare, consumer electronics, sporting, housewares, military, exhibits, and packaging.

TEACHING
Rob has taught as a full time professor, adjunct professor and visiting instructor at institutions including the following: Art Center Pasadena, Art Center Europe, Yale School of Architecture, Pepperdine University, Loyola University, Cranbrook Academy of Art, Pratt, Otis, a faculty member at SCA and UTS Sydney, Chair of Product Design and Furniture Design at the College for Creative Studies in Detroit, then the largest product design school in North America, Cal State San Jose, Escola De Artes e Design in Oporto Portugal, Instituto De Artes Visuals, Design e Marketing, Lisbon, Southern Yangtze University, Jiao Tong University in Shanghai and Nanjing Arts Institute in China.

AWARDS
Designs that Rob has managed and designed have been recognized with IDSA IDEA Awards, Good Design Awards UK, Australian Design Awards, and a number of best of show innovation Awards at CES Consumer Electronics Show. His designs are in the Permanent collection of the Powerhouse Design Museum. In 2013 Rob was nominated for the Advanced Australia Award. The Awards celebrate Australians living internationally who exhibit "remarkable talent, exceptional vision, and ambition." In 2015 Rob was selected with a group of leading international industrial designers to provide opening comments for the International Congress Of Societies Of Industrial Design Conference ICSID in Korea.

www.ingramcontent.com/pod-product-compliance
Lightning Source LLC
Chambersburg PA
CBHW051050230426
43666CB00012B/2639